JACQUELYN A. OTTMAN

THE
NEW RULES
OF
GREEN
MARKETING

Strategies, Tools, and Inspiration
for Sustainable Branding

785266 000297

Greenleaf
PUBLISHING

$\overline{\text{BK}}$

Berrett–Koehler Publishers, Inc.
San Francisco
a BK Business book

Published in the United States and Canada by
Berrett-Koehler Publishers, Inc.
235 Montgomery Street, Suite 650
San Francisco, California 94104-2916, USA
Tel: +1 415 288-0260 Fax: +1 415 362-2512 www.bkconnection.com

Published in the UK by
Greenleaf Publishing Limited
Aizlewood's Mill
Nursery Street
Sheffield S3 8GG
UK
www.greenleaf-publishing.com

Cataloging information is available from the Library of Congress.
  ISBN-13: 978-1-60509-866-1

British Library Cataloguing in Publication Data:
  A catalogue record for this book is available from the British Library.
  ISBN-13: 978-1-906093-44-0

FSC
www.fsc.org
MIX
Paper from
responsible sources
FSC® C013604

Printed in the United Kingdom
Printed on acid-free paper using vegetable-based inks by
CPI Antony Rowe, Chippenham and Eastbourne

Cover by LaliAbril.com

The New Rules of Green Marketing should serve as the definitive text for any organization that is looking to brand itself or its products as green or sustainable.

L. Hunter Lovins, president, Natural Capitalism

Jacquelyn will inspire you about the potential of green marketing not only to generate growth but to feel better about yourself and your career as you help improve the health of the planet.

Adam Lowry and Eric Ryan, Co-founders and CEOs, method

A must-read for marketers working to make green mainstream and moving markets toward a cleaner, more sustainable future.

Cathy L. Hartman and Edwin R. Stafford, Center for the Market Diffusion of Renewable Energy and Clean Technology, Jon M. Huntsman School of Business, Utah State University

. . . Jacquelyn Ottman has been and still is the undisputable # 1 advocate of the green marketing concept, pointing us at the absolute necessity to develop greener products and services that enable consumers to adopt a more sustainable lifestyle . . . A must for all product design and marketing students and professors as well as the product industry. Maybe the time is right for the establishment of "The Jacquelyn Ottman Academy"?

Dr Han Brezet, Research Director of the Faculty of Industrial Design and Design for Sustainability Professor, Delft University of Technology

This is a must-read for every marketer in their quest to add value to their existing business flow.

Hiro Motoki, Deputy Chief Executive, E-Square Inc.; Lecturer, Tohoku University Graduate School of Environmental Studies,

Jacquie Ottman has always been at the forefront in bridging the gap between the sustainable marketing theorists and visionaries, and the practical marketing world of competitive pressures and constraints. With her new book she has taken that bridge-building ability to a whole new level.

Professor Ken Peattie, Director, BRASS Research Centre, Cardiff University

Ms. Ottman's books and articles have been some of the key go-to works I have used to serve my clients and students for over a decade.

Wendy Jedlicka, author of *Packaging Sustainability*

Green marketing is the future and Jacquie Ottman is our guide. A high-energy, straight-talking book filled with useful pointers for anyone interested in smart, sustainable brand communications.

Brian Dougherty, author of *Green Graphic Design*

Every entrepreneur involved in sustainable consumer products should read this book.

CJ Kettler, Entrepreneur, Founder and CEO of LIME Media

Green marketing pioneer Jacquelyn Ottman delivers the "New Rules" in a comprehensive, engaging, and readable book sure to become another classic . . . Everything a green marketing professor (and her students) could ask for!

Fredrica Rudell, Associate Professor and Chair of Marketing, Hagan School of Business, Iona College

From the guru of green marketing, Jacquelyn Ottman's *New Rules of Green Marketing* provides an indispensable strategy for the marketing of products and services in the critical times ahead.

Jon Naar, author of *Design for a Livable Planet*

Jacquie Ottman is still the oracle on the subject . . . Jacquie continues to teach us all where responsible green marketing has come from. And, more importantly, where it will be in the next 20 years. Enjoy.

Sol Salinas, Former Director of Marketing and Planning, ENERGY STAR; Federal Sustainability Lead, Accenture Sustainability Services NA

In this new volume, [Jacquie] has once again integrated compelling data and keen observations into an engaging and insightful treatise on the topic.

Michael V. Russo, author, *Companies on a Mission*

Jacquie's latest book provides a highly readable, thoughtful, yet practical route map through often complex and challenging issues.

Martin Charter, Director, The Centre for Sustainable Design, UK

. . . in her new book Jacquie shows us what the next big thing is in the green marketplace.

Ichin Cheng, Director & Partner, Sustainable Innovation Lab, UK

Jacquelyn Ottman has yet again written an indispensable book about green marketing . . . *The New Rules of Green Marketing* is a must-read for every marketer.

Jennifer Kaplan, author of *Greening Your Small Business*

Finally, the book that we need for a 21st-century approach to marketing.

Mary McBride, Design Management Graduate Program, Pratt Institute

This book will become a key reference "rule book" for anyone who wants to participate in this new Green World reality.

Tukee Nemcek, Director, New Brand Initiative, BISSELL Homecare Inc.

Everyone who wants to participate in the sustainability space should read this book.

Ron Buckhalt, Manager USDA BioPreferred program

The New Rules of Green Marketing should be the compass for the business navigating on the odyssey of sustainability.

Jay Fang, CEO, Green Consumers' Foundation, Taiwan

Jacquie Ottman takes her 25 years of experience in green marketing and gives insightful data and helpful checklists for practitioners in the field.

Shelley Zimmer, Environmental Initiatives Manager, HP

The New Rules of Green Marketing is brilliant. A must-read for anyone interested in sustainability.

Laurie Tema-Lyn, Principal, Practical Imagination Enterprises

Ottman's *The New Rules of Green Marketing* is a wonderful, highly valuable resource.

Valerie L. Vaccaro, Associate Professor of Marketing, Kean University

Anyone who buys, designs, or sells *anything* can use this book to make better choices for a lasting and prosperous future.

Pamela J. Gordon, author of *Lean and Green*

Ottman's done it again. Jacquelyn doesn't just have her finger on the pulse of green marketing: she is the pulse.

John Rooks, author of *More Than Promote*

Other books by the author

Environmental Consumerism: What Every Marketer Needs to Know (with Eric Miller; Alert Publishing, 1991)

Green Marketing: Challenges and Opportunities for the New Marketing Age (NTC Business Books, 1993)

Green Marketing: Opportunity for Innovation (McGraw Hill, 1998)

**For my Geoff,
the original recycler**

Contents

Foreword

Over the past decade few marketing topics have been more dynamic than that of "green" or "sustainability". In a few short years we have witnessed consumers shift from being highly skeptical about the performance of green products to the commoditization of green in many categories.

The recent explosion of green media, products, services, and marketing has brought with it a sea of confusion and a lack of trust, all of which risk undermining the entire green movement and returning us to an era of consumer apathy.

Further complicating the green movement is the arrival of Gen Y who, now in their twenties, are taking center stage in the arena of consumerism. This generation's formative years were the prosperous '90s where they had so many choices that values often became the brand differentiator. Sustainability and green values are a generational characteristic for this 80-million-strong cohort that will influence their lifetime brand loyalty. Not only do they bring these deeply rooted values to the forefront of our economy, but also the tools to support or expose companies in the form of social media.

As this book goes to press we are seeing some of the world's largest polluters also rank high as some of the most "environmental" companies, according to consumer perception. This misalignment between public perception and true environmental impact is being fostered by mass marketing that frequently highlights a handful of "green halo" products or initiatives. But this won't last. The transparency of the Internet and the openness of social media tools will ruthlessly expose the differences between a company's private and public face. With this will come a shift in green marketing from what you say . . . to what you do.

As we move to a future where green marketing cannot remain separate from a business's operations, the role of the marketing team and its internal influence will evolve as well. At the heart of green marketing is a mission bigger than your own brand – the planet. It's about a higher purpose that will require marketers to change their role in an organization to one that influences the organization's actions and accurately reflects its true environmental impact. Is there a difference between green marketing and a green company? Today? Yes. Tomorrow? No.

Jacquelyn Ottman's *The New Rules of Green Marketing* is a timely arrival that will enable us to navigate this changing world. She will help you move from "green" as a niche opportunity to its being a core part of any company's marketing and overall corporate philosophy. Jacquelyn will inspire you about the potential of green marketing not only to generate growth but to feel better about yourself and your career as you help improve the health of the planet.

As we built the *method* brand over the past few years we undertook a pioneering journey bringing green home care into the mainstream. We have navigated these shifts within "green" by maintaining at the heart of our organization a true dedication to building a green and sustainable company called "People Against Dirty". At *method* we do not sell a product; we sell a philosophy. By following our values and beliefs we have created not only a financially rewarding brand, but a higher level of satisfaction and happiness in work – knowing that we are part of something bigger than ourselves. After all, who wants to just make soap when you can save a planet? We hope you find yourselves on a similar journey.

Adam Lowry and Eric Ryan
Co-founders and CEOs, **method**
San Francisco, California

Preface

This book is about the new rules of green marketing that increasingly characterize the purchasing sensibilities of billions of consumers around the world. It took over 20 years of my career advising leading businesses on green marketing strategies (and 15 more years than I had projected), but few would now question the facts that green is mainstream and the rules of the game for marketers are rapidly changing. Is every consumer making every purchase decision a green one? No. Far from it. But are awareness, concern, and intent to purchase the right thing squarely on the radar screens of most consumers in the developed world today? Is green also changing the agendas of the manufacturers and service companies that meet consumers' needs, as well as shaping the agendas of government officials, NGOs, church leaders, the news media, educators, Hollywood celebrities, and every other important force in society? The answer to both of these questions is an emphatic Yes!

This book is also about the strategies needed to play by the new rules. Reflecting the changing attitudes and behaviors of today's consumers, these strategies cover greening current products and inventing sustainable ones; communicating credibly and impactfully, and working proactively with a variety of stakeholders in order to extend one's resources and address consumer needs authentically and thoroughly. I illustrate these strategies by telling the stories of the sustainability leaders – brands with green ingrained in their DNA. Included are stories from Seventh Generation, Timberland, and Stonyfield Farm, companies that are swiftly growing their businesses by extending their appeal from a once very fringe audience to now mainstream consumers. Also included are the stories of the big multinational brands such as GE, HSBC, Starbucks, Nike, Procter & Gamble, Toyota, and Wal-Mart who are quickly adapting to the new rules. This book is also about these two forces coming together to open the doors for young, innovative upstarts such as Method to go green *and* mainstream from their very beginnings – and what everyone can learn by studying their ingeniously unique strategies.

Driven by fears for the future, consumer demand for sustainable products is built on trust. Unfortunately, as I write, the term "green marketing" bears the perceptual brunt of "greenwashing" – players within the industry who overstate or otherwise mislead consumers about the environmental attributes of their offerings. I personally believe that much so-called greenwashing is unintentional and even understandable in a fast-growing industry still finding its sea legs. Green marketers today largely operate without the light of a strong governmental sun or established self-governance. (The U.S. Federal Trade Commission executed zero cases of green claims during the Bush Administration of 2000–2008!) There is no form of certification for green marketing practitioners, and few, if any, courses about sustainable branding are available in community colleges, business schools, or corporate training programs. Nevertheless, I am encouraged by the many sincere efforts to communicate the benefits of legitimate sustainable products that are on the market today; it is these stories and strategies that I recount and celebrate from my many years deeply involved in this industry.

The goal of this book is to help every well-intended marketer to understand the strategies needed to adapt to the new rules of green marketing and to find a profitable, low-risk path to meeting consumer needs in a truly sustainable fashion – indeed, to be inspired to become a leader in his or her own right. Written primarily from the perspective of my native U.S., it nonetheless contains rich content from around the world. I wrote this book for sustainability directors and brand executives at consumer product manufacturers and service providers and their advertising and PR staff and agencies. It is also a valuable tool for entrepreneurs and venture capitalists, professors and students, and representatives of trade associations, NGOs, and government agencies.

I start by making the case for the mainstreaming of green and the ways in which the rules are quickly changing (Chapter 1). In Chapter 2, I describe two ways for segmenting green consumers before characterizing their swiftly changing buyer motives and psychology. Then I describe the new green marketing paradigm (Chapter 3) and provide an in-depth look at one company that superbly exemplifies this paradigm, Method. I move on to discuss what it takes to address the new green marketing paradigm, starting with the strategies for greening one's products (Chapter 4). This is followed by an introduction to sustainable innovation together with five practical strategies for forging an exciting path for significantly reducing one's environmental and sustainability impacts while improving one's top line far into the future (Chapter 5).

With legitimately greener products in hand, readers will be ready to learn about the new strategies of green consumer communications and how to deliver the benefits of their wares with impact (Chapter 6). An entire chapter (Chapter 7) follows devoted to the full complement of strategies for establishing trust and avoiding greenwash. I then offer in Chapter 8 the new strategies for collaborating with various key stakeholders – an essential step in ensuring the legitimacy and completeness of one's efforts in a complex world where one company cannot possibly garner the resources and the expertise necessary for the task.

I close with Chapter 9, which encompasses the in-depth stories and strategies of two sustainability leaders, Starbucks and Timberland, which exemplify a deep understanding of the new rules of green marketing and are laudably showing the way toward integrating environmental and social considerations successfully and profitably into their businesses. I then conclude (Chapter 10), followed by a full complement of resources from around the globe.

Enjoy reading this book and the examples of successful green marketing efforts being conducted by many sustainability leaders including, I am proud to say, some of our clients. I hope you find, as intended, that you will keep it within reach as a useful resource, practical guide, and source of ongoing inspiration.

I'd love to hear your comments, your questions, and the details of your own journey and successes. Send them to me via our company's website, www.greenmarketing.com, and indicate if you'd like to be added to our mailing list. Use the many articles and links there, as well as my blog, www.greenmarketing.com/blog, as supplementary guidance for your efforts and as updates to the material contained within this book.

I wish you much success addressing the **new rules of green marketing**.

Jacquelyn A. Ottman
New York, New York
Fall 2010

Acknowledgments

In the same way it takes a village to raise a child, it took an army of colleagues and associates whom I've met over my 22 years as a green marketing consultant to write this book.

At J. Ottman Consulting we regularly track the most successful greener products and campaigns for our clients. Several interns and other colleagues helped to further research and write many case examples referred to throughout this book. They include: David Aigner, Ann Amarga, James Blackburn, Catie Carter, Brynne Cochran, Marjorie Dunlap, JC Darne, Ling Feng Fu, Laura Gardner, Alana Gerson, Laura Kortebein, Lisa Martin, Isabelle Mills-Tannenbaum, Michael Mintz, Emily-Anne Rigal, Kyle Weatherholtz, and Margot Wood. Veronica Gordon, Sydnee Grushak, Sarah McGrath, Candela Montero, Alexandra San Romàn, and especially Elizabeth Weisser need to be singled out for particularly significant contributions to the text.

In addition, I am grateful to the many representatives of the sustainable corporate leaders, including some of our clients, who reviewed passages of this book for their accuracy. They include: Steve Davies of Natureworks, Clifford Henry and Laura Thaman of Procter & Gamble, Kate Lewis of the USDA's BioPreferred program, Steven Mojo of BPI, Katie Molinari of Method, Anastasia O'Rourke of Ecolabel Index, Ben Packard of Starbucks, David Rinard of Steelcase, Nicole Rousseau of HSBC, Cara Vanderbeck of Timberland, Jill Vohr of the U.S. EPA's ENERGY STAR program, and Shelley Zimmer of HP.

Special thanks to Gwynne Rogers of the Natural Marketing Institute who provided several proprietary charts, and Martin Wolf of Seventh Generation who guided the passages on life-cycle assessment as he has so ably done in my two previous books.

Several esteemed colleagues reviewed sections of the manuscript and provided valuable input and critique including: Martin Charter, Fred Curtis, Joy Fournier, Ann Graham, Wendy Jedlicka, Byron Kennard, John Paul Kusz, Birgitte Racine, Inês Sousa, Edwin Stafford, Pamela van Orden, Rudy Vetter, and particularly John Laumer. Special thanks to Mark Eisen who painstakingly made one last thorough edit towards the completion of the manuscript, and Stephanie Tevonian for her invaluable design assistance.

A final note of thanks goes to my publishers, Greenleaf Publishing in the UK and Berrett-Koehler in the U.S., and in particular to Dean Bargh, Jeevan Sivasubramaniam, and Johanna Vondeling for their significant contributions. Finally, my especial appreciation to John Stuart of Greenleaf for embracing this project with enthusiasm, intelligence, and grace.

The 20 New Rules of Green Marketing

1 **Green is mainstream.** Not too long ago, just a small group of deep green consumers existed. Today, 83% of consumers – representing every generation, from Baby Boomers to Millennials and Gen Ys – are some shade of green. Moreover, there are now finely defined segments of green consumers.

2 **Green is cool.** Once a faddish preoccupation of the fringe, green is not only mainstream, it's chic. In fact, green consumers are early adopters and leaders who influence purchasing behavior. Celebrities and other cool types generally are espousing green causes. People show off (and self-actualize) by tooling around in a Toyota Prius (or soon, we predict, in a Nissan LEAF electric), and carry cloth shopping bags to look the part.

3 **Greener products work equally or better – and are often worth a premium price.** Thanks to advances in technology, we've come a long way since the days when greener products gathered dust on health food store shelves because they didn't work as well and were not a good value. Organics, hybrid cars, and safer cleaning products now command a price premium.

4 **Green inspires innovative products and services that can result in better consumer value, enhanced brands, and a stronger company.** Savvy managers no longer consider the environment to be a burden that represents added cost and overhead – but an investment that can pay back handsomely.

5 **Values guide consumer purchasing. Historically, consumers bought solely on price, performance, and convenience.** But today, how products are sourced, manufactured, packaged, disposed of – and even such social aspects as how factory and farm workers are treated – all matter.

6 **A life-cycle approach is necessary.** Single attributes such as recyclable, organic, or energy-efficient matter greatly, but don't mean a product is green overall. Recycled products still create waste, organic strawberries can travel thousands of miles, and CFLs contain mercury. So a more thorough, life-cycle or carbon-based approach to greening is necessary.

7   Manufacturer and retailer reputation count now more than ever. In addition to looking for trusted brand names on supermarket shelves, consumers are now flipping over packages, saying, "Who makes this brand? Did they produce this product with high environmental and social standards?"

8   Save me! Scrap the images of planets! Bag the daisies! Nix the babies! Even the greenest consumers no longer buy products just to "save the planet." Today's consumers buy greener brands to help protect their health, save money, or because they simply work better. That's why products such as organics, natural personal care and pet care, and energy-efficient products are leading the way in sales.

9   Businesses are their philosophies. It used to be that companies were what they made. International Business Machines. General Foods. General Motors. Now, businesses and brands are what they stand for. Method. Starbucks. Timberland.

10   Sustainability represents an important consumer need, and is now an integral aspect of product quality. Green is no longer simply a market position. Products need to be green. Brands need to be socially responsible. Period.

11   The greenest products represent new concepts with business models with significantly less impact. If we simply keep greening up the same old "brown" products we've been using forever, we're never going to get to sustainability. With time running out, we've got to "leap" to service replacements for products, and adopt entirely new ways of doing business.

12   Consumers don't necessarily need to own products; services can meet their needs, perhaps even better. Consumers historically met their needs by owning products, but concepts like Zipcar and ebooks are starting to prove that utility and service are what really matters.

13   The brands consumers buy and trust today educate and engage them in meaningful conversation through a variety of media, especially via websites and online social networks. Talking "at" consumers through traditional media and paid advertising can't build loyalty among empowered consumers in a connected world.

14   Green consumers are strongly influenced by the recommendations of friends and family, and trusted third parties. With rampant cynicism about traditional forms of advertising and a backlash in place against perceived greenwashing, savvy marketers leverage purchase influencers and third parties like NGOs and especially eco-labelers.

15 Green consumers trust brands that tell all. BP, ExxonMobil, and SIGG learned this lesson the hard way. It's no longer enough to have a well-known name. Today's brands become trusted by practicing "radical transparency," disclosing the good – and the bad.

16 Green consumers don't expect perfection. Just like there's no more whitest whites, there's no greenest of the green. Consumers expect that you'll set high goals (i.e., perform beyond mere compliance), keep improving, and report on progress.

17 Environmentalists are no longer the enemy. Recognizing the power of the marketplace to effect change, many environmental advocates willingly partner with industry, offering useful guidance and expertise.

18 Nearly everyone is a corporate stakeholder. No longer confined to just customers, employees, and investors, publics of all stripes are now corporate stakeholders: environmentalists, educators, and children – even the unborn.

19 Authenticity. It's not enough to slap on a recycling logo or make a biodegradability claim. Brands viewed as the most genuine integrate relevant sustainability benefits into their products. That's why HSBC and Stonyfield Farm aim to reduce the carbon impacts of their operations.

20 Keep it simple. Plato was an environmentalist: "Simplicity is elegance." Today's consumers are cutting out the needless purchases, and getting rid of the gadgets and gizmos that don't add value to their lives. That's why they are migrating to brands that help express these values – Method, Starbucks, Timberland. It's just that simple.

785266 000297

Green is now mainstream

Back in the 1960s, trying to lead an environmentally conscious lifestyle, and especially integrating green into one's shopping, was a very fringe phenomenon. But it's now decidedly mainstream – and changing the rules of the marketing game in a very big way. Set in motion by Rachel Carson's seminal book *Silent Spring* (1962), the clichéd forerunners of today's green consumers lived off the nation's electric grid, installed solar-powered hot-water heaters on their roofs, crunched granola they baked themselves, and could be spotted wearing hemp clothing, Birkenstocks, and driving a Volkswagen bus. Whatever greener products were available – mostly from fringe businesses, and sometimes manufactured in basements and garages – gathered dust on the bottom shelves of health food stores for good reason: they didn't work, they were pricey, and they sported brand names no one had ever heard of. Not surprisingly, there was little demand for them. The natural laundry powders that were introduced in response to the phosphate scare of 1970 left clothes looking dingy, first-generation compact fluorescent light bulbs sputtered and cast a green haze, and multigrain cereals tasted like cardboard. If you were motivated to recycle, you lugged your bottles and daily newspapers to a drop-off spot inconveniently located on the far side of town. Green media was limited to treasured copies of *National Geographic*, PBS specials of Jacques Cousteau's underwater adventures, and the idealist and liberal *Mother Jones*, *Utne Reader*, and *New Age* magazines.

That was then. Times have changed – a lot, and with them the rules of green marketing. Today, mirroring their counterparts around the world, 83% of today's American adults can be considered at least some "shade" of green.[1] They enjoy a lifestyle where sustainable choices are highly accessible, attractive and expected. Thanks to advances in materials and technology, today's "greener" products (defined as having a lighter impact on the planet than alternatives) and today's more "sustainable" products (those that add a social dimension, e.g., fair trade) now not only work well, they likely work better and more efficiently than their "brown" counterparts.

Moreso, the channels of distribution have changed. Today, sustainable products are readily available in conventional supermarkets such as Fred Meyer and Safeway, brightly lit emporiums such as Trader Joe's and Whole Foods Market, and of course online. Once confined to rooftops, solar power is now mobile, fueling a modern-day, on-the-go lifestyle embedded in cell-phone chargers, backpacks, and even the latest fleet of powerboats. Once confined to the tissue boxes or wrappers of days gone by, recycled content is now good enough for Kimberly-Clark's own Scott Naturals line of tissue products and Staples' EcoEasy office paper, not to mention an exciting range of many other kinds of products from Patagonia's Synchilla PCR (post-consumer recycled) T-shirts made from recycled soda bottles, and even cosmetics packaging like that made from recycled newsprint which embellishes Aveda's Uruku brand, to name just a few.

The green market is not just here to stay, it will also grow and mature, evolving the rules of engagement even further. Knowing how best to cater to today's green consumers will bring significant opportunities to grow your top-line sales and revenue growth and increase your market share among the fast-growing numbers of green consumers, as well as to save money, enhance employee morale, and recruit and retain the brightest minds. As we'll discuss throughout this book, it will also stimulate game-changing innovation, and the ability to enhance your corporate reputation. Embrace sustainability – defined as acting today so that future generations can meet their needs – and enjoy long-term markets for your products, while safeguarding the sources of raw materials on which your very business depends.

Everyone is worried

Green has gone mainstream because more people are worried about sustainability-related issues than ever before. Reflecting awareness that has been steadily building over the past 20 years, the general public is beginning to comprehend the impact these issues will have on their lives now, and in the years ahead – and is starting to act.

Figure 1.1 **Top environmental issues of concern**

% U.S. adults indicating that the following issues concern them

	2009 %	2005–09 % change
Water quality	67	–1%
Hazardous, toxic, and nuclear waste	61	–6%
Pollution from cars and trucks	54	+2%
Water conservation	53	+10%
Deforestation	52	+8%
Global warming or climate change	50	+2%
Overpopulation	50	+28%
Reliance on fossil fuels	47	+18%
Lack of open space or urban sprawl	37	+42%

Source: © Natural Marketing Institute (NMI), 2009 LOHAS Consumer Trends Database®
All Rights Reserved

Historically, green marketers believed that people worried about the environment because they felt the planet was hurting – and their communications reflected as much. (Recall all the ads of days gone by featuring babies, daisies, and planets.) But today's marketers increasingly realize that consumers really fear the planet is losing its ability to sustain human life; they fret about their own immediate health, and that of their children. (Keep in mind that the planet will always be here!) That's why health-related issues such as water quality, hazardous waste and air pollution, water availability, global warming, and overpopulation top the list of environmental concerns consumers fear most (see Fig. 1.1).

This fear has been building for a long time. Toxic waste poisoning the water and community of Love Canal in New York State and the Cuyahoga River's catching fire in Cleveland, Ohio in 1972 put air and water quality at the top of Americans' worry list. Throw in the plight of the Mobro garbage barge that in 1987 searched in vain for a port, and packaging became a worry, too. The devastation wrought by Hurricane Katrina to New Orleans in the summer of 2005, Al Gore's 2006 Oscar-winning movie *An Inconvenient Truth*, and a steady stream of news reports that the Earth is warming and the ice caps are melting introduced the frightening prospect of climate change into living rooms. As I write, America deals with the aftermath of the BP oil spill in the Gulf of Mexico with projections of devastation worse than the *Exxon Valdez* oil spill of 1989.

Toxics – whether they are generated far away in industrial plants or reside in cleaning products tucked under the kitchen sink – are firmly planted on the list, too, fanned by a steady spate of scares over such chemicals as asbestos, PCBs and their dioxin and hormonal effects, perchloroethylene ("perc") used in dry cleaning, polyvinyl chloride (PVC), phthalates, the softening agent in plastic toys, and, most recently, bisphenol A (BPA), which was linked to fetal developmental problems, a discovery that led water bottles and baby products to be whisked from retailer shelves.

Limited supplies of natural resources and rapid population growth bring up the rear on the list of top scares. Save a watt! Save a tree! Save a drop! Consumers fret about dwindling resources of fossil fuels and increased dependence on foreign sources, depleting supplies of fresh water, and deforestation and, increasingly, its link to climate change. Gas prices in the U.S. spiked to over $4 a gallon during the summer of 2008 and many drivers fear such price increases may be just the beginning.

Every generation is green

One's behavior reflects one's values, and "sustainability" – caring for nature and the planet and the people who live here now and in the future – is now a core value of every living generation, starting with the Baby Boomers who led the green charge back in the mid to late 1960s. As important as Baby Boomers are to environmental activism as the nation's primary household shoppers and societal leaders, the potential impact to be made by the Internet-savvy Generations X, Y, and Z may be the most significant yet.

Baby Boomers: The first modern green generation

The heads of millions of U.S. households, the Baby Boomers, have long led the green movement through the values and attitudes they have instilled upon society and have imparted to their children and grandchildren. Born between 1946 and 1964, and ranging in age from 46 to 64 in 2010, the oldest Boomers, as college students and young adults, led the anti-Vietnam war, anti-big business, and pro-environment activist movements of the late 1960s and early 1970s. The brainchild of the then senator Gaylord Nelson, Earth Day was first celebrated by the Baby Boomers in 1970 followed by the first Solar Day in 1971. Their demonstrations of concern gave rise to the National Environmental Policy Act of 1969, the founding of the U.S. Environmental Protection Agency in 1970, the Clean Air and the Clean Water Acts that same year, and the Endangered Species Act of 1973.

Then came the Middle East oil embargo, marking the beginning of the energy crisis of 1973–75, which sharpened the Baby Boomers' focus on the need for smaller, more fuel-efficient cars and renewable forms of energy. In 1979 the release of the fictional *The China Syndrome*, a movie about safety cover-ups at a nuclear power plant, serendipitously opened two weeks prior to the partial core meltdown at the Three Mile Island nuclear-generating station near Harrisburg, Pennsylvania. Today, over half (54%) of Baby Boomers are considered to be "socially conscious shoppers."[2] That's 40 million green Boomers who choose organics, pluck resource-conserving products off the shelf, boycott the products of companies that pollute, and "pro-cott" the products of companies that give back to the community.

Generation X: Eyes on the world

Raised during the emergence of CNN which brought global issues into living rooms 24/7, Generation Xers (Gen Xers, also known as the Baby Bust generation) were born between 1964 and 1977 and are 33–46 years old as of 2010. Counting among them actors Leonardo DiCaprio and Cameron Diaz as two of the most outspoken environmentalists of their generation, Gen Xers see environmental concerns through a lens that aligns social, educational, and political issues.

In 1984, the Gen Xers witnessed the fire in a Union Carbide plant in Bhopal, India, which took over 3,000 lives and is thought to be still causing serious health problems today.[3] In 1985, the Live Aid concert organized by musicians Bob Geldof and Midge Ure broadcast the need for famine relief in a desperate Ethiopia to an unprecedented 400 million worldwide – and opened the eyes of millions of Gen Xers residing in developed nations to the horrors taking place in developing countries. In 1986, Gen Xers also experienced the aftermath of the explosion in the Chernobyl nuclear power plant. And in 1989, their same televisions showcased the devastation wrought by the *Exxon Valdez* oil spill in Prince William Sound, Alaska, and they were likely aware of events such as the Rio Summit of 1992.[4]

Generation Y: Digital media at their command

The likely new leaders of the modern-day green movement are the Generation Ys, born between the early 1980s and the early 1990s, and in 2010 ranging in age from 20 to 30 years old. This tech-savvy generation of Gen Ys (also known as Millennials) grew up with computers and the Internet. Distrustful of government and authority, they are quick to challenge marketing practices they deem to be unauthentic or untruthful. With the ability to express their opinions through blogging, texting, and social networks, they are capable of mustering immediate responses from millions around the globe. The offspring of the Baby Boomers whose social and environmental values they share, today's young adults lived through the Hurricane Katrina in 2005 and the BP Oil Spill in the Gulf of Mexico in 2010, and share awareness of the Great Pacific Garbage Patch, a mass of plastic trash whose exact size is estimated to be bigger than the state of Texas. Like their counterparts in other generations, Gen Ys believe that global climate change is caused by human activities and they are almost twice as likely to buy more green products than those consumers who think climate change is occurring naturally.[5]

Green is an integral part of this generation's college experience. Many schools have signed the American College & University President's Climate Commitment,[6] and legions of students are engaged in newly created environmental studies programs and in campus sustainability initiatives. Reusable water bottles and coffee mugs are ubiquitous on college campuses where many savvy companies are reaching out with sustainability messages to students who will soon become householders with significant incomes. Not content to sacrifice all for the almighty dollar, Gen Ys seek to balance "quality of life" and the "quest for wealth";[7] they seek to work for socially conscious employers.

Generation Z: Green is a natural part of their lives

Suggesting that green is here to stay are Generation Z; the first generation to be brought up in an environmentally conscious world, green is a part of their everyday life. Generation Zs, those currently under the age of 16, think nothing of living in solar-powered homes with a hybrid car in the driveway. Learning about environmental issues in school, they were likely exposed to *The Story of Stuff*, a 20-minute animated video that divulges the environmental impact of our daily consumption. For Gen Zs, sorting paper and plastic for recycling is as natural a daily activity as taking out the trash was for their parents. In school and at home the 3Rs of waste management, "reduce, reuse, and recycle," are as common as the 3Rs of "reading, writing, and 'rithmetic." Environmentally sensitive cleaning aids, locally grown produce, and recycled-paper goods top their parents' shopping lists. Clothes made from organically grown cotton and biobased fibers are part of the Gen Z uniform.

Green behavior: A daily phenomenon

With every generation now espousing sustainable values, environmentally considerate behavior is becoming the norm. As detailed in Figure 1.2, in 2009 nearly all (95%) of Americans are involved in various types of, albeit mostly easy, environmental activities they can do at home, from dropping empties in the recycling bin (recycling is now accessible to 87% of Americans),[8] to replacing an incandescent light bulb with a compact fluorescent lamp (CFL), or light-emitting diode (LED). (A scheduled phase-out of incandescent bulbs will begin in the U.S. in 2012.) They turn off the lights, nudge the thermometer down a degree or two, and turn off the tap when brushing their teeth.

Driven by higher gas prices and corporate carpooling programs, as of 2009, 23% of U.S. adults now claim to share rides to work (thanks in part to corporate rideshare programs), nearly one in four consumers takes the bus or subway, and 31% now claim to walk or ride a bike instead of driving a car. Thanks to new awareness of the harm caused by plastic shopping bags that choke marine life or wind up as litter, and incentivized by monetary rewards at the checkout, peer pressure, and even a desire to make a fashion statement), as of 2009, nearly half (48%) of U.S. adults claim to regularly take reusable shopping bags to the grocery store, up 30% from 2006. Importantly, almost half (46%) of consumers maintain that they regularly boycott a brand or company that has environmental or social practices they do not like, up

Figure 1.2 **Top consumer environmental behaviors**

% U.S. adult population indicating they regularly (daily/weekly/monthly) do the following:

	2009 %	2006–09 % change
Conserve energy by turning off lights	95	NC
Turn off electronics when not in use	90	–1%
Conserve water	85	+2%
Recycle all or most plastic bottles, jars, etc.*	65	+9%
Recycle all or most paper (e.g., newspapers)*	61	+3%
Take own bag to the grocery store	48	+30%
Boycott a brand or company that has practices I don't like	46	+17%
Walk or ride bike instead of driving a vehicle	31	+5%
Compost kitchen scraps and garden waste	27	+2%
Carpool	23	+8%
Take public transportation (e.g., bus, train, etc.)	17	+4%

* Change versus 2007. Recycling behavior measured in quantity not in frequency.

Source: © Natural Marketing Institute (NMI), 2009 LOHAS Consumer Trends Database®
All Rights Reserved

17% since 2006. Big-name companies have become easy targets for activist groups. Exxon, McDonald's, Coca-Cola, Wal-Mart, and Kimberly-Clark are just a few of the big brands that have all been castigated by Greenpeace and other activists for deficient environmental or social practices, including excess packaging, high sugar content, unfair labor practices, and unsustainable forestry operations. Once negative perceptions are created, they are almost impossible to reverse. Who still fails to link Nike to unfair labor practices or Exxon to the Alaskan oil spill?

Green voters and citizens

Concern over the state of the environment has swayed an unprecedented number of voters and has prompted citizens to volunteer in their communities. Broad swaths of citizens voted with the environment in mind when they supported Barack Obama in 2008 for taking even greener positions at the heart of his platform than had Al Gore. Support for such issues as mitigating global warming, curbing nuclear power, limiting offshore drilling, reducing ethanol production, and improving food and product safety have helped to propel green Congressional candidates in both the 2006 and 2008 elections.[9] To boot, since 2006, over 80% of candidates endorsed by the League of Conservation Voters have won seats in the House or Senate, while 43 out of 67 candidates identified as anti-environmental were defeated.[10]

Earth-shattering events that have occurred since the start of the new millennium such as the terrorist attack on 9/11, Hurricane Katrina, the wars in Iraq and Afghanistan, and the Indian Ocean tsunami have led to a sky-rocketing number of applications to service organizations such as Ameri-Corps and the Peace Corps – and the BP oil spill in the Gulf of Mexico now materializing will likely trigger a similar outpouring. Applications to Teach for America, an organization that serves neglected urban and rural areas, reached almost 19,000 in 2006, almost triple the number in 2000; in 2005 the Peace Corps added almost 8,000 volunteers (the largest group in 30 years), from 11,500 applications, up 20% over the year 2000; and AmeriCorps VISTA (Volunteers in Service to America) had a 50% increase in job applicants from 2004 to 2006.[11]

Shopping goes green

The rules are changing – and shopping lists along with them. An overwhelming majority (84%) of shoppers are now buying some green products from time to time, fueling mass markets for clothing made from organically grown fibers; organically produced foods; cold-water and ultra-concentrated detergents; natural cleaning, personal-care, and pet-care products; air- and water-filtration devices; low-VOC (volatile organic compounds) paints; portable bottled water containers; and biological pesticides and fertilizers. Thanks to a massive campaign from Wal-Mart during 2007 and intensive promotion by local utilities, purchases of CFLs top the list, followed by energy-efficient electronics and appliances, and natural/organic foods and cleaning products.

As of 2008, U.S. consumers invested an estimated $290 billion in a wide range of products and services representing such sectors as organic foods,

Figure 1.3 **Green purchasing behavior**

% U.S. adult population indicating they have purchased products within the last 3 years,[1] 12 months,[2] 6 months,[3] 3 months,[4] and those that own/lease a hybrid vehicle.[5]

	General population %
Any	84
CFLs[2]	51
Energy-efficient electronics and appliances[1]	34
Rechargeable batteries[3]	33
Natural foods/beverages[4]	29
Organic foods/beverages[4]	26
Natural/organic personal care[3]	25
Natural household cleaning products[2]	21
Natural/organic pet food[2]	19
Home water purifiers[1]	18
Low-flow toilets[1]	16
Energy-efficient windows[1]	15
Non-toxic or low fume paint[1]	12
Solar-powered lights[1]	11
Clothing made from organic cotton[3]	10
Eco-friendly lawn and garden[2]	9
Hybrid vehicle[5]	3
Furniture made with sustainable materials[1]	2
Environmentally friendly carpet[1]	2
Solar panels for my house[1]	1

Source: © Natural Marketing Institute (NMI), 2009 LOHAS Consumer Trends Database®
All Rights Reserved

natural personal care, ENERGY STAR-labeled appliances, hybrid cars, eco-tourism, green home furnishings and apparel, and renewable power, up from $219 billion in 2005.[12] This market will only magnify over time, reflecting further advancements in design and technology and an ever-expanding range of high-quality green products with trusted brand names that are readily accessible at mass merchandisers and supermarkets.

Interest in green shopping holds steady, even in a recession; indeed, some recession-driven behaviors are making green downright fashionable: 67% of Americans agree that "even in tough economic times, it is important to purchase products with social and environmental benefits."[13] It's one thing to express interest verbally, and another to demonstrate interest with one's credit card. While all shopping, including green, has been hit hard by the recession, many classes of green products have fared remarkably well, thanks in part to the health and cost-saving benefits that they bestow. For instance, according to the Organic Trade Association, in 2008 organic food sales grew by 15.8% to reach $22.9 billion (accounting for 3.5% of all food products sales in the U.S., up from 2.8% in 2006). Sales of organic non-foods (organic fibers, personal-care products, and pet foods) grew by 39.4% to $1.6 billion.[14] Burt's Bees, the line of natural cosmetics now owned by Clorox, continued to rack up annual sales of $200 million despite recessionary times.[15] During its 2008 market debut, Clorox's Green Works line of natural cleaning products grabbed $123 million in sales, representing a leading share of this burgeoning market, while Seventh Generation's sales of household products grew by more than 20% in 2009 over the previous year to $150 million – and will only multiply with distribution in Wal-Mart, announced in the summer of 2010. Toyota's fuel-efficient Prius sold at a brisk 140,000 vehicles in the U.S. in 2009, while Honda, who make a fuel cell vehicle and a natural gas Civic, reintroduced the Insight during fall 2009 with the goal of selling 500,000 units worldwide by early next decade.[16] And in 2008, General Electric saw a 21% gain in revenue for its portfolio of environmentally sustainable consumer and industrial products, to $17 billion.

Sensing the opportunities are now ripe for picking (and likely fearing that greener competitors will steal their lunch), mainstream consumer-products giants are introducing new green brands. They are skewing advertising dollars, beefing up their websites and quickly getting up to speed on the latest social media networks to educate their own eco-aware consumers about the environmental benefits of their products. Some notable examples include: Kimberly-Clark's Scott Naturals (household paper products made from recycled material), Reynolds Wrap foil made from 100% recycled aluminum, and Church & Dwight's Arm & Hammer Essentials laundry products. Having spent the past 20 years addressing consumer concerns mostly via reduced packaging, the mighty Procter & Gamble (P&G) have themselves started to play by the new green rules. They have pledged to develop and market by 2012 at least $20 billion in cumulative sales of "sustainable inno-vation products," which they define as "products with a significantly reduced environmental footprint versus previous alternative products."[17] Toward that end, in spring 2010, they inaugurated in the U.S. a multi-brand, multi-platform green campaign dubbed "Future Friendly." Its goal is to place their greenest offerings in 50 million U.S. homes by year-end. The effort, started in the UK and Canada in 2007, will be bolstered by educational messages con-ducted with conservation groups and will feature P&G brands such as Dura-cell Rechargeable batteries, Tide HE (high-efficiency) laundry powder and Tide Coldwater, and PUR water filtration products.[18] As the manufacturer of several billion-dollar brands, P&G's campaign builds on research showing that consumers are looking to understand how the brands they already know and trust can help them reduce their impact on the environment.

Another sign that the rules are rapidly changing: well-established mass marketers are also now acquiring leading sustainable brands with the adjudged potential for mass-market expansion. Just a few examples include The Body Shop (acquired by L'Oréal), Stonyfield Farm (now 40% owned by Danone), Tom's of Maine natural personal-care products (Colgate-Palmolive), Aveda cosmetics (Estée Lauder), Green & Black's organic chocolates (Cad-bury, now part of Kraft), Ben & Jerry's ice cream (Unilever), Cascadian Farm cereals (General Mills) and Burt's Bees personal-care line and Brita water fil-ters (Clorox).

Expect more supermarket shelves to be lined with green choices in the future. In 2007, the U.S. Patent and Trademark Office saw more than 300,000 applications for green-related brand names, logos, and tag lines. According to Datamonitor, as of April 2009, there were more than 450 sustainable prod-uct launches for the year, on track to represent triple the number of launches in 2008, which was in itself more than double those in 2007.[19] Retailers are demanding greener alternatives from their suppliers and are giving greener products preferential shelf treatment. Leading the charge is the Sustainability Consortium Wal-Mart announced during the summer of 2009, and formed in conjunction with the University of Arkansas and Arizona State University. The Consortium is tasked to understand the best way to label products with life-cycle-based data to inform consumer purchase decisions – no doubt raising the green bar for the products they stock in the future.

Finally, over $4 billion in venture capital – more than ever before – is being invested in the cleantech industry to support the development of solar and wind, biofuel, geothermal, and other renewable alternatives to fossil fuels.[20] More money is being invested in renewable energy than for conventional power, and cleantech is now the largest U.S. venture capital category, representing 27% of all venture funds.

Media turns green

Green stories now run in all sections of the *New York Times* and the *Washington Post* and other major dailies each day, and are featured on the covers of *Vanity Fair*, *Newsweek*, *Wired*, and the *Sunday New York Times Magazine*, among many others. Big-budget ad campaigns such as those for Apple's "Greenest Laptops," Kashi cereals' "Seven Whole Grains on a Mission," and Scott Naturals' "Green Done Right" run on primetime television. Discovery Channel, Planet Green, Sundance, and other eco-cable channels target the sustainability-aware viewer. At NBC, attention is paid to green via the special programming and "Green is Universal" campaign. With nearly five million subscribers, *Good Housekeeping* magazine has even introduced its own green seal accompaniment to its venerable Good Housekeeping seal. Such organizations are not only committed to addressing the green interests of their viewers and readers, they are greening themselves, some through the Open Media and Information Companies (Open MIC) initiative dedicated to making corporate management practices of the media industry more transparent and responsible.[21]

Many of the uncountable daily messages and images that fan the mainstream consumer's green lifestyle are supported behind the scenes by the Environmental Media Association (EMA), a Hollywood-based nonprofit group with the goal of securing primetime television and movie exposure for the environment. Helping EMA to paint green as cool, accessible, and something people want to emulate, are many Hollywood celebrities including Bette Midler, Brad Pitt, Julia Louis Dreyfus, Cameron Diaz, Leonardo DiCaprio, and the father of Hollywood green, Ed Begley Jr., who among other celebrities walked the green carpet from his Toyota Prius into the Academy Awards in 2006.

Meanwhile the Internet is fast changing the media landscape, becoming the interactive medium for information-seeking aware consumers. Websites such as Discovery's treehugger.com and greenamerica.org empower visitors with the latest new green products and green living tips. Do an Internet search of the words, "green," "environment," or "eco" and you will find that entire communities of tweeters and bloggers are passing along trusted recommendations about which products to buy and which companies to trust. Is your sustainable brand part of this digital conversation? (See the Further Information section on page 199 for the names of more consumer-focused websites and media.) Finally, according to J.D. Power & Associates, conversations on sustainability-related blog posts and discussion boards more than doubled between January 2007 and December 2008. By the end of 2008, more than 70% of online contributors indicated that they were concerned about the environment and nearly half reported that they were actively doing something about it: e.g., driving less, recycling – and buying green products.[22]

Governments take action

Any politician who believes that green is inconsistent with a robust economy may soon be unelectable. In stark contrast to the Bush administration, which failed to lead on global climate change and many other key environmental matters, the Obama administration is fast changing the green rules by making green jobs, green energy, and green infrastructure a focal point of its national agenda. Among its first out-of-the-box initiatives: the 2009 Economic Stimulus Package, which included more than $30 billion in funding focused on energy efficiency grants for state and local budgets, weatherization for low-income housing, retrofitting and modernization of federal buildings, investments in the "smart grid" for electrical power, and "clean coal" carbon capture and sequestration projects. The highly successful Cash for Clunkers program launched in July 2009 aimed to take inefficient, high-emission cars off the road and to stimulate the struggling automobile industry through the purchase of newer, more fuel-efficient cars. A special White House office for green jobs spearheads a national initiative that actively works to educate, train, and prepare a labor force prepared for tomorrow's green technologies.

Although mostly symbolic in nature, it is still telling that in one of her first acts as First Lady, Michelle Obama planted a "slow food" garden at the White House to help educate Americans about the benefits of healthy, locally grown fruits and vegetables.

In response to Americans' sustainability concerns, leaders at the municipal, state, and federal levels are creating more sustainable cities and towns characterized by more green spaces for city dwellers and reduced inner-city congestion (e.g., closing Broadway to traffic in New York City); bike paths and hiking trails built over old railroad tracks (including New York City's new High Line); mandated hybrid taxis and natural gas "clean air" buses; composting by residents (in San Francisco among others); and giving a boost to farmers' markets and community-supported agriculture.

With a history of internal mandates on green purchasing, governments at all levels are now taking steps to skew the mammoth consumer economy toward a greener shade by creating (or promoting more established) eco-labels that favor energy-efficient (ENERGY STAR), organic (USDA [U.S. Department of Agriculture] Organic), and water-efficient (WaterSense) goods; and as of this writing, the USDA is readying a voluntary consumer label to accompany its BioPreferred program for federal purchasing of biobased products. If California's Senator Dianne Feinstein has her way, the U.S. will one day soon have a multi-attribute eco-label resembling Europe's Eco Flower, Japan's EcoMark, and Brazil's "Qualidade Ambiental."

The specter of rising sea levels is fast changing the rules in the many cities that have banned bottled water (whose transportation-related fuel use is now linked to global warming), from government meetings or are incentivizing the construction or upgrade of green buildings and the products (office equipment, carpeting, etc.) that furnish them. With an eye toward reducing greenhouse gas emissions linked to energy generation, many government buildings must now be benchmarked according to the EPA's ENERGY STAR building guidelines or meet the U.S. Green Building Council's Leadership in Energy and Environmental Design (LEED) certification.

Far-reaching business opportunities

Consumer demand for greener products and services creates opportunities for businesses to promote their greener offerings, and introduce profitable new ones, all the while building their top-line sales, enhancing their image, and bolstering the morale of employees newly engaged in a higher purpose.

Higher profits

Polls indicate that consumers are willing to pay a premium for green. However, empirical evidence is demanded by skeptical businesspeople to justify the investments in new technology, special materials or ingredients, and high start-up costs of introducing new greener products. A key new rule of green marketing: people will now pay a premium for such brands as Aveda, Burt's Bees, Method, Stonyfield Farm, and Toyota Prius, all discussed in this book, indicating that today's consumers have higher expectations for the products they buy and that environmental soundness is a new dimension of quality. To the extent that businesses can meet or exceed these new consumer expectations, they will enhance their products' image and ability to command a premium.

According to the old rules, consumers didn't expect ecologically preferable products to work well. However, as will be demonstrated throughout this book, and specifically in Chapter 4, thanks to advances in technology, today's greener products work far better than their predecessors that languished on health food retailer shelves; by definition, the current crop of greener products are perceived as healthier, less toxic, and capable of saving time and money, as well as contributing to a sustainable future. Just a few examples: faucet aerators and water-saving showerheads help slash water and energy bills, concentrated laundry detergents can be carried and stored with greater ease, and non-toxic cleaning products, pest control, and garden products are viewed as safer for children and pets.

Some greener products appeal to consumers for many reasons, suggesting the potential to win over more than one segment of the now enormous

Figure 1.4 **Green products offer mainstream benefits**

Product category	Consumer benefits
CFL lightbulbs	Save money, last longer
Hybrid cars	Quiet ride, fewer fill-ups, status
Natural cleaners	Safety, peace of mind
Organic produce	Safety, better taste
Recycled paper	Save money
Car sharing	Convenience, save money
Solar-powered cellphones	Extended use

Chart: J. Ottman Consulting, Inc.

market for green. Own a hybrid? You might because it's more fuel-efficient, but chances are you want to eventually save money (beyond the purchase premium) or to make fewer trips to the filling station. You may also want to drive in the HOV (High Occupancy Vehicle) or just to look good while tooling around town. And so it goes with so many other greener products, as demonstrated in Figure 1.4.

Expect the genuine value-added benefits of superior performance, convenience, cost savings, and increased health and safety to continue to propel the mass market for eco-inspired products in the years and decades ahead.

New source of innovation

Historically, going green helped to unearth efficiencies that beefed up a company's bottom line. Under the new rules, businesses are discovering the even more attractive eco-opportunity for innovation that boosts top-line revenues. That's because green means doing things differently. As will be demonstrated in Chapter 5, proactive companies are inventing new greener technologies, new business models, and new designs that are capturing media attention, grabbing new customers, and establishing a competitive advantage – if not changing the rules of the game altogether. Examples abound. Zipcar, the new time-sharing scheme for cars, is changing the models for vehicle ownership, leasing, and rental. Toyota's Prius has reawakened a truck- and SUV-focused Detroit to the future-saving possibilities of hybrid-engine vehicles, and a new generation of electric cars and fuel cells is right on Toyota's tail. Cargill's NatureWorks is proving that plastics don't have to rely on fossil fuels and can be recyclable and compostable as well. And "smart grid" technology, coupled with in-home energy meters and web-based monitoring systems, is creating exciting new business opportunities springing from increased consumer awareness about the ability to save money through efficient resource management.

The time for marketers to act is now

The condition of the environment is expected to worsen in the years and decades ahead. Despite conflicting reports and opinions, most scientists still predict that the average temperature will rise between 1.8 and 4.0 degrees Celsius during the 21st century due solely to the burning of fossil fuels.[23] By 2030, climate-change-induced calamities alone are projected to account for 500,000 deaths and $340 billion in damages, up from 315,000 and $125 billion today.[24] The fast-developing BRIC economies of Brazil, Russia, India, and China now attempt to meet their own escalating resource demands and will no doubt put further pressure on commodities. Over the past 50 years, fresh water consumption around the world has tripled;[25] it is projected that, by 2025, two-thirds of the world's people will not have access to potable water.[26]

Green touches the lives of all people around the globe. Businesses cater to myriad stakeholders, including customers, investors, and employees; so industry leaders that are sensitized to the new rules are greening up their products and processes. They know that projecting a company's image as a leader and an innovator, as well as being socially and environmentally aware, can only be positive. Influential customers want to do business with companies that have established their green credentials, so companies are launching hefty advertising and web campaigns, publishing extensively documented sustainability reports, cooperating with external sources to communicate transparently, and communicating their efforts internally.

Pick up any copy of *Fortune* or *BusinessWeek* or tune into a TV news program and you will likely see advertisements for multinational companies that are spending millions to project their commitment to sustainability and to create awareness for exciting new products and technologies: Dow Chemical's The Human Element campaign portrays its ability to address pressing global economic, social, and environmental concerns. Chevron's Human Energy campaign advocates for energy efficiency. General Electric's Ecomagination campaign underscores its commitment to solve pressing environmental problems while driving profitable growth through the development of more efficient jet engines, wind turbines, major appliances, and other technologies. Underscoring social benefits, SC Johnson takes great pains to let you know it is A Family Company while Toyota communicates its interest in enriching the community and being a good neighbor via its campaign We See Beyond Cars. Although some campaigns may be questionable (should General Electric be advocating "clean coal" technology? And few would argue now that BP's Beyond Petroleum campaign was markedly premature in light of the Gulf Oil spill and other recent environmental transgressions), the fact remains that companies now recognize opportunities and are attempting to seize them.

Communicating a company's embrace of sustainability can enhance corporate equity since investors seek to reduce risk and many "socially responsible" investors want to align their values with their savings. Recognizing the opportunity, more and more companies are communicating their green mission and progress. For example, according to a study conducted by SIRAN, a working group of the Social Investment Forum, as of 2007, 49 of the Standard & Poor's 100 issued sustainability reports, up 26% from 2005; and by 2008, 86 out of 100 had special websites detailing their efforts to address the triple bottom line – social, environmental, and economic – of sustainability, compared to 58 in 2005.[27] These reports often detail progress related to sustainability performance aligned with standards produced by the Global Reporting Initiative, along with glowing mentions of coveted green awards – credible third-party demonstrations of environmental and sustainable excellence. For instance, a list of winners of the World Environment Center's annual Gold Medal Award reads like a Who's Who of Corporate America: the Coca-Cola Company, Starbucks Coffee Company, S.C. Johnson & Son Inc., the Procter & Gamble Company, and IBM number among their ranks. Dozens of companies representing over 50 product categories have cherished their nod as U.S. EPA's "ENERGY STAR Partner of the Year," indicating their willingness to work positively with government to foster energy efficiency. Some companies, like our client Bissell ("Get a Little Greener" site), Patagonia ("ecofootprint" site), and IKEA Canada ("The IKEA Way"), have special websites with detailed information for consumers.[28]

On the product front, the Industrial Designers Society of America (IDSA) bestows special Industrial Design Excellence Award (IDEA) prizes that have been won by Nike, Timberland, Herman Miller, and many other leaders for eco-innovative product designs. Some examples are listed in Figure 1.5.

Figure 1.5 **IDEA award winners for design excellence**

Company	Product
Dell	Studio hybrid eco-conscious PC
Herman Miller	Leaf Lamp energy-efficient LED light
Nike	Trash Talk recycled shoe
Tesla	Roadster electric car
Timberland	Mion footwear
Tricycle	SIM carpet sample simulator

Chart: J. Ottman Consulting, Inc.

Finally, special green "Effies" – the advertising industry's Oscar equivalent for campaign effectiveness – have been awarded to General Electric (GE) ("Ecomagination"), our client HSBC ("There's No Small Change"), Wal-Mart ("Personal Sustainability Project"), and Frito-Lay's SunChips ("Compostable Bag").

Personal rewards, too

The rules are also changing as to what constitutes personal satisfaction at work. With customers and stakeholders of all stripes, from employees and plant neighbors to legislators and NGOs, clamoring for businesses to embrace sustainability in their products and their processes, smart CEOs know that sustainability offers a rare opportunity to integrate one's own values and vision into the workplace – and, as demonstrated by the ardor of the Gen Ys for work that balances making a living with making a difference, this is becoming essential in recruiting future generations of capable employees. Sustainable branding helps take that vision to one's customers through the prism of products that are more in sync with nature and via communications that are more in tune with consumers' own evolving values – all the while affording the unique opportunity to personally contribute to a brighter future for our children and grandchildren and sustain human life on the planet for generations to come.

Grasping the new rules of green marketing starts with an in-depth understanding of how today's mainstream green consumers differ markedly from yesterday's fringe activists in attitudes, behaviors, lifestyle, and corporate expectations. Let's start by discussing the full range of issues that concern today's consumers, their green purchasing motivations and behavior, and how this total broad swatch of consumers can be segmented for green marketing purposes – the subjects of the next chapter.

The *New Rules* Checklist

Use the following checklist to test your understanding of the mainstreaming of green and the need for your business to respond now.

- Is there an awareness within our company of the true extent of environmentalism within society today?

- What are the top environmental issues of concern to our consumers? Shareholders? Employees? Suppliers? Retailers? Community?

- What is our top environmental risk? Is there a PVC, BPA, or other chemical scare lurking in our brand's future?

- What are the natural resources that our brands depend on – and what are the long-term projections for their availability?

- To which generations do our consumers belong and what are the unique ways in which they express their environmental and social concerns?

- To what extent do environmental issues affect the way consumers engage with our brand and the products in our category in general?

- To what extent are our consumers politically and socially active about environmental issues?

- How has environmentalism affected the shopping habits of our consumers? What types of greener products and services are our consumers buying these days?

- What are our competitors' key sustainability-oriented initiatives? To what extent are they introducing or possibly acquiring new sustainable brands?

- What are the key sources of sustainability-related information on which our consumers rely?

- Which environment-oriented legislators and legislative initiatives affect our business?

- What opportunities do we have to grow our sales and enhance our image through greener products and green marketing campaigns?

- What personal rewards in going green might be meaningful in enlisting the support of colleagues and stakeholders in our company's sustainability efforts?

We are all green consumers

Since it was first ignited during the 1970s, the green consumer revolution has been led by women aged between 30 and 49 with children and with better-than-average education. They are motivated by a desire to keep their loved ones free from harm and to secure their future. That women have historically been in the forefront of green purchasing cannot be underestimated. They still do most of the shopping and make most of the brand purchasing decisions (albeit aided by tiny eco-cops riding in the front seat of shopping carts), and they naturally exhibit a nurturing instinct for the health and welfare of the next generation. Poll after poll shows that women weigh environmental and social criteria more heavily in their purchasing decisions than do men. This may also reflect the fact that men in general feel less vulnerable and more in control than women, and thus feel relatively less threatened by news of environmental gloom and doom.

However, with the mainstreaming of green, we are *all* green consumers now. Yesterday's activist moms have been joined by teen daughters searching out Burt's Bees lip balm made from beeswax while their "twenty-something" nephews opt to clean their new digs with Method cleaning products. Husbands boast of higher mileage, fewer fill-ups, and the peppy look of their new Mini Coopers or diesel-powered Jettas that get 50-plus miles to the gallon. The incidence of green purchasing is so prevalent throughout the U.S. population (and I would venture to guess the populations of all countries where greening is prevalent), that consumers need to be segmented psychographically, i.e., by lifestyle orientation and commitment to green, in order to zero in on one's most appropriate target customers. One such segmentation is provided by the Natural Marketing Institute (NMI) of Harleysville, Pennsylvania. Their research, based on interviews with over 4,000 U.S. adults and entitled *The LOHAS Report: Consumers and Sustainability*, is excerpted below.

Five shades of green consumers

According to the NMI, the vast majority of today's consumers – a whopping 83% of the U.S. population – can be classified as some shade of green, signifying their involvement in green values, activities, and purchasing. The balance, an estimated 17%, however unconcerned they may be about the planet, can be viewed as inadvertent greens if only because they must abide

Figure 2.1 **NMI's 2009 green consumer segmentation model**
% U.S. adults

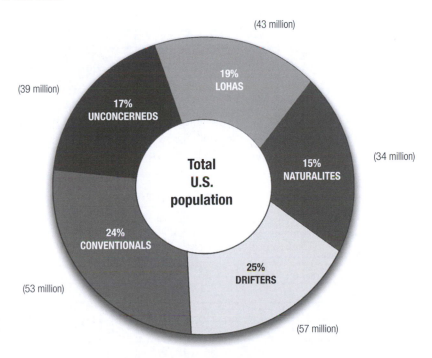

Figure 2.2 Demographic composition of five NMI consumer segments

Capital letters indicate significant difference between groups at 95%.
Percentages rounded.

	Total U.S. adults %	LOHAS (A) %	Naturalites (B) %	Drifters (C) %	Conventionals (D) %	Unconcerneds (E) %
Gender						
Male	48	39	40	49^{AB}	57^{ABC}	54^{AB}
Female	52	61^{CDE}	60^{CDE}	51^{D}	43	46
Age						
Mean (years)	47.3	48.6^{CE}	46.6	46.3	49.1^{BCE}	45.5
Generation						
Gen Y	24	21	27^{AD}	26^{AD}	19	30^{AD}
Gen X	20	19	19	22	22	18
Booomers	37	40^{C}	36	33	39	36
Seniors	19	19	18	19	21	17
Race						
White	78	80^{B}	72	77	82^{BC}	80^{B}
African-American	11	8	23^{ACDE}	10	7	11^{D}
Asian	2	2	1	4^{ABDE}	2	2
Latino	4	4^{B}	1	4^{B}	4^{B}	3
Employment status						
Employed	51	54^{B}	45	51	52^{B}	51
Retired	23	20	24	23	25^{AE}	20
Children in the household						
Children under 18	28	23	31^{AE}	33^{ADE}	26	25
Age 0–4	10	7	11^{A}	13^{AD}	8	9
Age 5–12	15	13	19^{ADE}	16	14	14
Age 12–17	12	10	13	14^{AE}	12	9
Education						
High School or less	44	33	53^{AD}	47^{AD}	39^{A}	50^{AD}
Less than College Grad	29	33^{C}	27	26	29	28
College and Post Grad	28	34^{BCE}	20	27^{BE}	32^{BCE}	21
Annual household income						
Median (US$000)	$59.6	$68.6	$43.3	$60.5	$69.4	$50.8
Geography						
Northeast	21	27	13	25	25	10
Midwest	22	21	23	20	23	27
South	33	29	48	27	26	45
West	23	24	16	28	26	19

Source: © Natural Marketing Institute (NMI), 2009 LOHAS Consumer Trends Database®
All Rights Reserved

by local laws requiring green behavior – and the consuming that goes with it, such as recycling. Led by the LOHAS (Lifestyles of Health and Sustainability)[1] segment (the deep greens), the NMI's segmentation of U.S. adult consumers into five distinct and mutually exclusive groups makes targeted marketing of mainstream consumers possible (see Fig. 2.1).

LOHAS

As their name suggests, the LOHAS (Lifestyles of Health and Sustainability) segment represents the most environmentally conscious, holistically oriented, and active of all consumers. Representing 19% of all U.S. adults or 43 million people in 2009, they see a universal connection between health and global preservation and use products that support both personal and planetary well-being. The segment that historically has held the most cachet for sustainable marketers, the typical LOHAS consumer, as depicted in Figure 2.2, tends to be a married, educated, middle-aged female. With the second highest income of all five segments, these consumers tend to be less sensitive to price than the other segments, and particularly so for greener products.

Active at home and in their communities, they readily pluck environmentally sustainable products off the shelf, support advocacy programs for a variety of eco and social causes, and are conscious stewards of the environment. They lead the pack in such behaviors as energy and water conservation, toting cloth shopping bags, and lobbying elected officials to pass environmentally protective laws (see Fig. 2.3). A great consumer for any marketer to snag, they are early adopters of greener technologies. Nearly twice as likely to associate their own personal values with companies and their brands, they are more loyal to companies that mirror their values than their counterparts in other segments. Influential in their communities, they recommend greener brands to friends and family.

Representing a change in the rules for their own purchasing, LOHAS consumers energetically seek out information to ensure the products they purchase synchronize with their discerning environmental and social standards. They scrutinize food and beverage labels, opt for foods with minimal processing, and consume more organically grown produce than any other segment. They also study up on corporate sustainability policies; an astonishing 71% will boycott a brand or company that has practices they do not like, almost twice as high as that of their cousins in other segments. Distrustful of paid media, they will consult the Internet and social among other sources of information. According to the NMI, 14% of the LOHAS segment reports that they purchase hard-to-find greener products online.

Naturalites

About one in six U.S. adults, or 34 million consumers, falls into the Naturalites segment. Assuming a very personal approach to the environment, Naturalites aim to achieve a healthy lifestyle and believe in mind–body–spirit philosophies in addition to the power of prayer. Motivated by buzzwords such as "antibacterial," "free of synthetic chemicals," and "natural," Naturalites are concerned about the harmful effects of chemicals in such products as paint, cosmetics, and food. They are quick to select what they perceive to be safer alternatives for themselves and their children. They are also more likely than any of the other segments (aside from LOHAS) to find it important for their stores to carry organic food, with 19% purchasing natural cleaning products in the past year.

Naturalites see themselves as committed to sustainability, but in reality, they are not as dedicated to green purchasing or behaviors including even recycling as their LOHAS or even Drifter cousins. Nevertheless, Naturalites do want to learn more and become more active in environmental protection and are receptive to education in this regard, especially when there is a personal connection to their health. Demographically, Naturalites are the least likely to be college-educated, and have the lowest incomes. Half of Naturalites live in the South (where recycling is not as prevalent as in other areas) and are much more likely to be African-American.

Drifters

Driven by trends more than by deeply held beliefs, Drifters are the second largest segment of the population, representing 25% of all U.S. adults or 57 million consumers. Younger and concentrated in coastal cities, unlike their LOHAS counterparts they have not yet integrated their values and ethics with their lifestyles. With green considered to be "in," catch Drifters making the scene at a Whole Foods lunch bar with a trendy cloth sack in hand, or driving a hybrid not to save money on gas, but for how they will look driving about town. They will boycott companies with questionable environmental reputations, but yield to information culled from the media rather than through their own research. Eager to pitch in on simple green activities they understand – they are avid recyclers and energy conservers – they are less apt than their LOHAS counterparts to engage in more nuanced eco-behaviors such as taking steps to reduce carbon emissions.

Demographically, Drifters tend to have larger household sizes with a third having children under the age of 18. Because Drifters are somewhat conscious of the effects that their actions have on the environment, and earn

Figure 2.3 **Consumer behavior by NMI segment**

% of each segment that regularly (daily/wekly/monthly) does the following:

Activity on a regular (daily/wekly/monthly) basis	LOHAS %	Naturalites %	Drifters %	Conventionals %	Unconcerneds %
Conserve energy by turning off the lights	99	94	95	96	92
Turn off electronics when not in use	96	88	90	90	84
Make extra efforts to reduce heating and cooling costs	95	85	85	89	74
Control thermostat to conserve energy	93	83	85	86	77
Conserve water	96	81	88	86	68
Recycle all/most newspapers	87	29	78	79	24
Slow down when I drive to save gas	79	67	67	66	47
Turn off my car when it's idle to save gas	74	66	64	61	50
Take my own bag to the grocery store or other stores I shop frequently	71	38	50	50	26
Boycott a brand or company that has practices I don't like	71	44	45	40	29
Walk or ride my bike instead of driving a vehicle	43	26	34	31	19
Encourage my elected officials to pass laws to protect the environment	43	23	19	17	8
Compost kitchen scraps and garden waste	41	21	30	28	12
Carpool	31	19	26	23	15
Take public transportation (bus, train, etc.)	21	15	19	16	10

a moderate income, they represent an attractive segment for green market-ers. According to NMI, nearly one-fifth think it's too difficult to consider the environmental impacts of their actions and nearly one-half of Drifters wish they did more to advance sustainability. Marketers who are able to commu-nicate the camaraderie and a sense of belonging that a green lifestyle brings to Drifters will enjoy exceptional returns.

Conventionals

Picture a practical dad directing his kids to pull on a sweater instead of turn-ing up the heat and constantly badgering them to turn off the lights and you get a feel for the Conventionals, the second largest segment represent-ing 53 million consumers who are driven to green for practical reasons. For instance, if LOHAS consumers spend the green for the sake of green, Con-ventionals will spend more for an ENERGY STAR-labeled fridge knowing it will slash their utility bills.

Characterized by good old Yankee ingenuity or midwestern values, Con-ventionals are adept at recycling, and they reuse and repurpose things in an effort to reduce waste and pinch pennies. They are aware of environmental issues but are not as motivated to purchase organic foods or other health-re-lated products as their LOHAS cousins for health or environmental reasons. Likely to be males in their mid-to-late forties with the highest incomes of all the segments, 25% of Conventionals are retired, more than other segments, and a sensible group: 45% of them always pay the entire balance on their credit cards every month.

Unconcerneds

In contrast to their LOHAS, Drifter, and Conventional counterparts, 17% of the population representing 39 million consumers, called the Uncon-cerneds, demonstrate the least environmental responsibility of all the seg-ments. Just over one-quarter will boycott brands made by manufacturers they do not approve of, versus upwards of 40% for their counterparts in other segments; and while 61% say they care about protecting the environ-ment, only 24% recycle. Demographically, the Unconcerneds skew towards younger males living in the South with slightly below-average incomes and lower education levels.

Segmenting by green interests

The rules for addressing the fears of green consumers just got tougher and more complicated. Whereas their counterparts in an earlier day fretted over a rather short list of eco issues topped by clean air and water, recycling, and conserving energy, today's green consumers fear a much wider range of environmental, social, and economically related ills that include carbon emissions and global climate change, fair trade, and labor rights. No one, of course, has the mental and psychological bandwidth, time, or resources to act on all of these issues. So, even the most eco-aware consumers tend to prioritize their environmental concerns, making it necessary to further divide green consumers into four sub-segments characterized by specific issues and causes: resources, health, animals, and the great outdoors. My colleagues and I at J. Ottman Consulting derived the segmentation depicted

Figure 2.4 **Segmenting by green interests**

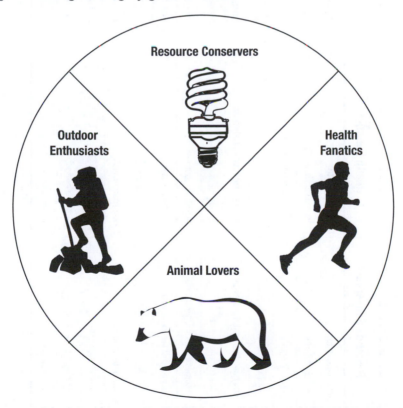

Figure 2.5 **Segmenting by green interests: in depth**

Resource Conservers	Health Fanatics	Animal Lovers	Outdoor Enthusiasts
Likely belong to:	**Likely belong to:**	**Likely belong to:**	**Likely belong to:**
American Rivers	Beyond Pesticides	Wildlife Conservation Society	Sierra Club
Green America	Organic Consumers Association	Defenders of Wildlife	Surfrider Foundation
Center for the New American Dream	Slow Food	People for the Ethical Treatment of Animals (PETA)	American Hiking Society
Likely environmental behavior:	**Likely environmental behavior:**	**Likely environmental behavior:**	**Likely environmental behavior:**
Conserve energy, water	Buy organic foods	Vegetarian/vegan	Use durable, reusable bottles and bags
Recycle bottles, cans, newspapers	Buy natural cosmetics	Boycott tuna, ivory	Avoid excessive packaging
Buy compact fluorescent bulbs	Buy natural cleaning aids	Boycott products tested on animals	Buy natural/biodegradable products for easy camping/hiking clean up
Use reusable shopping bags	Use sunscreens	Avoid fur	Purchase outdoor gear and clothing made with recycled materials
Likely read or visit:	**Likely read or visit:**	**Likely read or visit:**	**Likely read or visit:**
www.treehugger.com	HealthyStuff.org	*Animal Fair Magazine*	*Sierra magazine*
www.greenerchoices.org	*Natural Life magazine*	*Veg News Magazine*	*Backpackers Magazine*
www.earth911.com	*Natural Awakenings magazine*	*The Animals Voice magazine*	*Outdoors Magazine*

Chart: J. Ottman Consulting, Inc.

in Figure 2.4, with further depth provided in Figure 2.5, from empirical evidence, and offer it as a supplement to the NMI segmentation described above to help you add relevance and precision to efforts targeting the deeper green consumers.

Resource Conservers

Resource Conservers (author included) hate waste. Wearing classic styles that last for years, they can be spotted carrying canvas shopping bags and sipping water from reusable bottles. They take their used printer cartridges and electronics to the drop-off center at Best Buy. Once avid newspaper recyclers, they switched to online news services long ago. At home, they reuse their plastic food storage bags and aluminum foil. Ever watchful of saving their "drops" and "watts," they install water-saving toilets and showerheads and faucet aerators. They shun over-packaged products, knowing they will cost them more in "pay as you throw" municipal waste systems. They've swapped their incandescent lamps for CFLs long ago, and they plug their lamps and appliances into power strips, allowing them to save more watts while at work or during a weekend away.

Given the means to do so, they buy home composters to process food waste and install solar panels to save money on electricity. Resource Conservers relish the financial savings that result from these behaviors (it makes them feel smart), and share their experiences with their friends and family to help cut down on more waste. Organizations such as Green America and Center for the New American Dream keep them supplied with ever more tips on eliminating waste.

Health Fanatics

The rule of thumb for Health Fanatics is the consequences of environmental maladies on one's personal health. These are the folks who worry about sun-induced skin cancer, fear the long-term impacts on their children's health from pesticide residues on produce, and perk up to news articles about lead and other contaminants in children's toys and school supplies. Health Fanatics apply sunscreen, pay a premium for organic foods, non-toxic cleaning products, and natural pet care. Catch them bookmarking websites such as the Ecology Center's HealthyStuff.org and HealthyToys.org to keep abreast of the latest on toxic substances in such recently spotlighted products as school supplies, car seats, toys, automobiles, and pet products.

Animal Lovers

As their name suggests, Animal Lovers are passionate about all animals, whether it be their own pets or those in shelters, as well as those in the wild. Likely to be vegetarian or vegan, Animal Lovers are committed to a pro-animal lifestyle. They belong to People for the Ethical Treatment of Animals (PETA), boycott tuna and fur, and only buy products labeled as "cruelty-free" (not tested on animals). They perk up to news stories featuring animals in need, whether it be manatees or polar bears in faraway sites to strays in their neighborhood, and are most likely to volunteer at the local animal shelter. Out of concern for marine life, they eschew plastic bags. This group would favor the cause-related campaign currently being run by Dawn dishwashing liquid, discovered to be an excellent cleaner of oil-soaked wildlife.

Outdoor Enthusiasts

Outdoor Enthusiasts love the outdoors and spend much of their time actively engaged in such activities as camping, "bouldering" (rock climbing without the aid of ropes), skiing, and hiking. They vacation in national parks and enjoy reading about natural destinations around the world. Outdoor Enthusiasts are also actively involved in such organizations as the Sierra Club and the American Hiking Society, which preserve the pristine spaces they value so highly. Whether it's purchasing Dr. Bronner's castile soap to reduce the impact of washing dishes while camping, or reusing bottles and bags to avoid littering the trail, Outdoor Enthusiasts are serious about minimizing the environmental impact of their recreational activities. Their new purchasing criteria includes outdoor gear made from recycled materials, such as Synchilla PCR polyester from Patagonia, Timberland's Earthkeepers boots, and reusable water bottles from Klean Kanteen.

Green consumer motives and buying strategies

Although they express their environmental concerns in individual ways, all green consumers, no matter how "deep" or "light," are motivated by universal needs (see Fig. 2.6) that translate into new purchasing strategies with implications for the way authentic sustainable brands are developed and marketed.

Figure 2.6 **Green consumer motives and buying strategies**

Needs	Strategies
Take control	→ Take preventive measure
Get information	→ Read labels
Make a difference/ Alleviate guilt	→ Switch brands or stores
Maintain lifestyle	→ Buy interchangeable alternatives
Look smart	→ Buy "conspicuous" green

Chart: J. Ottman Consulting, Inc.

Take control

At least one fundamental rule of green consumerism has not changed and likely will not: consumers are looking to control a world they see as spinning out of control. Driven zealously to protect their health and that of their families, sustainability-minded consumers take control in the marketplace, scrutinizing products and their packaging and ingredients with a vengeance; as an added precaution, they also note the reputations of product manufacturers for eco and social responsibility. A key reason consumers are taking things into their own hands is because they tend not to trust manufacturers or retailers – the historical polluters – to provide them with credible information on environmental matters. (see Fig. 2.7).

Today's consumers are doing more at the shelf than just checking prices and looking for familiar brand names. They turn over packages in search of such descriptors as "pesticide-free," "recycled," and "petroleum-free." As depicted in Figure 2.8, the various buzzwords that consumers now use to guide their decision-making represent every phase of the product life-cycle. This suggests that, momentously, while such attributes as performance, price and convenience – once the only things consumers considered when shopping – continue to be important, today's consumers now want to know about the specifics of a product's full panoply of green bona fides such as where raw materials were procured, how a product was manufactured, how much energy is required during use, and whether a product and its packaging can be safely disposed of. Remarkably, as a result of green as well as social concerns (e.g., child labor, fair trade), today's shopping agendas now encompass factors consumers can't feel or see!

Figure 2.7 **Whom do consumers trust for information on global warming?**

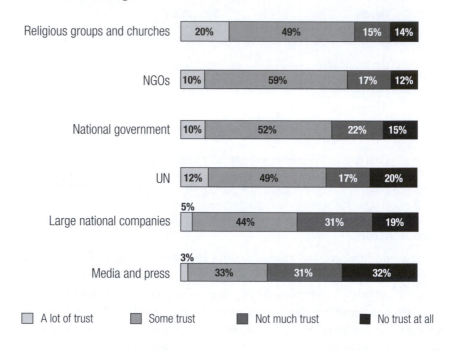

Source: Globescan report on issues and reputation, USA, 2009. Reprinted with permission

Figure 2.8 also references manufacturers – for good reason. Reflecting the deep-seated loyalties of the LOHAS segment, according to the new rules of green marketing, sustainability-aware consumers now look to see if branded product manufacturers can be trusted for eco and socially conscious practices. Consumers are asking such new questions as: Do they treat their workers well? Pay fair wages? Have a low carbon footprint? If the answers are "yes," the vast majority of consumers claim they will "pro-cott" or reward such companies. In a 2008 survey, 57% of respondents said they were likely to trust a company after finding out that it is environmentally considerate, and 60% said they were likely to purchase its products.[2]

Manufacturer (and retailer) reputations for environmental and social responsibility are also critical to consumers' purchasing decisions in another important way. In the absence of information on the package or shelf identifying a specific product as environmentally responsible in one way or another, today's consumers defer to their perceptions of a manufacturer's or retailer's eco and social track records as de facto eco-labels. The fact that

Figure 2.8 **Green purchasing buzzwords**

Raw materials

Sustainably harvested
Biobased
Fair trade

Manufacturing/ production

Unbleached
Pesticide-free
Carbon neutral

Distribution

Fuel-efficient
Local
Reusable packaging

Marketing

Ethical
Cause-related
Transparent

In-use

Low-fume
Resource-efficient
Durable

Packaging

Recycled
Non-aerosol
Minimal

After-use

Recyclable
Refillable
Reusable

Disposal

Landfill-safe
Compostable
Biodegradable

Manufacturer

Socially responsible
Low carbon footprint

Chart: J. Ottman Consulting, Inc.

there are so many corporate ads with green themes suggests that business leaders recognize this new reality and are responding accordingly.

As discussed in Chapter 1, following in the tradition of the Baby Boomers who first boycotted companies that invested in South Africa (and hence enabled apartheid social policies), today's greener and social-leaning consumers will also boycott suspected polluters, so a questionable reputation for environmental and social practices can also drive consumers away at the shelf.

Get information

Yesterday's consumers cared mostly about a product's performance and price. To help them take control of a world they increasingly see as risky, today's consumers are asking more penetrating questions. They are finding the answers offered in plentiful supply from a broad array of sources. For example, eco-shoppers can now consult any number of trusted environmental groups, including Green America and Center for the New American Dream. They can log onto favorite Internet sites and get the answers to frequently asked questions such as "What's all the fuss about bamboo?" and "What are some ways that I can save energy in my home?"[3] Consumers can also link to any number of other electronic sources, too, including the very detailed GoodGuide.com website and iPhone application for a peek into the health, environmental, and social impacts of over 70,000 food, toys, personal care, and household products; scores reflect data from nearly 200 sources, including government databases, nonprofits, academia institutions, and scientists on the Good Guide staff.

However, not all of this information is consistent, and consumers are having trouble sorting through it in their quest to tell the greener products from their "brown" counterparts, and find out which products and packages can be recycled or composted in their community. Confusion and distrust are setting in, and the reasons are understandable and many: greener alternatives don't always sport eco-sounding brand names – how can consumers tell by its name that the Method line-up of cleaning products may be greener than Palmolive or Mr. Clean? Alternative cleaners such as baking soda and vinegar may be even greener than Method but are not labeled as such.

As will be discussed in more detail in Chapter 7, today's greener consumers seek out trusted eco-labels such as ENERGY STAR and USDA Organic. In fact, at last count, there are more than 400 eco-labels and certifications in existence. However, only a small percentage of greener products actually carries an eco-label, and if they do, there's no guarantee that consumers will recognize or understand it. As depicted in Figure 2.9, awareness is high for such terms as "global warming" and "biodegradable," but falls off for newer concepts such as "carbon offset" and "socially responsible investments."

Figure 2.9 **Consumer awareness of environmental terms**

% U.S. adult population indicating which of the following terms they are aware of:

		2009 %	2007–2009 % change
Global warming		91	−1
Biodegradable		86	−1
Renewable resources		76	+5
Carbon footprint		69	+34
Sustainability		58	+10
Corporate social responsibility		48	−3
Carbon offset		34	+22
Socially responsible investments		32	−6

Source: © Natural Marketing Institute (NMI), 2009 LOHAS Consumer Trends Database®
All Rights Reserved

Making things worse, sometimes labels can be misleading – or even wrong. Products and packages marked "biodegradable" or "compostable" may be compostable in municipal composting programs, but may not in fact be compostable in backyard composters; those marked "recyclable" may not in fact be recyclable in one's own community if no facilities exist. (Some of this information is the result of intended or unintentional "greenwashing" by businesses looking to put their best green foot forward. See Chapter 7 for more details about greenwashing.)

Although environmental concern runs high and consumers say they are trying to educate themselves, there are still many issues that they don't fully comprehend. For instance, most consumers – and even many well-intentioned green marketers – still believe that anything "biodegradable" simply "disappears" – and will even do so in a landfill – rather than decomposing into soil or other nutrients under controlled conditions in a municipal composting facility, when the truth is that trash in landfills is simply entombed.

Make a difference/alleviate guilt

With the world seen as spinning out of control, green consumers want to feel that they can make a difference either as single shoppers or in concert with all the other users of the products they buy. Acutely aware of how humans are compromising their own health and that of the planet, an increasing number of consumers are now reassessing their own consumption and asking, "Do I really need another widget?" For those looking to pitch in, the mantra becomes, "What can I do to make a difference?" This is called "empowerment," and it underlies such bestsellers as *50 Simple Things You Can Do to Save the Earth*, the groundbreaking book that was revamped in 2006. It is now joined on the shelf by *It's Easy Being Green: A Handbook for Earth-Friendly Living; Gorgeously Green: 8 Simple Steps to an Earth-Friendly Life;* and *The Lazy Environmentalist: Your Guide to Easy, Stylish, Green Living*. And they're watching new television shows on cable such as those produced by Animal Planet, The Science Channel, and National Geographic Channel.

Electronically inclined consumers are also linking to other greens via social networks such as MakeMeSustainable.com, Care2.com, Zerofootprint. net, Carbonrally.com, Change.org, Celsias.com, and Worldcoolers.org. Care2. com, for instance, has a Care2 Green Living section and the Care2 News Network where members can post the latest green news stories.

As demonstrated in Figure 2.10, over half (56%) of consumers believe they are doing their bit to protect the environment and indeed perceive themselves as leading other societal groups in this regard, especially government and business. Yet a nearly identical amount (55%) think they should be doing even more – a sentiment that has been trending upward. Consumers' need to make a difference stems as much from a desire for control as from a corresponding need to alleviate guilt, so their greener purchases can make aware consumers feel good about themselves.

Figure 2.10 **Who should be doing more?**

% U.S. adult population stating the following organizations are either currently acting as a leader in protecting the environment or should be doing more:

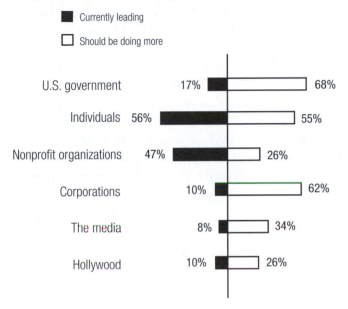

■ Currently leading

□ Should be doing more

	Currently leading	Should be doing more
U.S. government	17%	68%
Individuals	56%	55%
Nonprofit organizations	47%	26%
Corporations	10%	62%
The media	8%	34%
Hollywood	10%	26%

Maintain lifestyle

The environment may be on every consumer's shopping list, but it's rarely at the top – for a very understandable reason. Greener products still need to be effective, tasty, safe, sanitary, attractive, and easy to find in mainstream outlets – just like the "brown" counterparts consumers have been dropping into their shopping carts for decades. Although they are concerned about the planet, at the end of the day, shoppers of any stripe, green or not, will – and should – always prefer the laundry detergent that gets their clothes clean over the one that simply promises to "save the Earth." So it's imperative that, to be successful, sustainable brands deliver on performance, and why new entries from established brands (e.g., Clorox GreenWorks) perceived by consumers as treading lightly will always win the green day over the proverbial "Happy Planet" brand from an unknown entity.

Despite recessions that bring them back to stark reality, American consumers have been traditionally loath to save for a rainy day, preferring to spend today on short-term gains and pleasures. The same holds true for the environment. Consumers in general are more involved in buying products that will save them money or protect their health today, rather than seeking products that can ameliorate "big picture" issues such as global warming.

Similarly, it is not surprising that price tops the list of barriers to green purchasing (see Fig. 2.11). Likely sharing this with many types of products (most consumers cannot afford to pay premiums for any products, green or not), resistance to paying a premium for green is exacerbated by the facts that many greener products rely on untested materials, ingredients or technology, have unfamiliar brand names, and, in general, carry perceptual baggage left over from the 1970s when many greener products didn't work. So ensuring that products work as well as conventional ones, while pricing competitively with alternatives or justifying a premium price with a compelling value proposition, is the name of the game when attempting to meet the needs of the new mainstream green consumer.

Figure 2.11 **Barriers to green purchasing**

% U.S. adults indicating each of the following prevents them from using environmentally responsible products and services:

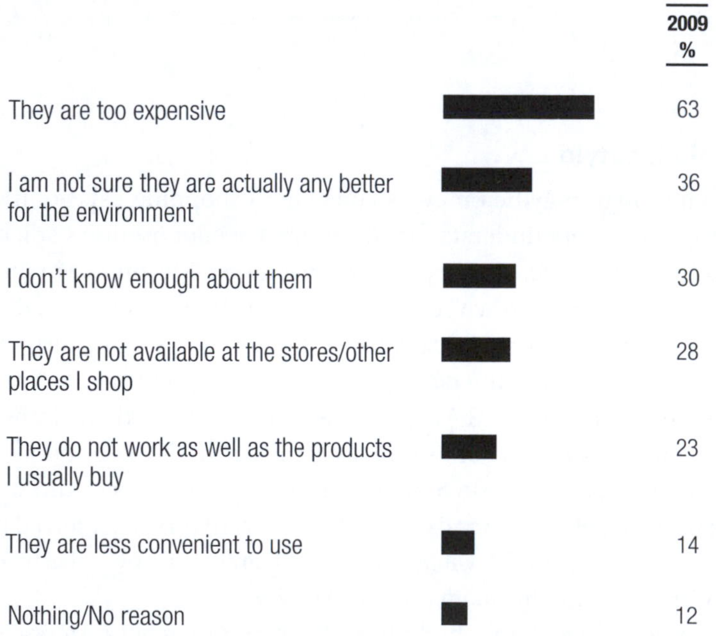
2009
%
They are too expensive
63
I am not sure they are actually any better for the environment
36
I don't know enough about them
30
They are not available at the stores/other places I shop
28
They do not work as well as the products I usually buy
23
They are less convenient to use
14
Nothing/No reason
12

Source: © Natural Marketing Institute (NMI), 2009 LOHAS Consumer Trends Database®

Despite the aforementioned, are there times when consumers *will* pay a premium for green? The answer to this $64,000 question of green marketing is a resounding "Yes!" Consumers will pay a premium if they know a product will save them money. That's why CFLs are flying off the shelves at Wal-Mart despite their significant premiums over 75¢ incandescent bulbs, and why Americans state they are three times more likely to pay more upfront for energy-efficient electronic equipment than they are to pay less for an energy-guzzling model upfront.[4] Consumers will also spend more for their health. Organic. Natural. PVC- and BPA-free. These are the reasons why sales of organic foods and clothing, natural personal care and pet care, and green cleaning products are growing so dramatically.

Lastly, consumers need to believe that brands are genuinely attempting to be more sustainable, a challenge for marketers with implications for education and efforts with the goal of establishing credibility for their messages, discussed throughout this book.

Look smart

It's the early 21st century. Green is trendy, and as such is part of many consumers' identity projection. There is a cachet in being green. Green is cool. Celebrities are into sustainability, and the fashionistas enjoy making stylish new clothes out of organic cotton, recycled soda bottles, and other hot materials perceived as greener. Method's teardrop-shaped bottle and the now iconic Anya Hindmarch "I'm not a plastic bag" reusable tote help outwardly focused Greens (read: Drifters, see above) project their values. Even with record levels of concern over climate change, a study of Prius owners conducted in 2007 found the number one reason why they bought their vehicle was "because of the statement it makes about me,"[5] rather than high fuel economy or lower emissions.

Environmental concerns have found their way into consumers' shopping decisions, and, in turn, are affecting all areas of marketing. Manufacturers and marketers looking to cater to aware and active consumers must adopt a new paradigm for green marketing, detailed in the next chapter.

The *New Rules* Checklist

Ask the following questions to assess the environment- and social-related issues that affect your products, branding, marketing, and corporate reputation.

○ Which segment(s) do our consumers fall into? Which consumer segment(s) likely represent the best target audience for our new sustainable brand?

○ What are the chief environment-related interests of our consumers? Are they motivated most by issues such as health? Saving resources? Protecting animals? Enjoying the outdoors and wildlife?

○ What are the chief environment-related behaviors of our consumers?

○ To what extent are our consumers likely to read labels? Take preventive measures? Switch brands or stores? Buy greener alternatives that fit their lifestyle? Buy "conspicuous" green goods?

○ To what extent are our consumers actively using the Internet to find environment-related product and corporate information?

○ Which product-related life-cycle issues concern our consumers? Raw materials? Manufacturing? Packaging? In-use consumption? Disposal?

○ To what extent are our consumers willing to boycott or pro-cott our own company's brands?

○ To what extent do our consumers believe that they should be doing more to help the environment? In what ways might they want to express this environmentalism?

○ What can we learn for our brand from all the various ways that environmentally conscious consumers act on their concerns?

785266 000297

The new green marketing paradigm

Conventional marketing is out. Green marketing and what is increasingly being called "sustainable branding" is in. According to the new rules of green marketing, effectively addressing the needs of consumers with a heightened environmental and social consciousness cannot be achieved with the same assumptions and formulae that guided consumer marketing since the post-war era. Times have changed. A new paradigm has emerged requiring new strategies with a holistic point of view and eco-innovative product and ser-vice offering.

Historically, marketers developed products that met consumers' needs at affordable prices and then communicated the benefits of their brands in a memorable way. Paid media campaigns characterized by ads with catchy slogans were de rigueur. Green or "sustainable" marketing and branding is more complex. It addresses consumers' new heightened expectations for businesses to operate and requires two strategies:

1. Develop products that balance consumers' needs for quality, perfor-mance, affordability, and convenience with the lowest impact possible on the environment, and with due concern for social considerations, e.g., labor, community.

2. Create demand for the resulting brands through credible, values-laden communications that offer practical benefits while empowering and

engaging consumers in meaningful ways about important environmental and social issues. These communications represent value to consumers for what they provide functionally and what they represent, and often positively reinforce the manufacturer's track record for sustainability as well.

The new rules being laid down by today's eco-conscious consumers cannot be addressed with conventional marketing strategies and tactics. Brand builders in the 21st century are accountable to tough new standards. Sustainability represents deep psychological and sociological shifts – not to mention seismically important issues – as did one of its predecessors, feminism, which forced marketers to develop more convenient products in step with two-income lifestyles and to portray women with a new respect. Meeting the challenges of today's level of green consumerism presents its own mandates for corporate processes, branding practices, product quality, price, and promotion.

To realize that the rules of the game have changed in a big way, one need only recall the unsavory backlash that is now occurring over what is perceived by environmentalists, regulators, and the press as inconsistent and often misleading eco-labels and messages. The resulting deluge of skepticism, confusion, and regulatory nightmares that spurious green claims – dubbed "greenwash" – are spawning in the marketplace proves that environmental marketing involves more than tweaking one or two product attributes and dressing up packages with meaningless and often misleading claims. Too many marketers are learning the hard way that leveraging environment-related opportunities and addressing sustainability-related challenges requires a total commitment to greening one's products and communications. Green marketing done according to the new rules also affects how a corporation manages its business and brands and interacts with all of its stakeholders who may be affected by its environmental and social practices (see Chapter 7 for more on this).

The new green marketing paradigm

A new paradigm is being forged by sustainability leaders that are creatively, authentically, and distinctively addressing the new rules of green marketing. Basic assumptions about how to best cater to consumer needs are being shattered. To successfully market to environmentally and socially aware consumers credibly and with impact requires first that one no longer view people as mere "consumers" with insatiable appetites for material goods, but as human beings looking to lead full, healthy lives. To follow the new rules means to project one's values, and to be sensitive to how one's customers, employees, and other stakeholders interact with nature; to be cognizant of how the production and consumption of material goods impacts lives positively as well as negatively, short-term as well as long-term (see Fig. 3.1).

In the age of sustainability, products are ideally designed to travel in endless loops; when their useful lives end, materials are not heedlessly disposed of in a landfill, but thoughtfully recaptured for recycling, reuse, or remanufacturing. Consciousness is growing for the benefits of sourcing one's materials locally, and about products that do a better job of fitting regional environmental considerations or the specific environmental needs of different segments of consumers. Under the new rules of green marketing, yesterday's resource-intensive products are being replaced by eco-innovative ones with radical new designs and technologies. Some products are even being shunted aside by services representing exciting new business models that allow forward-looking businesses to be profitable and ecologically responsible while increasing value and convenience for consumers.

Today's more sustainable product and service brands are marketed with communications that derive added value from the empowering educational messages that they impart, the values they project, and the communities – increasingly online as well as offline – of users they build. Many ecologically sound brands are so appreciated by consumers in the vanguard of environmental and social consciousness, they do not have to be advertised at all; rather, they make their way to the top of influential consumers' shopping lists based solely on the power of word of mouth. Goodwill propels many sustainable brands; today's consumers feel empowered when they reward companies they see as positively impacting people and the planet; and environmentally and socially aware consumers who spot gross infractions of this new paradigm will be quick to boycott as well.

The new rules of green marketing call for businesses to excel by being proactive. Aiming to surpass minimal compliance standards, they set the standards by which they and their competitors will be judged; they are not afraid of disclosing their ingredients and swinging open the doors of their factories in order to build a lasting relationship with green consumers ready to reward them with their loyalty.

Ecologically and socially responsible corporations are akin to nature's processes – interdependent. They ally with the panoply of corporate envi-

Figure 3.1 **The new green marketing paradigm**

	Conventional marketing	**Green marketing**
Consumers	Consumers with lifestyles	People with lives
Products	"Cradle to grave"	"Cradle to cradle"
	Products	Services
	Globally sourced	Locally sourced
	One size fits all	Regionally tailored
Marketing and communications	Product end-benefits	Values
	Selling	Educating and empowering
	One-way communication	Creating community
	Paid advertising	Word of mouth
Corporate	Secretive	Transparent
	Reactive	Proactive
	Independent and autonomous	Interdependent/ allied with stakeholders
	Competitive	Cooperative
	Departmentalized	Holistic
	Short term-oriented/ profit-maximizing	Long term-oriented/ triple bottom line

Source: J. Ottman Consulting, Inc.

ronmental stakeholders in cooperative, positive alliances and work hand in hand with suppliers, retailers, and local governments to manage environmental and social issues throughout their products' value chain. Cross-functional corporate teams convene with a web of external stakeholders to find the best possible holistic solution to sustainability challenges. These stakeholders are willing partners in the quest to innovate, communicate, and challenge the company to achieve ever-higher levels of sustainability. Long-term rather than short-term in orientation, these companies manage with an eye on a triple bottom line – one each for profits, the company's contribution to society, and the planet.

The seven strategies for green marketing success

Under the new rules, the currency of sustainable branding is innovation, flexibility, and heart. I have formulated seven strategies which I believe can help businesses address these deep-seated and lasting changes in consumer sensibility. Reflecting our learning from working with sustainability leaders over the past 20-plus years, they can be summarized as follows:

Ottman's seven winning strategies for green marketing

1. Understand the deeply held environmental and social beliefs and values of your consumers and other stakeholders and develop a long-term plan to align with them.
2. Create new products and services that balance consumers' desires for quality, convenience, and affordability with minimal adverse environmental and social impacts over the life of the product.
3. Develop brands that offer practical benefits while empowering and engaging consumers in meaningful ways about the important issues that affect their lives.
4. Establish credibility for your efforts by communicating your corporate commitment and striving for complete transparency.
5. Be proactive. Go beyond what is expected from stakeholders. Proactively commit to doing your share to solve emerging environmental and social problems – and discover competitive advantage in the process.
6. Think holistically. Underscore community with users and with the broad array of corporate environmental and societal stakeholders.
7. Don't quit. Promote responsible product use and disposal practices. Continuously strive for "zero" impact.

Source: J. Ottman Consulting, Inc.

Many enlightened companies, too numerous to mention, have already awoken to this new green marketing paradigm. They are putting these seven winning strategies into practice in their own ways, thus forging their own brands to fit the new consumer sensibility. Many of their stories illustrate the strategies described later in this book. One such story focuses on eco-entrepreneurs Eric Ryan and Adam Lowry, founders and co-CEOs of Method, who have created a much-talked-about sustainable brand and set a greener pace that others must follow.

**Addressing
the New Rules**

Method makes a difference by being different

The Method difference

In 1999, in what they considered the dirtiest apartment in San Francisco, long-time friends Adam Lowry and Eric Ryan, both under 30, decided to clean up their act – and everyone else's. Sensing the opportunity to transform household cleaning from a chore to something fun, Lowry and Ryan combined their expertise – Lowry in chemical engineering and Ryan in marketing – and founded Method. Their goal: create "a line of environmentally friendly cleaning and personal-care products that are safe for every home and every body." Today, with a loyal and growing following among engaged young adults, and an enlightened approach to sustainability, they are proving themselves as deliberate change agents in a sleepy category with such entrenched entries as Tide, Wisk, and Palmolive.

With a fast-growing line of household and personal-care products that spans body lotions and hand sanitizers to air fresheners and mops, and distribution in over 25,000 retail locations such as Lowe's, Target, and Whole Foods Market, they have achieved over $100 million in revenues despite prices that can be up to 30% more than their well-known competitors. In 2008, their market share increased in all product categories, most notably a near 18% growth in sales over the previous year for the all-purpose cleaner, one of their most popular products, representing $5 million in sales alone.

In stark contrast to the big "soapers," P&G, Unilever, and Colgate-Palmolive, who follow the old rules and just sell *products* – and even the drudgery associated with cleaning one's home and dishes – Method serves up an entire cleaning *experience*, characterized by fun and social awareness. Eye-catching, museum-quality design – previously unheard of in their industry

– draws in their youthful customers; an appreciation of Method's demonstrated commitment to sustainability, and their other brand hallmarks of efficacy, safety, environment, and fragrance, keep them coming back for more.

Customers who want more than clean

Lowry and Ryan know their customers won't settle for positive reinforcement for a job well done (you won't catch them admiring their reflections in plates made shiny by Joy liquid). Unlike the customers of "Madge the manicurist," the historical television spokesperson for Palmolive dishwashing liquid, Method users are hip, young, aware, and desirous of solving problems in the world. In contrast to clunky bottles of conventional dishwashing liquids that are typically hidden under the kitchen sink, Method's sleekly designed bottles stay perched on the countertops, adding to the kitchen decor and helping to project their consumers' values to others.

According to Method, its users are young, professional females whom they dub "progressive domestics." Whereas the venerable Seventh Generation brand attracts a loyal following of "deep green" (LOHAS) consumers, Method draws from the larger band of light green, the "Drifters" who view eco-awareness as popular and hip; to them, Method represents something easy to do about issues they care about. The Method brand makes them feel good about their purchases and themselves. In Method they find everything they want in a personal-care or household-cleaning aid – efficacy, fragrance, and chic design in addition to a lighter environmental footprint and low toxicity. Even the name "Method" doesn't sound deep green like "Seventh Generation" (reflecting an Iroquois slogan about preserving the Earth for the next seven generations), but is non-specific yet provocative, even scientific, ensuring mainstream appeal.

A company with a conscience

The company's deep-seated environmental and social values have translated into state-of-the-art green operating and manufacturing processes with the accolades to prove it. For starters, they have green offices (including one that's certified to the U.S. Green Building Council's LEED standards) and a factory that doesn't emit a drop of waste-water. They achieve a lofty goal of carbon neutrality in all manufacturing, office operations, and employee travel through a combination of energy efficiency, biodiesel fuel in transport trucks, and use of renewable energy such as wind and solar; their remaining carbon is offset by buying Renewable Energy Certificates (RECs)[1] (from

*Native*Energy, a nonprofit that supports projects to capture methane and energy from three Pennsylvania dairy farms).

Method's environmental consciousness is partnered with a social one, marked by support for numerous service projects that help to foster good community relations. Employees get three paid days per year to volunteer, enabling them to pitch in on projects like Park(ing) Day, an annual event where volunteers transform parking spaces in cities around the world into parks for the day; Save the Bay, removing litter, testing the water's phosphate levels, and planting native seedlings in the San Francisco Bay Area; and cleaning, repainting, and installing new furniture at the local family shelter run by San Francisco nonprofit Compass Community Services.

To help monitor their progress, in June 2007 Method underwent certification as a B Corporation by the B Lab, a Philadelphia-based nonprofit organization that provides third-party audit ratings of a company's commitment to social and environmental issues.

Figure 3.2 **Method's B Impact Report**

Summary	Certified: June 2007	
	Points earned	**% Points available**
Environment	36.9	80%
Employees	33.6	80%
Community	14.4	33%
Consumers	29.2	60%
Leadership	14.4	75%
Composite B Score	128.5	66%

▷ 80 out of 200 is eligible for certification
▷ 60% points available = Area of excellence

Source: BCorporation.net. Reprinted with permission from Method

Companies that score highly in the ratings are eligible for B Corporation certification (which also includes a legal expansion of corporate responsibilities to include consideration of stakeholder interests). B Impact Reports for all Certified B Corporations are publicly available on B Lab's website. One

Figure 3.3 **Method "teardrop" bottle**

Reprinted with permission from Method

thousand other progressive companies in 54 industries, including Seventh Generation, Numi Tea, and Dansko footwear are also rated.[2] Publishing these results shows customers that Method values transparency and is willing to receive constructive criticism on the functioning of its company. Method's B Corp rating (Fig. 3.2) reflected a composite score of 128.5 placing it in the top 10% of all B Corporations (the bar for eligibility is 80 points, and B Corporations have an average score of about 100 points). Method's high scores reflect the company's wide-ranging social and environmental commitments; the relatively lower scores for "Community" and "Leadership" do not indicate that the company is not doing good things, but rather that Method has not chosen those topics as a focus of its business.

Five product hallmarks

In tune with their desire to make cleaning fun, Method products step out from the cobwebbed cleaning products category and claim a strong aesthetic sensibility. To meet their youthful customers' demands, they strike a balance for efficacy, environment, safety, design, and fragrance – and fun. As one example, the Method baby + kid line features hypoallergenic, pediatrician-tested, and "never tested on rubber duckies" bath-time formula in penguin-shaped bottles.

Packaging is sleek and trendy – and easy to spot on the retail shelf. In keeping with a Method moral that each product has a past, present, and future, packaging is minimal and uses recycled or recyclable materials. For example, as of 2008 all packaging for surface cleaners, floor cleaners, specialty sprays, and other cleaning products is made from 100% recycled and recyclable PET (polyethylene terephthalate) plastic – with the goal of extending this recycled and recyclable plastic packaging to all Method products.

Naturally appealing fragrances and colors such as pink grapefruit and lime-green cucumber distinguish the Method experience by reinforcing the natural aura of the products and making them fun to use. The line is spiced up during the holiday season with special scents such as winterberry and frosted fir.

When choosing ingredients, Method follows a paraphrased "precautionary principle": "if there's a chance it's bad, don't use it." Product formulations start with the non-toxic and biodegradable ingredients on Method's "clean list"; their "dirty list" includes items they will never use such as phosphates and chlorine.

Method's bottles are sculpted by noted designers to make the brand stand apart from competitors and help to reach a wider group of consumers than simply the deep greens. One, a now-famous "teardrop" bottle, is shown in Figure 3.3.

At Method, good design is very much a deliberate "added plus" to a focus on sustainability – that element that helps to distinguish their brands from competitors. (As discussed in Chapter 6, this strategy is known as "bundling" additional benefits to add value to sustainable products. As co-founder Adam Lowry explains:

> One of the big goals with Method, and why design and sustainability are inextricably linked in our brand, is that if you don't have the design element, you're only going to appeal to people who are already green, so you're not actually going to create any real environmental change . . . To us, "sustainability" and "green" are just aspects of the quality of our product – they are not a marketing positioning . . . I mean everything should be that way. Just build it into the quality of the product and let the experience of the product be the real hero.[3]

Credible, impactful green marketing

In stark contrast to the old rules for marketing household products, Method's marketing platform is built on three essential hallmarks: limited or no paid advertising, transparency, and community. All three work synergistically to create loyal followers.

Unlike the primary focus on paid advertising invested by their competitors each year, Lowry and Ryan have historically targeted their users through direct consumer education and engagement that reinforces the fun experience of using the brand and underscores Method's credibility. To demonstrate the inherent safety of their products and underscore fun, sales brochures feature models cleaning a house in the buff. Bold package design gets noticed on the shelves and reinforces the brand within the home. Indeed, the quality of the experience of using, owning – even discovering – the product, generates word of mouth among excited users who immediately link the brand to fun and authenticity.

Method's first paid media campaign, launched in 2010 to support their revolutionary 8X concentrated laundry liquid, takes direct aim at mainstream laundry aids that, in their words, feed a household's heinous "jug habit."[4] Cheeky-tone ads executed in print and online attempt to provoke change and begin a new conversation by imploring presumably "addicted" consumers to "Say no to jugs" or to support a "jug-free America," position the brand as a David to Tide's Goliath, and encourage consumers to rethink ingrained habits.

Pluck a bottle of any major brand of dishwashing liquid off the shelf and you might find a statement indicating that the product is phosphate-free or possibly packaged in recycled plastic. But Method, in line with its commitment to transparency, discloses its ingredients on its website. As the nude campaigners photographed in their sales brochures prove, it is clear that Method has nothing to hide!

In addition, Lowry and Ryan have opened their doors to outside auditors. Their products are certified by the EPA's Design for the Environment (DfE) label and the Cradle to Cradle (C2C) certification. DfE has assessed over 50 Method product formulas to date to ensure that the company uses only environmentally responsible ingredients. Method has already earned C2C certification on 20 of its products and, as of this writing, is in the process of certifying 20 more.

Have you ever seen anyone wearing a T-shirt that has the brand name of a popular brand of household cleaning products on it? Of course not! But some fiercely loyal Method consumers gladly sport T-shirts that they buy on the company website with the Method brand name emblazoned on the front, accompanied by silly slogans such as "Cleans like a mother."

An important aspect of Method's approach to green marketing is engaging their users, which the company does offline and, increasingly, online. Facebook page fans make suggestions about products and practices, and participate in contests to win free Method products. At last count, over 6,000 users were following "methodtweet" on Twitter, while Flickr visitors keep up to date on goings-on inside the company – on moving day, employees were pictured walking down the street with office supplies in hand, followed by a mariachi band.

One of Method's most popular outreach activities is their People Against Dirty campaign, with over 5,300 advocates united in a common passion for Method and its cleaning mission. A blog informs readers of topics related to design, sustainability, and environmental awareness. After signing up on the Method website, and uploading their photo, members receive updates, previews of new Method products, and even an "Advocacy Kit," including three individual pass-along kits they can give to friends and family. Method is now working on ways that users can interact with one another through the site.

To equip consumers with the information they seek to make responsible product choices Lowry and Ryan wrote *Squeaky Green: The Method Guide to Detoxing Your Home*, giving home-cleaning tips and exposing the "dirty little secrets" of traditional cleaning products. Method also runs Cleaning Tours in Chicago, Boston, New York, and other cities, setting up pop-up shops on street corners where customers can swap an old toxic cleaning product for a free Method one. While on tour, staffers throw "detox parties" in consumer homes. Guests receive a "plastic bag rehab" tote filled with Method products.

Cleaning up at the checkout

Method's rule-breaking approach to cleaning not only builds fierce brand loyalty and free word-of-mouth advertising, it also helps it clean up at the cash register – while sprucing up their competitors.

Besides fast-growing sales and extensive retail distribution, Method's proverbial trophy shelf is crammed with such accolades as being named in November 2008 a "Champion" of the Safer Detergents Stewardship Initiative of the DfE program, commending Method for its voluntary commitment to use safer surfactants (ingredients that help remove dirt from surfaces and do no harm to aquatic life). In 2006, Method was ranked seventh on *Inc.* magazine's annual list of the 500 fastest-growing private companies in the U.S.; that year, too, annual revenues grew 80% in an industry that is normally lucky if it sees 4% growth, and PETA named Lowry and Ryan as "Persons of the Year" for creating a revolutionary line of home-cleaning supplies that are free of animal-derived ingredients and are not tested on animals.

Perhaps Lowry and Ryan's biggest gold star relates to achieving the goal they set for themselves at their company's founding: to revolutionize and provoke change in the cleaning-products industry. No longer content to follow age-old rules, key competitors now offer their own greener cleaning products: Palmolive's pure + clear range contains "no unnecessary chemicals and no heavy fragrances," while P&G's Pure Essentials Dawn dishwashing liquid has no added dyes or superfluous ingredients and is packaged in a bottle made with 25% post-consumer recycled plastic. Madge has finally cleaned up her act. What a nice reflection on Method.[5]

The rules have changed. A new green marketing paradigm has arrived, characterized by my seven strategies that will be integral to consumer products marketing for decades to come. Successfully adapting to the new rules and executing the strategies outlined as part of this new green marketing paradigm starts with taking a life-cycle approach to one's product offering – the subject of the next chapter.

The *New Rules* Checklist

Use the following checklist to assess how well your organization understands and addresses the new green marketing paradigm.

- Do we strive to offer a product that balances consumers' traditional needs with minimal impact on the environment and addresses social considerations?

- Do our communications offer practical benefits while empowering and engaging consumers in meaningful ways about important issues that affect their lives?

- Do we have a short- and long-term plan of environmental and social-related improvements for our products?

- Do we view our consumers with respect as human beings concerned about their health and the state of the world around them?

- In what ways can we express our sensitivity to how our customers, employees, and other stakeholders interact with nature?

- Do we know how the production and consumption of our products impacts human lives negatively as well as positively? Long-term as well as short-term?

- Are we taking pains to ensure that our products are designed for an afterlife versus a landfill? Materials are sourced locally? Our products address regional considerations?

- Are we taking advantage of opportunities to use eco-innovative designs and technologies? Are we looking at new business models?

- How do our consumers feel about our brand? Do they reward us with their loyalty (pro-cott)? To what extent are they willing to boycott?

- Are we sufficiently aware of and linked with our various environmental and social stakeholders?

- Are we taking advantage of opportunities to engage employees to help manage and magnify the sustainability aspects of our brand?

- Do we have our eyes sufficiently on the longer-term sustainability aspects of our brand?

785266 000297

Designing greener products
A life-cycle approach

It used to be that consumers simply expected the products they bought to work well, sport a familiar brand name, be sold in a nearby store, and be affordably priced. The rules have changed. Today, that once seemingly short checklist includes minimizing the environmental impacts of those products at every phase of their life-cycle, starting with the impacts associated with mining, growing, or otherwise processing the raw materials right through to the impacts linked to a product's eventual disposal. And now, throw in for good measure a number of social considerations such as fair working conditions and whether or not laborers receive a living wage (even perhaps in some equitable proportion to the salaries of the highest-paid managers), use of child labor, whether prices paid to producers are deemed fair (can coffee growers afford to send their children to school?), and whether the manufacturer is a good member of the community. This presents to businesses looking to develop highly marketable and legitimately sustainable brands the need to juggle traditional product considerations with an extremely varied and highly complex list of issues involving the entire supply chain.

These issues also include the harnessing and consumption of natural resources such as water and energy, as well as the protection of natural habitats and endangered species. It is generally not the brand manager's job to be responsible for a product's environmental and social impacts. However, given that they sit on cross-functional teams, and their consumers are increasingly favoring brands based on their track records for managing these issues, this chapter is included as a primer on green product design. Its relevance to marketers is illustrated with numerous examples of how green product benefits can be associated with business success; in successive chapters we will deal with the strategies for communicating these various benefits with credibility and impact.

Consider the entire life-cycle

Designing products and packaging for minimal impact can be tricky. What may appear to be an ecological benefit may actually result in little or no added environmental value. Some plastic plates made from cornstarch, for example, may decompose in a municipal composting facility but not in backyard composters, where conditions are not likely to be so hot and steamy. Hybrid cars save energy but the batteries they contain represent a potentially significant source of hazardous waste.

Sometimes the presumed greening of a product can actually increase overall environmental impact. CPC, the makers of Mueller's pasta, found that converting to recycled carton material would actually add about 20% to the width of their package material and this would at least partially offset savings to the environment, considering the extra energy needed to ship the new boxes. Because of the energy it takes to transport recyclables to a processing facility, it may be that a product with a very high degree of recycled content may represent greater impact than one with less recycled content.

It can even be argued that there is no such thing as a truly "green" product, because every product, no matter how thoughtfully designed, uses resources and creates waste. Therefore, "green" is a relative term, with some products being greener for certain reasons or in certain circumstances (and hence my preference for the term "green*er* products" throughout this book).

So, in order to address consumers' various sustainability-related product concerns discussed in Chapter 2, and to prevent backlash from consumers, environmental groups, and other stakeholders, all of whom may be quick to point out the shortcomings of products and packaging touted as green, a thorough approach to improving the environmental profile of one's products/services and processes is required. A tool called life-cycle assessment (LCA) can help by examining all the environmental issues involved in designing a greener product:

Green product design issues

Raw materials acquisition and processing

- Conservation of natural resources
- Use of renewable resources; sustainable use of resources
- Use of recycled and recyclable materials
- Protection of natural habitats and endangered species
- Water conservation
- Energy conservation
- Waste minimization and pollution prevention, especially the use of toxics and release of toxics to air, water, and land
- Transportation

Manufacturing and distribution

- Minimal use of materials
- Waste minimization and pollution prevention, especially the use of toxics and release of toxics to air, water, and land
- By-product management
- Energy conservation
- Water conservation

Product use and packaging

- Conservation of natural resources
- Energy efficiency
- Water efficiency
- Consumer health and environmental safety
- Packaging efficiency
- Packaging recycled content
- Packaging recycle rates

After-use/disposal

- Recyclability; ease of reuse, remanufacture, and repair
- Waste minimization
- Durability
- Biodegradability/compostability
- Safety when incinerated or landfilled

Source: Martin Wolf, Seventh Generation Inc. Printed with permission

The first step in conducting a full life-cycle analysis of a product is to define the functional unit and the product system. For instance, in conducting an LCA of a toothbrush, you need to decide whether to analyze just the toothbrush, or include the package, too. What about the water and toothpaste used throughout the life of the toothbrush? Conducting an LCA also requires you to set boundaries on the data to be collected for analysis; for instance, should you consider the environmental impacts associated with making the trucks needed to transport the toothbrushes to stores? Likely not! But factoring in the energy used in transportation would be totally appropriate.

Your study may encompass the product's complete life-cycle, from raw material extraction to disposal ("cradle-to-grave" analysis), or it may be limited to the processes from raw materials extraction to product production ("cradle-to-gate" analysis). Ideally, it would look at the impacts associated with a "cradle-to-cradle" point of view,[1] and take into account various options for recycling or otherwise responsibly turning your product into useful new material or energy.

Your study may take into account the materials, energy, and emissions to produce a kilogram of product, or to produce enough product for 1,000 uses.

Once the boundaries and assumptions are determined, quantify the use of energy, resources, and emissions associated with raw-material procurement, manufacturing and production, packaging, distribution, and in-use (e.g., use of energy, water, or other consumables) straight through to after-use (e.g., recycling and recovery) or final disposal. Then, analyze the data, identify problems and opportunities, and allocate the resources to address them in priority.

An LCA of a washing machine, for example, would quantify the environmental impacts associated with fabricating the metal, along with pollutants and energy from the mining process (which can be significant). It would consider the energy needed to manufacture the machines and transport them to stores. Then it would factor in the water, energy, and detergent needed to run the washer over an estimated lifetime (likely measured in years), making assumptions regarding such things as number of washings per week, water temperatures, and size of loads. Finally, it would consider the impacts associated with collecting and recycling the machines, and/or eventual disposal in a landfill or incinerator.

LCAs can help assess particular impacts: for instance, energy, which is often a key component in all products. The Procter & Gamble Company has conducted life-cycle assessments of many of their company's products. Some of their results through 2006 are summarized in Figure 4.1. As can be seen, areas of greatest energy usage vary greatly by life-cycle stage and product category. An LCA of a laundry detergent, for instance, shows that the greatest energy impacts by far occur during the usage stage, considering all the energy needed to heat the water. It was this type of assessment that spurred P&G to introduce Tide Coldwater (discussed in Chapter 6), a product that P&G estimates could help to save the equivalent of 3% of total U.S. energy consumption, and over 8% of the CO_2 reduction target for the U.S. set in the Kyoto Protocol.[2]

Figure 4.1 **Product energy usage from a life-cycle perspective**

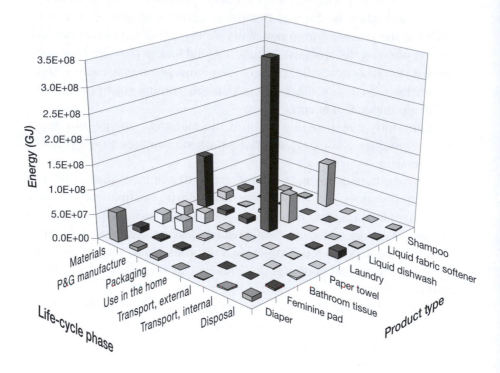

Energy's contribution to so many products during use represents a key reason why the U.S. government has devoted so much attention to the ENERGY STAR label (discussed in more detail in Chapter 7). It was an LCA, too, that prompted the move by makers of soft drinks in the 1970s to save energy by shifting from returnable glass bottles that required two-way transport by grocers to one-way disposable PET (polyethylene terephthalate) bottles.

LCA is a valuable tool for addressing the new rules of green marketing, as it can be very useful for:

- Comparing the costs associated with energy and resource usage and environmental emissions associated with existing product designs, manufacturing and packaging methods and their alternatives

- Identifying significant areas for reducing energy use, water use, and waste

- Comparing energy and resource usage and environmental emissions associated with competitive products, i.e., as the basis for manufacturing claims.

Many organizations around the world have performed LCAs in industries ranging from automotive, paper, paperboard, glass, steel, lighting, energy, aluminum, plastic beverage containers, and delivery systems to building materials and transportation products. Many different methodologies have evolved, both quantitative and qualitative; some allow businesses to conduct their own LCAs with the aid of sophisticated software tools such as SimaPro, GaBi, and Umberto programmed with estimates of the environmental impacts for various materials and processes.

Use caution when attempting to use life-cycle assessment as a marketing tool! The transparency afforded by LCA is highly desirable but challenges abound. For instance, it's one thing to report to consumers the results of an LCA conducted on one's own product, as Timberland does with its Green Index (see Chapter 9), but comparisons with competitors' products can be tricky. Comparisons that favor a study sponsor can easily be criticized – and held suspect. Besides, it is not easy obtaining accurate data on competitors' products!

Moreover, try comparing the environmental impacts of two different concepts that meet the same consumer need. Take diapers as an example. What's more important to society: landfill space or water and energy associated with laundering cloth? Also tricky – LCAs of two products based on the same technology can yield very dissimilar results, making comparisons for marketing purposes unfair. For instance, two competitive products might have been made in different countries (or even different states or provinces) with different types of energy, each with their respective pollutants. For instance, an LCA of a washing machine conducted in the U.S. may likely be based on coal, the predominant type of energy used in the U.S., whereas in France it may be nuclear. Consumers, at least for now, are not knowledgeable enough about LCA to ask the right questions when presented with comparative results.

Experts in industry, government, and academia are working to legiti-mize the use of LCA and other approaches as marketing tools. The EPA has created an online resource called LCAccess, designed to "promote the use of LCA to make more informed decisions through a better understanding of the human health and environmental impacts of products, processes, and activities."[3] Businesses looking to use LCA data to more easily compare competitors and alternatives may want to consider a standardized system of analysis such as the economic input–output LCA software developed by Car-negie Mellon University's Green Design Initiative and available on the web (www.eiolca.net).

Among its shortcomings, LCA does not adequately address certain environmental and social concerns. According to Martin Wolf, Director of Product and Environmental Technology, Seventh Generation, an expert on life-cycle inventory and green product development, an LCA must be aug-mented with a holistic evaluation of a product's total environmental and social impacts. Renewable or sustainable resource use, habitat destruction, biodiversity depletion, odors, visual pollution, noise pollution, toxicity, bio-degradability, and social issues such as fair trade, labor practices, and com-munity responsibility of import to environmentalists, consumers, and others in society cannot be evaluated by the quantitative approach of LCA and must be considered separately.

Representing a new development in product LCA, carbon footprint-ing has emerged as an alternative to LCA. Given the fact that LCAs can be extremely complex, and that energy can represent a good proxy for an LCA given that so much of any product's life-cycle impacts are energy-related, calculating the carbon footprint of a product, rather than conducting a full LCA, is becoming popular. Similar to conducting an LCA, one would deter-mine a product's carbon footprint by calculating the amount of energy con-sumed at each stage of the product life-cycle, then converting it into the amount of emissions associated with each stage, before arriving at a total carbon footprint.

One product that is watching its carbon footprint these days is Pep-siCo's Walkers Crisps, a brand of potato chip sold in the UK. Since 2007, the Walkers package has sported a Carbon Reduction Label developed by the Carbon Trust (see Chapter 7 for more detail). Pepsi worked with the UK-based not-for-profit to develop the carbon footprint of Walkers Crisps – and learned a lot in the process. From 2007 to 2009, PepsiCo has been able to reduce the carbon footprint of Walkers Crisps by 7%, saving about 4,800 tons of emissions. This has paid off at the point of sale, with about 52% of those polled in the UK saying they were more likely to buy a product carrying the Carbon Reduction Label. Pepsi has since put the label on UK-based packages of Quaker Oats, as well as Oatso Simple Original and Oatso Simple Golden Syrup.[4]

Strategies for sustainable product design

Many marketers now grow their businesses and attempt to minimize their environmental and health-related risks by addressing the specific environmental and social issues most relevant to their consumers and other stakeholders. Proactive green marketers keep an eye on the future with a phased plan for managing potential risks 5–15 years hence. In the process, they often save money and enhance brand image while ensuring future sales for existing and new products. A plethora of strategies, ideally considered as part of a holistic effort to manage one's brand rather than incorporated in isolation, exist to inspire profitable new and improved products and packages that address the new rules of balancing consumers' needs with sustainability considerations. These are examined below.

15 strategies for sustainable product design

1. Sustainable harvesting and mining practices
2. Recycled content
3. Source reduce
4. Organically grown
5. Fair trade
6. Reduce toxicity
7. Think global, grow local
8. Responsible manufacturing practices
9. Energy- and fuel-efficient
10. Water-efficient
11. Extend product life
12. Reusable and refillable
13. Recyclable
14. Compostable
15. Safe for disposal

1 Sustainable harvesting and mining practices

Sustainability has established itself as a buzzword in the business world, but it has become particularly important for manufacturers whose supplies of raw material are threatened. What is abundant today may become scarce tomorrow, wreaking havoc for manufacturers whose designs are dependent on specific types of raw materials. Herman Miller's Eames lounge chair and ottoman, the design icon introduced in 1956, originally featured Brazilian rosewood which is now endangered; however, taking great care to protect its authentic design sensibility, since 1991 Herman Miller has produced the chair with cherry and walnut wood from sustainably managed forests.

C.F. Martin & Company

With supplies of rosewood, spruce, and mahogany all scarcer in recent years due to unsustainable logging practices, Christian F. Martin IV is the first generation of Nazareth, Pennsylvania-based guitar makers C.F. Martin & Company, to worry that his family company's supply of wood would soon become exhausted. With an eye on the future, in 2007 Martin teamed up with three other leading U.S. producers of guitars and Greenpeace to form the Music Wood Coalition to promote better logging practices in the areas where these rare woods are grown. One thing the coalition learned was that the last old-growth Sitka spruce tree from a temperate rainforest in Alaska, which had been an important source of wood for the guitar industry, would be harvested within the decade. So, C.F. Martin led the industry in the use of more plentiful, alternative woods such as birch and cherry.[5]

Tiffany & Company

Blood diamonds, meet dirty gold. Gold mining can wreak havoc with water supplies, violate human rights and decimate an area's natural surroundings. Production of just one gold ring can generate 20 tons of waste.[6]

Tiffany & Co., the legendary jewelers, recognized the issue of dirty gold early on and took out a full-page ad in the *Washington Post* asking the Federal Government to halt construction of a controversial silver mine that threatened Montana's Cabinet Mountains Wilderness and called for important mining reforms.[7] The first jeweler to respond to NGO Earthworks' call for responsible mining, Tiffany embraced the DC-based environmental group's No Dirty Gold campaign calling for jewelers to pledge to work only with those mining companies that adhered to Earthworks' high standards of social and environmental responsibility.[8]

By taking an early definitive stance against destructive mining, Tiffany has defended its sterling reputation and protected market share among its discriminating customers. Michael J. Kowalski, Tiffany's chairman and CEO, says it best in Tiffany & Co.'s sustainability report: "Tiffany & Co. is committed to obtaining precious metals and gemstones and crafting our jewelry in ways that are socially and environmentally responsible. It is simply the right thing to do: Our customers expect and deserve nothing less."[9]

2 Recycled content

Recycling is the most popular eco-design strategy, and for good reasons. It can save the energy needed to mine, ship, and produce new materials, in turn preventing the air pollution associated with the generation of new energy. For instance, creating aluminum cans from recycled content uses 95% less energy than constructing new ones from virgin material. Some materials, such as glass and aluminum, can be recycled in a theoretically endless loop while most plastics and paper are simply "downcycled" into less valuable uses. Recycling also spares valuable materials from ending up in a landfill and prevents toxins from leaching into underground water. Along with these environmental benefits, recycling can save businesses money, so it is great for the bottom line, too. And, of course, it's relatively easy for consumers to pitch in.

HP inkjet cartridges

Materials such as newspapers, packaging, magazines, books, clothes, and toys – what we all throw away every day – are considered "post-consumer waste." This includes the 700 million inkjet and toner printer cartridges that are used yearly across the U.S.[10] Uncomfortable with these numbers (which represent future risk), Hewlett-Packard now makes more than 200 million of its inkjet cartridges with post-consumer plastics. Their process combines various kinds of recycled plastics, from used inkjet cartridges to common water bottles, with a variety of chemical additives. HP used 12 million pounds of recycled plastic in 2008, more than double what it used the previous year.[11] Helping consumers to close the loop, HP includes a pre-paid return envelope in its packages; they have also arranged for consumers to take used cartridges to recycling centers and many office supply stores such as Staples, Office Depot, and OfficeMax.

Recycline

Recycline Inc. of Waltham, Massachusetts, founded in 1996, manufactures the Preserve brand of toothbrushes, razors, tongue cleaners, and tableware made exclusively from recycled feedstocks. The Preserve toothbrush, Recycline's premier product, is made of 100% recycled polypropylene plastic, the majority of which comes from Stonyfield Farm's yogurt containers as well as old or broken grocery store carts and toys.

Until 2007, Recycline's products were sold principally at specialty green-type stores, but with mainstream consumers ready for a recycling step forward, Recycline's Preserve toothbrushes are now sold by Wal-Mart and on Amazon.com, as well as by their primary retailer, Whole Foods Market. In 2007, Recycline won Forbes.com's Boost Your Business contest over nearly 1,000 other small businesses from around the country.[12]

3 Source reduce

Recycling has much to recommend it ecologically, but does have its drawbacks. It still takes energy to transport the recyclables to a processing facility, topped off by the energy used to recycle those materials. Sometimes such factors weigh *against* recycling. While recycling is most often preferable to landfilling, source reduction and reuse of products usually have less environmental impact than recycling – hence the mantra "Reduce, Reuse, and Recycle." In assessing the feasibility of recycling polystyrene clamshells, for example, McDonald's found that the amount of energy needed to transport the super-lightweight yet bulky materials (requiring multiple trucks) made the operation infeasible. They decided against recycling in favor of very thin "quilt wraps" – a form of source reduction – which were landfilled after one use.

Source reduction, a strategy most often associated with packaging, was originally referenced in the U.S. Pollution Prevention Act of 1990 with a statement that "pollution should be prevented or reduced at its source whenever feasible." Since the cost savings derived from source reduction are often parallel to the amount of materials eliminated, the tenets of this law are not only good for the environment, they are good for business.

Dropps dissolvable laundry capsules

Many large corporations are seizing opportunities to source reduce, prodded by a Wal-Mart pledge to skim 5% of all packaging from its supply chain by 2013, along with nearly 700,000 metric tons of carbon emissions and $3.4 billion. Accordingly, Wal-Mart is giving preferential shelf treatment to such innovations as Sun Products' "All small & mighty," a detergent that is three times more concentrated than traditional All. The environmental benefits? Smaller bottles requiring less plastic to produce, fewer boxes to ship, less water – and less weight for the same number of loads – as well as fewer trucks to ship them. Such benefits are desirable in and of themselves, but Dropps, a Philadelphia-based start-up, has an even better idea.

Instead of a bulky plastic container, the folks at Dropps have decided to sell their laundry detergent packed inside dissolvable one-inch square capsules dubbed "Dropps," packed 20 in a stand-up pouch. According to the company, the collapsible plastic pouches are so thin, it would take 292 of them to equal the plastic represented by one empty jug of All. Representing pre-measured portions of six-times concentrated detergent, tossed into the wash, they leave behind nothing but clean clothes. In addition, the super-concentrated formula means that there is very little water being shipped with the detergent, reducing transportation costs and maximizing the retailer's shelf space efficiency. Beyond its own formula for super source reduction, Dropps' low-suds formula is free of chlorine, NPE (nonylphenol ethoxylate – a stain-fighting additive found to be an endocrine disruptor[13]) and phosphate. A sure-to-be-rising star of the concentrated detergents market, Dropps can now be found on the shelves of Publix, Safeway, and Target stores.

4 Organically grown

Since the deadly effects of DDT were first publicized in Rachel Carson's 1962 watershed book *Silent Spring*, society has fretted about the potential health threats of using pesticides and fertilizers in crops. So started the organic foods movement over 40 years ago. Today, organic is everywhere. Hershey makes organic chocolate. The Gap produces organic clothing. Even Target, Wal-Mart, and 7-Eleven stock a huge range of organic foods, cleaning products, and make-up. Free of artificial preservatives, coloring, irradiation, pesticides, fungicides, and hormones, organic products chalked up $24.6 billion in consumer purchases in the U.S. in 2008, an increase of 17.1% over 2007.[14] The organic movement even has its own government seal. (To learn about the USDA Organic seal, see Chapter 7.)

Safeway's O organics line
Safeway's USDA-certified "O" brand line, with 300 organic products in more than 30 categories, and thus appealing to a wide array of consumers, has enjoyed such success that the products are now carried by other food chains.

In addition to milk, bread, and other staples, the line consists of frozen dinners, snacks such as popcorn and chips, and even ice cream bars. The line is especially targeted at new mothers seeking to provide their children with healthier food without spending much more. With prices comparable to conventional alternatives, James White, president of Safeway's Lucerne Foods division, says the brand is "making organics available to everyone," and with the spread of the line into other supermarkets, this may soon be true. In its first year, 2005, the line brought in $150 million, sales doubled to $300 million in 2007,[15] and were projected to be $400 million for 2008.[16]

Earth's Best organic baby food

New mothers are especially concerned about how synthetic pesticides can affect the development of young children. One company offering an alternative to conventional baby foods is Earth's Best, an organic baby food launched in 1985 and now in the hands of Hain Celestial Group, the largest manufacturer of natural food products with brands that are increasingly being embraced by mainstream consumers such as Celestial Seasonings Tea, Arrowhead Mills, Health Valley, and Terra Chips, Earth's Best is USDA-certified organic and delivers flavorful taste without any preservatives, salt, refined sugar, or modified starches.

With a product line-up including jarred food, cookies, frozen meals, cereal, and body care, sales in 2006 were up almost 50% from the previous year.[17] According to Philip Tasho, manager of the Aston/TAMO Small Cap Fund that owns Hain shares, "The natural and organic food industry is broadening and becoming more mainstream. Overall consumer spending may decline, but consumers aren't going to scrimp on products for their health."[18]

Nike Organics

Although 100% cotton may suggest 100% natural or 100% organic, both are far from true. For starters, producing 2.5 pounds of cotton takes anywhere from 2,000 to 8,000 gallons of water.[19] Cotton also requires the extensive use of herbicides and pesticides – more than any single crop. And if that's not enough, cotton crops are sprayed with a chemical defoliant to prevent leaf staining, and the resulting fiber is saturated with bleach or dyed with any number of potentially toxic chemicals.

All of this impact is not lost on Nike, one of the world's largest manufacturers of cotton clothing. To address this issue, Nike has become the world's largest buyer of organic cotton and, in 2005, they launched Nike Organics, a full line of clothing made from 100% organic cotton in the spirit that "one shouldn't have to decide between style and nature." The USDA certifies Nike's cotton as organic, documenting the process all the way from the farm to the finished garment. Nike's commitment stretches further than this one line: 9% of all the cotton they used in 2007 was organic – no small amount at 11 million pounds[20] – and the company aims to blend 5% organic cotton in all of its cotton garments by 2010.[21] Nike is not alone in playing by different cotton rules. According to the Organic Exchange, a trade organization, global organic cotton sales rose from $245 million in 2001 to $4.3 billion in 2009. Riding a 40% average annual growth rate since 2001, projections for 2010 are close to $5.1 billion.[22]

5 Fair trade

The rules of the game are fast changing when it comes to labor practices and resulting in favorable impacts on worker wages and living standards, and none too soon. According to UNICEF, one-sixth of the world's children aged 5–14, 158 million in all, are engaged in child labor, vulnerable to exploitation and the poverty that accompanies a lack of education.[23] Such conditions can persist throughout a lifetime, especially for women, who account for 70% of the more than one billion people living in extreme poverty worldwide.[24]

Several certification programs run at the national/regional levels by groups such as Oakland, California-based TransFair USA and the UK-based Fairtrade Foundation have sprung up to address the issue. Progress is being made. According to the World Trade Organization, over 7.5 million disadvantaged producers and their families are estimated to benefit from fair-trade-funded infrastructure and community development projects.[25] In 2008, worldwide sales of fair trade products such as coffee, cocoa, tea, herbs, spices, fruit, and sugar skyrocketed to over $4 billion, an increase of 22% over 2007.[26] One of the top volume sellers of Fair Trade Certified coffee in the U.S. is Starbucks, whose Café Estima brand helps to create a positive impact on the lives of farmers in Latin America and Africa.

Divine Chocolate Limited

"Heavenly Chocolate with a Heart" is the slogan of Divine Chocolate Limited, a fair trade chocolate manufacturer that is owned (45%) by the members of the Kuapa Kokoo cooperative in Ghana, who not only receive fair trade prices for their cocoa but also sit on the board of directors and share in the profits.[27]

Launched in the UK in 1998, Divine Chocolate is now available in many U.S. grocery stores including Wegmans, Fairway, and Whole Foods in addition to specialty chocolate stores throughout the country. Representing U.S. sales of $2 million in 2008, Divine Chocolate has won accolades for its socially conscious practices, winning the Social Enterprise Coalition (the UK's national body for social enterprise) award for Best Social Enterprise in 2007 and UK *Observer* newspaper's Best Ethical Business award in 2008, as well as *Good Housekeeping*'s Favorite Fair Trade Product in 2008.[28]

Following the example of committed companies such as Divine, chocolate industry leaders are beginning to follow new rules themselves. UK-based Cadbury, one of the world's largest confectioners (now owned by U.S. conglomerate Kraft), purchased the organic chocolate company Green & Black's in 2005 and launched its own fair trade product in July 2009 as the new Cadbury Dairy Milk chocolate – a commitment that translates to tripling the amount of fair trade cocoa bought from Ghana. Not to be left behind, a month after Cadbury's announcement, competitor Mars Inc. publicized its goal to produce candy from only sustainable sources by 2020.[29]

Ben & Jerry's Fair Trade Certified Chunks and Swirls

Since 1978, Ben & Jerry's, the Vermont-based wholly owned subsidiary of Unilever known for its super-premium ice cream, has been operating its business on a three-part mission which emphasizes product quality, economic reward, and a responsibility to the community. In 2010, Fair Trade Certified ingredients became part of that mission, when the company announced its decision to go fully Fair Trade across its entire global flavor portfolio by the end of 2013.

Ben & Jerry's Fair Trade commitment, the first in its industry, means that every ingredient in its ice creams and confections that can be sourced Fair Trade Certified, now or in the future, is Fair Trade Certified. Globally, this involves working across diverse ingredients such as cocoa, banana, vanilla, and other flavorings, fruits, and nuts. It also means coordinating with Fair Trade cooperatives representing a combined membership of over 27,000 farmers.

Rob Cameron, Chief Executive of Fairtrade Labelling Organizations International, believes Fair Trade Certified is consistent with the Ben & Jerry's brand. In his words, "Ben & Jerry's, like all of us in the Fair Trade movement, believe that people can have fun standing up to injustice and campaigning against poverty while enjoying some of Ben & Jerry's best-selling favorites like Phish Food and Chocolate Fudge Brownie, how cool is that."[30]

Clarins beauty products

Taking an alternative approach to fair trade certification, Clarins, the France-based manufacturer of upscale skin care, make-up and perfumes, opts to rigorously screen their suppliers of precious botanical ingredients themselves, and commit to fair trade agreements and hands-on community development projects in indigenous communities. [31]

In Madagascar, Clarins supports over 2,500 families by offering agricultural jobs for harvesters. Additionally, Clarins reinvests 5% of all of its profit from a harvest back into local community projects.[32] For example, they helped to install an infrastructure system to supply a village in Marovay with clean drinking water and renovated a village school. Clarins also pledged to replant 10,000 native Katafray trees, and to teach local farmers how to remove the bark used in their products, sustainably.[33]

In Vietnam, Clarins has set up fair trade agreements to purchase Vu Sua, a fruit used for Clarins firming lotions, which is the main source of revenue for the village of Vin Kim.[34] Clarins also helped to finance and remodel one of the area's schools.

To help promote further socially responsible projects and protect the sources of its brand-distinguishing botanicals, Clarins recognizes outstanding individuals with company-sponsored service awards, such as the Dynamic Woman Award[35] started in 1997, and the ClarinsMen Environment Award, first given to Jean-Pierre Nicolas, an ethnopharmacologist, in 2004 for his organization Jardins du Monde, which brings alternative medicine to communities where conventional medicine is unavailable or too expensive.[36]

6 Reduce toxicity

Toxicity affects products at every stage of their life-cycle: for example, chemical spills on highways, fires and lethal toxin leaks at chemical plants such as the one in Bhopal, India, in 1984, and such issues as asbestos risks to workers and arsenic-laden mine tailings. Phthalates, a compound used as a plastics softener in children's toys, is believed to have adverse effects on the endocrine system and to be linked to birth defects in males.[37] Mercury and other toxic metals leach from batteries and cell phones as they languish in landfills long after their useful lives. Some chemical agents in common cleaning products, such as butyl, are also thought to pose a significant risk to children and pets.

Heeding consumer demand for healthier products, governments and corporations are taking action. The U.S. Congress passed the Consumer

Product Safety Improvement Act in August 2008 banning phthalates in children's toys. Wal-Mart, Target, and Toys R Us began requiring suppliers to follow similar standards for all children's products by January 2009.[38]

Reducing toxicity is good for business. It reduces the liability associated with risks to workers, and safer alternatives can enhance productivity and cut workers' compensation claims. Less (or non-) toxic materials save money on handling costs, while speeding time to market since there may be fewer legal hurdles to navigate. And, of course, there's the opportunity to market to the growing number of mainstream consumers looking for safer alternatives.

Nike's Considered shoe line

Working toward the elimination of noxious adhesives needed to join uppers and lowers on its sports shoes, in 2005 Nike launched its Considered line. A unique weaving process now holds the pieces together while lending the boot a unique moccasin-like aesthetic – and helping it to earn a coveted gold IDEA award from the Industrial Designers Society of America. Targeted toward "deep green" consumers, Considered helped illustrate Nike's commitment to sustainability – as exemplified through its impressive reductions of 61% in manufacturing waste, 35% in energy consumption, and 89% in the use of solvents.[39]

Nike has since sought to make the concept more universally appealing. The new Air Jordan XX3 is constructed using material from old recycled sneakers, manufacturing scraps, and jigsaw-like components resulting in an inner construction that uses less glue. This shoe even inspired the invention of a sewing machine designed to produce sneakers using more stitching and fewer chemical-based glues. Testament to the universal appeal of green, the new Air Jordan is targeted toward the same audience as the rest of the Air Jordan line, with the emphasis placed on performance. The green factor is included as an added bonus for those who are interested. Consumers are buying. Nike brand chief Charles Denson reported that during the first quarter of 2009, the company's basketball shoe division grew by double digits, propelled by Air Jordan sales.[40]

Marmoleum flooring from Forbo

For over half a century, vinyl has been the cheapest, easiest-to-install kind of flooring. However, it fades and scuffs and eventually needs to be replaced and sent to landfills. If incinerated, the scrapped vinyl (short for polyvinyl chloride – PVC) releases dioxins into the air. The vinyl manufacturing process also creates dioxin, one of the deadliest toxins on the planet, so constantly replacing vinyl exacerbates the situation.

Propelled by growing awareness for the environmental drawbacks of vinyl, old-fashioned natural linoleum is making a comeback. Produced from linseed oil, rosins, wood flour, and natural pigments with a backing made from jute, linoleum is an ecological alternative to vinyl. Leading the charge is Forbo Flooring, the industry leader, headquartered near Zurich, Switzerland. Its star product, Marmoleum, is helping to reinvent the image of linoleum. The company asserts that Marmoleum comes in an array of colors and styles and installs as easily as vinyl, but mounts using a safe water-based adhesive. To help combat the fact that the linoleum tiles are significantly costlier than vinyl, usually about $6 to $8 per square foot as opposed to prices that can run as low as $0.99 per square foot, the company emphasizes the fact that linoleum is healthier, antistatic, and does not promote the growth of bacteria, mold, or mildew. Also notable is the longer life of Marmoleum, which the company maintains does not sustain water damage, rip, gouge, or develop gaps, but ages gracefully, staying more richly colored, cushiony, and quieter than vinyl.[41] Someone is listening, as Forbo rides the green building and green home wave, enjoying net sales of over US$1.8 billion worldwide in 2009.[42]

Seventh Generation household cleaning products

Typical household cleaning products contain any number of synthetic chemicals including ammonia, chlorine, and parabens.[43] However, with the Burlington, Vermont-based Seventh Generation line-up, there is less worry about child-proofing the kitchen cabinet: although some of the company's products require trace amounts of preservatives, Seventh Generation products typically use plant-based ingredients that are biodegradable as well as chlorine- and phosphate-free, and the resulting products are just as effective as their conventional counterparts. Seventh Generation's cleaning products are also "not acutely toxic" as defined by the Consumer Products Safety Commission, by oral, dermal, or inhalation exposure.[44]

To reinforce their safer stance, Seventh Generation's product labels and website include ingredient lists for every product, as well as Material Safety Data Sheets. The website also includes a Corporate Responsibility Report and a blog by CEO Jeffrey Hollender on all things green. Thanks to this combination of safety, efficacy, and transparency, since 1989 Seventh Generation has grown from a catalog founded to serve the green niche directly, to one of the most trusted names in cleaning products found on the shelves of Whole Foods, Target, and many mainstream supermarkets.[45]

7 Think global, grow local

On average, commercially produced meals travel from 8 to 92 times farther from field to plate than locally grown meals,[46] and much of that food is carried on airplanes – the most carbon-intensive form of transportation.[47] Today, in a world watching its carbon consumption, buying and producing locally helps to minimize transportation costs and impacts, while supporting local farmers and strengthening communities. Mainstream consumers are starting to get the point. According to the NMI, in 2009 39% of U.S. consumers noted "buying products that are made locally" as an area of concern, up from 31% three years before.[48]

All across the U.S. the number of local farmers' markets is growing in response to consumers' desire for local produce, and gourmet chefs are writing new rules for their menus, promoting high-quality local produce. According to the USDA, the number of farmers' markets in the U.S. was 6,132 in 2010, versus 1,755 in 1994, and up 16% from 2009 alone.[49] Local purveyors such as Oregon-based New Seasons Market, a grocery store chain with seven locations throughout the state, to the 280-unit Whole Foods chain now make local sourcing a priority. Whole Foods even runs special Native Growers and Producers Events where local growers and producers of products including artisan snacks, vegan treats, and small batch soaps can learn about packaging and labeling guidelines, operations, and logistics support, as well as a local loan program. This is not just confined to the U.S.: UK supermarkets are increasingly bringing local food in, with one of the latest entrants being Waitrose, who as, this book was going to print, started a trial of local suppliers in its Saxmundham, Suffolk branch.

Wal-Mart

Even Wal-Mart is demonstrating a commitment to local sourcing, racking up annual sales of $400 million in locally grown produce from farmers throughout the country in 2008, making the retail giant the largest single purchaser of local produce in the United States. In 2008, the company increased local partnerships by 50% over 2006, and purchased more than 70% of its produce from U.S.-based suppliers.

Senior Vice President Pam Kohn says that this commitment saves on fuel costs and enables Wal-Mart to offer fresh products at low prices.[50] Demonstrating the potential to eliminate thousands of food miles that contribute to greenhouse gas emissions and air pollution, in 2008, by expanding their peach sourcing from just South Carolina and Georgia to 18 different states and selling locally, Wal-Mart slashed 672,000 food miles – translating to savings of 112,000 gallons of diesel fuel and more than $1.4 million.[51]

8 Use responsible manufacturing practices

Sometimes it's what consumers don't see that can have the most impact: the energy use and emissions from the manufacturing plant being a case in point. Recognizing this, a number of manufacturers are taking steps to reduce their plant emissions, green their energy sources, and curb their use of water, among other measures.

Kettle Foods

In keeping with its commitment to using all-natural ingredients, Kettle Foods makes its full line of snacks including potato chips, tortilla chips, nuts, and trail mix with an eye toward minimizing impact on the environment. "Walking their talk" as a producer of healthy snacks, Kettle Foods cooks its chips in sunflower and safflower oils; afterwards it converts 100% of the waste vegetable oil into biodiesel, which in turn runs a growing fleet of company vehicles and prevents 8 tons of CO_2 from being emitted each year.

In 2003 Kettle Foods Inc. partnered with Portland General Electric and Energy Trust of Oregon, a nonprofit organization, to install 600 solar panels atop their manufacturing plant, representing one of the largest arrays in the Pacific Northwest. The 120,000 kWh of electricity per year that is generated is enough power to produce 250,000 bags of Kettle Chips each year and eliminates 65 tons of CO_2 emissions per year when compared with fossil-fuel-based methods. Kettle Foods also offsets 100% of the plant's electricity use through wind power, which is the equivalent of taking 1,000 cars off the road or planting 1,600 acres of trees.

In 2000, when Kettle Foods Inc. moved its headquarters and production to its five-acre Mill Creek site in Salem, Oregon, it chose to restore the wetlands on the property. It introduced native and aquatic plants and built a two-acre trail system for people in the community to enjoy. They now see herons that faithfully return each year. In 2007, Kettle opened a second factory in Beloit, Wisconsin. It was the first U.S. food manufacturing facility to earn LEED gold certification. The factory has 18 wind turbines on its roof and is surrounded by prairie land that the company is restoring to its native state.[52]

Kettle Foods Inc.'s all-natural product produced in a natural way has helped the company generate a loyal following among consumers around the world who are prepared to pay premium prices versus more mainstream chips.[53]

9 Energy- and fuel-efficient

Electricity is needed to heat and light buildings and streets as well as to power all kinds of products, from those that plug into the wall to those that are fueled by batteries. However, the generation of electricity represents the single largest source of air pollution and greenhouse gas emissions in the United States. Nationally, power plant emissions are responsible for spewing significant amounts of carbon dioxide (CO_2), sulfur dioxide (SO_2), nitrogen oxides (NO_x), and mercury (Hg) into the air, not to mention particulate emissions that can be particularly harmful to athsmatics and other sensitive individuals. These four pollutants are the major cause of such serious environmental problems as acid rain, smog, mercury contamination, and global climate change.

Happily, much of this pollution can be avoided through simple actions and intelligent design. For example, "standby power," which enables televisions to be turned on instantly, accounts for approximately 5% of total residential electricity consumption in America, adding up to over $3 billion in annual energy costs.[54] Cutting down on standby power is one benefit of the ENERGY STAR label (see Chapter 7), which can now be found on more than 50 kinds of energy-using product, including homes and commercial buildings.

Bosch appliances

German-based Bosch is the only manufacturer selling appliances in the U.S. to have an ENERGY STAR label on all of its models. Bosch received ENERGY STAR recognition in 2008 and 2009, and was named ENERGY STAR's Partner of the Year in 2010. Bosch appliances, including the Nexxt clothes washer and Evolution dishwasher, are also competitively priced, ensuring their appeal to the mass market.

Bosch's "Nexxt" clothing washers benefit from multiple new technologies: a computer sensor that optimizes the water level for each wash, an internal water heater that monitors water temperature for efficiency, an inclined drum that cleans clothes with less water, and a final washer spin at 1,200 rpm that quickens the drying process. Using these washers which exceed ENERGY STAR guidelines by 102%[55] instead of top-loader washers, can save $150 a year in water and energy bills.[56]

The company's EcoSense Wash Management System for dishwashers provides similar sensors that cut energy use by 20%; dishwashers also offer effective water heating systems, condensation drying techniques, and the option for users to select an energy- and water-sipping half-load wash. At 190 kWh per year, the SH_98M model is the most efficient available in the U.S.[57]

Smart-Grid-enabled appliances

Many electric utilities, electrical product manufacturers, government, software manufacturers, and other organizations including Google and Microsoft are now working jointly to transform the nation's power grid into one digitally controlled "Smart-Grid" network that can convey electricity to consumers more efficiently, cutting pollution and electric bills in the process.

General Electric and Whirlpool are even readying "smart appliances" that are Smart-Grid-compliant: that is, they can be controlled from afar by the power company, who can lower thermostats, switch into energy-saver mode, or shut them down entirely during times of peak demand. Whirlpool predicts it will put one million smart clothes dryers on the market during 2011. Offering the potential for significant energy and cost savings, a smarter clothes dryer may help Whirlpool climb out of recession-induced sales slump, while also benefiting the environment: an electric dryer that tumbles without heat uses only about 200 watts of electricity, in comparison to the 500 watts used by one that's set on maximum heat. Multiplied by one million, this results in the equivalent of six big coal-fired power plants.[58]

Nokia's mobile phones

Approximately two-thirds of the energy used to power mobile phones is wasted when the charger remains plugged in or when the phone has finished charging but energy is still flowing – the "no-load" mode. To combat this, Nokia has reduced the no-load demand of its chargers by 70% over the decade preceding 2006, and aims to further reduce the demand by an additional 50% by 2010. Their most efficient charger uses just 0.03 W, beating the ENERGY STAR requirement by 94%.

In 2007, Nokia was the first cell phone manufacturer to build in alerts to encourage users to unplug when the phones are fully charged. The potential energy savings? If the owners of all one billion Nokia phones in use around the world unplugged their chargers when alerted, it would save enough energy to power 100,000 homes.[59] To save even more energy, users can turn off extraneous sounds such as keypad tones, dim the screen, and set backlight standby time to a minimum.

Toyota Prius

Representing a now iconic greener product, the now globally distributed Toyota Prius hybrid sedan combines smart design and a new brand of marketing (discussed in more detail in Chapter 6) with an exceptional rate of fuel efficiency gauged at 50 miles-per-gallon overall (city 51/highway 48). All of this adds up to fewer trips to the gas pump, less money spent on gasoline, and less pollution than competitive sedans.[60] Indeed, many U.S. states allow hybrid cars to use High Occupancy Vehicle (HOV) lanes even if there is only one person in the car, offering a competitive edge against popular sedans such as the Nissan Altima and Honda's Accord. To Toyota's credit, the Prius dashboard even includes a feedback display that promotes more efficient driving. Anecdotal reports indicate that Prius drivers have fun challenging themselves to get way beyond the estimated 50 mpg in fuel efficiency every time they drive. (The device has been so successful that Ford recently unveiled its own dashboard device, Smart Gauge, which is set to debut in its gas-electric hybrid cars in 2010.)[61]

10 Water-efficient

The United Nations Environment Programme predicts that 1.8 billion people will be living in places with severe water shortages by 2025, and two-thirds of the world's population could be subject to some water scarcity.[62] Due to a near tripling of per capita water usage in the past few decades, General Accounting Office anticipates water shortages in 36 U.S. states by 2013,[63] likely leading to price spikes and treacherous implications for crops, livestock, and other water-intensive industries.

In an effort to spur the market toward water-conserving showerheads, faucets, toilets, urinals, and even landscape irrigation practices and newly built homes, the EPA offers the WaterSense label, the H_2O-saving counterpart to its ENERGY STAR label. With the availability of xeriscaping, a water-efficient landscape that has been found to use up to 75% less water, the amount of turf grass allowed on newly built homes could be government's next target.[64] Meanwhile, if the San Francisco-based Carbon Disclosure Project, a nonprofit group that has persuaded major corporations to disclose greenhouse gas emissions, has its way, water-intensive industries, such as auto manufacturing, electric utilities, food and beverage manufacturing, mining, and pharmaceuticals, will become water-efficient. The group is now surveying major corporations about their water use and discharges into nearby water bodies, as well as water-related risks, opportunities, and strategies.

Caroma dual-flush toilets

The average household uses 350 gallons of water per day, over 40% of which is used in the bathroom.[65] The latest development from Brisbane, Australia-based Caroma, one of the world's leading plumbing product companies, is a new dual-flush toilet that is a pioneer in water-saving technology. The toilet has two different buttons – one for liquid waste and one for solid, using 0.8

and 1.6 gallons of water per flush, respectively. This single product with its half-flush and full-flush technology reduces water usage by up to 67% compared with traditional toilets, which use almost 3 gallons per flush.[66] Caroma toilets are distributed all across the world and bearing the EPA's WaterSense logo they are used by universities, hotels, companies, and homes throughout North America.[67]

A new rule in the making: product water-footprints. As reflected throughout this book, water efficiency is usually referred to about products in use. But a lot of water goes into the making of many consumer products. For instance, because of the water consumed in cotton growing, it takes 10,855 gallons of water to make a pair of jeans, and 15,5000 for a kilogram of beef.[68] With expected pressure on water supplies in the not-too-distant future, expect consumers to start to demand information about your product's water footprint, similar to the nascent carbon footprint.

11 Extend product life

Consumers have long valued brands such as Maytag, Volvo, and Zippo for their high quality and long life. With the mainstreaming of green, durable products are being valued anew for their low environmental impact, eliminating the stigma often associated with used products. As just one example, Lexus gives their high-end cars a second life as "certified, pre-owned" cars, attracting a clientele usually in the market for new cars.

Stokke Tripp Trapp chair

Smart designers have created cribs that transform into regular beds as the child grows. Stokke, a Norwegian-based furniture manufacturer specializing in versatile baby products, has designed a highchair that grows with the child. With an adjustable seat and footrest, their Tripp Trapp chair evolves over time from a safe seat for a small child to comfortable seating for an adult. Constructed primarily of sustainably harvested beech wood with formaldehyde-free varnish, the chair is durable and easily cleaned with a damp cloth. Underscoring the company's commitment to durability, the Tripp Trapp Chair comes with a seven-year warranty on all the wooden components.[69]

12 Reusable and refillable

Reusable materials and refillable packaging reduce waste and save businesses money. Mainstream shoppers are getting the hang of reusability, thanks to the efforts of eco-conscious retailers that sell reusable bags in their stores rewarding consumers who bring their own bags, and penalizing those who don't. IKEA and Whole Foods Market encourage shoppers to bring their own tote bags by giving them five and ten cents off their purchase, respectively.

Reusable water bottles

Advertising for bottled water often showcases pristine springs bubbling up from deep within the earth, but behind the scenes loom the environmental impacts associated with its transportation and packaging, which together consume about 17 million barrels of oil per year.[70] In 2006, over 30 billion bottles of water were consumed in the United States[71] – 86% of the bottles subsequently became litter or sent to landfills; when incinerated, they create chlorine gas and harmful by-products.[72] A backlash is already in place among local governments and concerned consumers, creating opportunities for Nalgene and Klean Kanteen among other manufacturers touting a reusable solution. Nalgene has teamed up with Brita water filter company in an innovative partnership to promote the benefits of bottling one's purified water at home. Meanwhile, sales of Klean Kanteen's sleek stainless steel water bottles have skyrocketed from $2.5 million in 2007 to $18 million in 2008.

ecoEnvelopes

Online bill paying is fast becoming the norm, but each year, more than 81 billion return envelopes are still enclosed in utility bills, credit card statements, and other mailings.[73] Ann DeLaVergne, a former organic farmer based in Minnesota, is attempting to rewrite the rules for assisting in bill collection: she has invented the ecoEnvelope, a reusable mail solution, which in February 2008 was approved by the U.S. Postal Service. Users zip open the ecoEnvelope by lifting a tab and pulling along a perforated strip. They then insert their response, moisten, and close the flap.

ecoEnvelopes are manufactured exclusively on FSC- and SFI (Sustainable Forestry Initiative)-certified recycled paper from sustainably managed forests, and use soy and water-based inks. Not only do ecoEnvelopes cut down on waste, they can also help companies project an ecologically conscious image to their customers and save 15% to 45% on mailing costs.[74] Companies such as the Land Stewardship Foundation, Fresh Energy, and Renewable Choice Energy are already using ecoEnvelopes, saving money while literally sending a message to their customers about their commitment to sustainability.

13 Recyclable

It's great if products are made from recycled content, but those same products need to be easy to disassemble in order to keep labor costs down so recycling can be economically feasible. Done correctly, designing for disassembly can lead to business success.

Herman Miller Mirra work chair

Introduced in 2003, the Mirra work chair from Herman Miller has it all. It is made from a high percentage of post-consumer and post-industrial aluminum. With a minimum number of parts – and taking all of 15 minutes with normal household tools – it is easy to disassemble for recycling. Parts are coded for recycling according to American Society for Testing and Materials standards. Because it is easy to disassemble, the chair is also a cinch to repair.

Representing a holistic approach to environmental design, the Mirra chair eschews PVC. It is made in a manufacturing plant that is LEED-certified and powered by 100% renewable energy, and it comes with a 12-year warranty. The design has received positive publicity, as well as accolades for environmental and ergonomic performance, not to mention being well on its way toward becoming a design icon.

Patagonia Common Threads recycling program

A product designed for easy disassembly and made of recyclable content must also be easy for consumers to return for recycling, whether by bringing used products back to store or sent to another location, or picked up, or handed over to a retailer or other third party who will recycle them.

Patagonia's Synchilla PCR fleece and Capilene fabrics are made using recyclable fibers that are easily broken down to their original monomers, a process that eventually results in new fibers equal in quality to the originals. Seizing an opportunity to make new garments from old ones and satisfy customer demands for recycling, in 2005, Patagonia launched the Common Threads Recycling Program, a garment take-back program driven by in-store collection of used garments made from polyester. Reusing old garments to manufacture new Capilene (polyester) garments saves 76% of the energy associated with making a new garment from scratch.[75] Representing a true closing of the loop, since spring 2007 Capilene fabrics have included old Capilene garments which have been recycled into virgin-grade polyester collected through the Common Threads Recycling Progam.[76] With the instigation of a new chemical recycling process in the summer of 2008, Patagonia can now collect and recycle nylon products, too.[77]

14 Compostable

In nature, everything is recycled – waste for one organism becomes food for another. According to the EPA, approximately 30% of solid waste, mostly food, is biodegradable material that can be effectively composted into humus, an organic matter that can enrich gardens and agricultural soils, but only a small amount of consumers have access to municipal or backyard composters. So most waste winds up in landfills, where it will be entombed forever or, even worse, slowly degrade, creating methane gas, which is highly flammable and 21 times more powerful than CO_2 as a global warming gas. Composting, which typically involves the use of new biobased materials, will need to play a big part in future waste disposal scenarios. Happily, a number of new products and packages designs are appearing in the market, encouraging more composting activity. Innovative designers are now developing compostable products and packages with this idea in mind.

VerTerra dinnerware

Sometimes the inspiration for a new material can come from an existing material that may be old or overlooked. Michael Dwork, founder and CEO of VerTerra, Ltd., an enterprising firm located in New York City, on a trip to Asia saw that fallen palm leaves from plantations were being burned. He noticed that a woman had taken some of the fallen palm leaves, soaked them and pressed them into shape with a crude waffle iron and used them as plates.[78] That provided the inspiration to repurpose the plates on a larger scale as the basis of attractive, functional, and compostable line of plates, bowls, and trays.

The leaves, which otherwise would have been burned, are steamed, heated, and pressed in a local factory. No chemicals, glues, lacquers, or bonding agents are used in the manufacture of the products. In 2008, VerTerra salvaged 1.5 tons of leaves per month. In 2009 that monthly average jumped to nearly 12 tons; annual production and sales tracked in similar fashion up nearly eight times. The waste from the process is powdered and traded back to the farmers as mulch in exchange for more leaves. Compostable and biodegradable, VerTerra's food service line has earned the BPI logo, and is currently used by major universities such as Columbia University in the City of New York, by major sports stadiums such as that of the Dallas Cowboys, and by Evelyn Hill Inc., concessionaire for the Statue of Liberty and the Playboy Mansion. In early 2009 VerTerra launched a retail line that is now available at natural and specialty stores across the country such as Whole Foods Markets and numerous health food stores and Internet websites; a set of eight plates starts at $3.99.[79]

Frito-Lay SunChips packaging

Launched in 1991, SunChips, a multigrain snack made with sunflower and with 30% less fat than potato chips, has appealed to consumers looking for healthier alternatives. But after the brand team realized that its health-conscious clientele care seriously about the environment as well, they launched a program propelled by greener marketing, production, and packaging strategies – and once-flagging sales have nearly doubled from $172 million in 2007 to $308 million in 2009.[80]

As part of its synergistic strategy of "healthy for me" and "healthy for the planet," the SunChips plant in Modesto, California, which cranks out 145,000 snack bags daily, is powered by the sun, and all of Frito-Lay's carbon emissions in the U.S. are offset by the purchase of green energy credits.[81] In 2010, Frito-Lay rolled out across the U.S. new chip bags made largely of Ingeo by Natureworks LLC. Made from polylactic acid (PLA) derived from corn fermentation, it is compostable in industrial composting facilities and, since it is quite thin, over a longer period of time in backyard composters, thus representing the potential to reduce landfill waste and the greenhouse gases associated with the production of petroleum-based packaging.[82] The bags are noisier than conventional chip bags – an issue the brand is working through as this book goes to press – but judging by nearly 50,000 YouTube views of a SunChips 30-second commercial showing time-lapsed decomposition, consumers are excited by the bag's compostability, and Frito-Lay is demonstrating a firm commitment to perfecting this innovative new material and disposal method.

Harvest Collection by GenPak

As the use of disposable cutlery and tableware has become more common in the home as well as at picnics, parties, and other gatherings, compostable products are emerging to replace the tons of plastic cutlery that end up in landfills. One such line is the Harvest Collection by GenPak, which includes compostable plates, cups, and food containers. These products are made from renewable resources such as corn, rice, and wheat, which are either grown or recovered as crop residue. All Harvest Collection cutlery and dinnerware is completely heat- and water-resistant and will break down within months of being composted.[83]

Compostable products are beginning to appear more frequently on store shelves, but, as mentioned above, not all products that claim to be so are actually compostable. To deal with this issue, the Biodegradable Products Institute (BPI) created a eco-label to help consumers and compost facility operators easily identify plastic products that will actually compost completely and safely in the proper facilities.[84] BPI's label is designed to facilitate composting by eliminating the need to sort food scraps from tableware. This is especially useful for picking up after large gatherings. The entire waste stream – food, tableware, and cutlery – can be composted, rather than land-filled.[85] In addition to finished products, BPI certifies producers of resins, the raw materials that can be converted into a plethora of products including bags, food serviceware, and packaging.

Figure 4.2 **BPI logo**

15 Safe for disposal

With the potential for disposable batteries, cell phones, iPods, and other ubiquitous electronic equipment to contain toxic substances that can leach into underground water supplies from landfills, the call for reduced tox-icity is fast changing the rules for business. In 2006, the European Union passed the Restriction of Hazardous Substances (ROHS) directive prohibit-ing sales of new electrical and electronic equipment containing more than agreed-on levels of lead, cadmium, mercury, hexavalent chromium, poly-brominated biphenyl (PBB), and polybrominated diphenyl ether (PBDE) flame retardants. As Sony learned the hard way, not complying with such legislation is one game with very high stakes. In December 2001, the Sony Playstation was rejected for sale in the European Union and $162 million worth of merchandise was impounded because the power cord exceeded the allowable amount of cadmium, causing Sony to miss the all-important Christmas sales season.[86]

Philips Alto II fluorescent lamps

Even though CFLs represent a game-changing step forward in energy effi-ciency, all compact fluorescents contain a tiny, yet highly toxic amount of mercury. Once in landfills, it can contaminate underground water supplies.

Indeed, many states prohibit the disposal of CFLs (and all fluorescent lighting) in regular trash. Even without laws, the value of this mercury, as well as the energy embodied in CFLs, behooves lamp manufacturers to collect the bulbs for recycling.

One bulb that is raising the bar for product disposal is Philips Alto fluorescent lamps. Easily spotted by their bright green end caps, the Alto II fluorescents have the lowest mercury content on the market, and use a lead-free solder.[87] They pass the EPA's Toxicity Characteristic Leaching Procedure (TCLP) test, thus classifying the bulbs as non-hazardous waste and relieving commercial customers of regulatory burdens associated with disposing of fluorescent bulbs. Their longer life saves money on bulbs and labor-intensive change-outs. There are over half a billion Alto lamps in operation.[88]

As demonstrated in this chapter, the new rules of green marketing now require businesses to adopt a life-cycle approach to their products and packages. Doing so not only minimizes environmental and social impacts and risks, and helps to meet consumer needs, but it can be also be a sure route to innovation. However, greening can present even greater opportunities for businesses that want to change the rules of the game to innovate further. Many of the strategies and tools being used by sustainability leaders for "sustainable product innovation" are discussed in the next chapter.

The *New Rules* Checklist

Use the following checklist to explore the myriad opportunities for refining your products or developing new ones to environmental imperatives and satisfy consumers' primary demands for quality/performance and affordability.

- Do we know the full range of environmental and social issues that are associated with our product or service? Can we consider a "cradle-to-gate" or "cradle-to-grave" or even a "cradle-to-cradle" life-cycle assessment for our products?

- How do our products' environmental and social impacts compare to our competitors?

- Do we have a short- and long-term plan of environmental and social-related improvements for our products?

○ What environmental improvements do we anticipate competitors introducing? Are we prepared with a response?

○ In what ways do environmental enhancements improve our product or service's overall performance and quality?

○ Are there opportunities to use environmental enhancements to extend our brand?

Raw material use and procurement

○ Are we using the minimum amount of raw materials possible, i.e., taking advantage of opportunities for source reduction?

○ Are we ensuring that procurement processes for our raw materials avoids tropical deforestation? Clear-cutting? Land stripping? Oil spills?

○ Can we use renewable resources or resources that are sustainably managed and harvested? Organically grown?

○ Can we use locally procured raw materials to keep energy shipping costs to a minimum and assist local farmers?

○ Are our suppliers certified by such organizations as TransFair, Rainforest Alliance, or the Fairtrade Foundation for sustainable harvesting and fair labor practices?

○ What steps are we taking for reducing the use of toxic chemicals in our products?

Manufacturing and distribution

○ What steps can we take to prevent or otherwise reduce the production of solid and hazardous waste in our manufacturing processes? How can we reduce our use of water? How can we reduce our emissions to air and releases to waterways?

○ Can we use solar or wind or other forms of renewable energy to power our manufacturing plants?

○ Are we manufacturing close to our markets so as to create local jobs and minimize transportation energy and costs?

Packaging

○ Can we redesign our packages to reduce materials? Make them from recycled content? Make them recyclable?

○ Can we use alternative materials such as bioplastics to make them compostable?

Use

○ Can we redesign our products to make them more energy- fuel- or water-efficient and thereby reduce consumers' operating costs and carbon footprint?

○ Might we provide real-time information that informs consumers of their environmental impact as it relates to a product?

○ Can we use alternative ingredients that help to minimize risks to health and the environment?

After-use

○ Can we design our products to be durable? Refillable? Reusable? Repairable? Remanufacturable? Rechargeable?

○ Can we design our products so they can be easily disassembled for recycling?

○ Are we designing our products from materials that are easily recyclable and do facilities exist for recycling in consumers' communities?

○ Can we take back our products for recycling? Can we create reverse distribution logistics and strategies?

Disposal

○ Can we use materials and ingredients that are biodegradable or compostable?

○ Can we make our products and packaging safer to landfill or incinerate?

785266 000297

Innovate for sustainability

Almost daily, new scientific data become available, suggesting that humans will need to tread significantly more lightly on the planet to meet our future needs sustainably. In short, all signs point toward present modes of production and consumption being unsustainable. This issue is especially critical for U.S. consumers whose lifestyles are the least sustainable on the planet and, to boot, are emulated or aspired to by billions of other consumers in emerging economies and developing nations. According to the U.S. EPA, in 2006 American households threw away more than 251 million tons of trash. The bulk of this waste ended up in landfills, consuming vast quantities of energy to transport and potentially adding toxic leachate to underground water supplies, not to mention using millions of pounds of raw materials that will take untold quantities of new resources and energy to replace. Some experts go so far as to estimate that, to achieve significant reductions in our energy and natural resource use over the next several decades, we will need to radically alter our entire means of production and consumption by a factor of four. One way to address this critical problem is through innovation.

Innovating for sustainability brings with it exciting opportunities for businesses to help grow their top-line sales and even evolve and transform their business models – indeed, their entire company – to better compete within the rules of a more sustainable future. That this represents a opportunity for marketers to lead the way is unquestioned. Brand managers and marketers – those responsible for the development and communications of products and services – are closest to their brands and often the lead the way toward creative new products that can best meet their consumers' needs. This chapter is aimed at managers and marketers who want to understand how the quest for sustainability can help them discover the next big idea leading to meaningful new products and more satisfied consumers.

Beyond eco-design to eco-innovation

It is one thing to use the most authentic green design principles, such as those described in Chapter 4, to create products with a lower impact. But the rules are quickly changing. To stay competitive and meet the challenges of sustainable development, forward-thinking businesses will need to combine innovation with ecology, through the power of what's known (especially in Europe) as "eco-innovation." Eco-innovation can be defined as innovating at the concept stage, or developing entirely new products and services (including materials and technologies) capable of performing the same function as existing ones only with significantly less environmental impact. As will be seen in many of the examples to follow, it represents the opportunity to at once solve pressing environmental issues while superbly meeting consumer needs, and even to transform one's company – profitably.

Figure 5.1 **Sustainable product innovation**

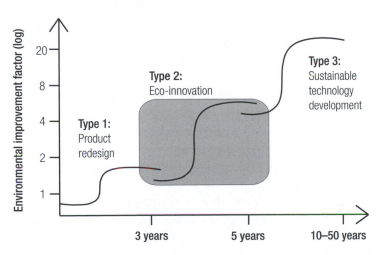

Source: TNO Science and Industry, The Netherlands

As can be seen in Figure 5.1, denoting the progression of three "S" curves of sustainable product innovation, existing products can only be tweaked (eco-designed) so much before it becomes necessary to leap to an entirely new product concept in order to meet the same consumer need with significantly reduced environmental impact. At the end of even the most thoroughly executed process, greening a product by making adjustments in raw materials, packaging, and so forth, leaves you, by definition, with pretty much the same concept as when you started. Your toothbrush is still a toothbrush, but now uses recycled materials. Your water bottle is still a water bottle, only the shoulders are a little shaved off, or it is made from aluminum instead of plastic. Even at the end of a series of multiple iterations aimed at greening, at some point you will find yourself at the end of the first "S" curve labeled "Type 1: Product redesign," unable to achieve greater environmental improvement; you are limited by your product concept.

In order to achieve significant, not just incremental, reductions in eco-impact, you must jump-shift to an entirely new product concept. This is called "eco-" or "functional innovation," represented by the second "S" curve labeled "Type 2: Eco-innovation." To develop new product concepts that perform the same function as existing products but with significantly less impact, start by questioning fundamental assumptions. For instance, to further reduce the environmental impact of a toothbrush, first consider modifying the task from merely "greening a toothbrush" to, let's say, "cleaning teeth without a toothbrush." This might trigger a new product concept such as a specially treated chewing gum that will clean teeth without the need for a toothbrush (and also the toothpaste, water, and the packaging!).

To proceed from the second to the third "S" curve labeled "Type 3: Sustainable technology development," you must redefine your task more radically – for instance, from "cleaning teeth" to "preventing the plaque from forming in the first place." This might lead to developing, say, a benign food additive that would accomplish the task. Moving up and across the three "S" curves in this graph starting with a product concept of a toothbrush made of recycled materials, then evolving to chewing gum, and finally to a food additive, shows how eco-innovation can inspire new products and new business models with significantly reduced environmental impact – and economic benefit as well.

Among its many attractive business and green marketing opportunities, eco-innovation represents the potential for significantly enhanced consumer benefits. In the case of the chewing gum, one can imagine significant cost, convenience, and even efficacy plusses (not to mention ending the problem of getting the kids to brush). Rather than simply focusing on eco-efficiency and its desirable but less exciting effect on the bottom line, moving along these "S" curves of sustainable innovation represents the potential for changing the rules of the game, and, as GE experienced with its Ecomagination initiative, the ability to project an image as a leader, innovator, and socially responsible corporate citizen, all rolled into one. Finally, many sustainably innovative companies gain competitive advantage by anticipating future changes in the market. Innovating for sustainability before it reaches the radar screens of others in your industry allows companies to anticipate market changes. Eco-innovative products, such as the ones described in this chapter, put their developers, designers, and producers way ahead of the curve, often yielding a first-mover advantage that neatly translates into a better brand image for their products and companies.

Five strategies for eco-innovation

There are several strategies that forward-looking companies can use to eco-innovate. Let's take a closer look at five of them.

Five strategies for eco-innovation

1. Innovate at the system level
2. Develop new materials
3. Develop new technologies
4. Develop new business models
5. Restore the environment

1 Innovate at the system level

No one is an island, and no product stands alone, either. Products are part of a larger system from which they draw resources and deposit by-products and wastes. The most successful businesses understand, appreciate, and leverage the system in which their products operate. Changing the system in which products are developed and/or delivered allows innovators to expand their business and redefine their industry. Following are three of many ways to change a product's system in order to minimize its environmental impact: changing the elements in a product system, dematerializing the product, and creating a new product system.

Change individual elements within an existing product system

Changing a product system is a big task – but starting small and rethinking the individual elements of an existing product system not only gets you started, it can also achieve some pretty big results in and of itself. For example, a lot of water is still used even if consumers use low-flush toilets and turn off the water while brushing their teeth or washing their hands. But if one first considers the fixtures in a bathroom as working together in one unified system, rather than as individual standalone units, exciting new business opportunities arise.

AQUS greywater recycling system

Take the AQUS system by WaterSaver Technologies of Louisville, Kentucky. This ingenious technology makes use of a concept called "greywater". Run-off water from the bathroom sink feeds into the toilet, and is then used for flushing. The water works twice at no additional cost! Given that about 40% of all water used in households is used to flush toilets, combining the sink and toilet in such a unique new product system saves the typical two-person household between 10 and 20 gallons a day, or about 5,000 gallons per year.

Soladey toothbrush

Japanese company Soladey took a step back and decided that the tooth-brushing system as we know it didn't need as many elements. So they built a photocatalytic titanium dioxide rod into the handle of their toothbrush. Brushing teeth with this toothbrush in a bright room causes chemical reactions to break down tooth plaque, eliminating the need for toothpaste.[1] By combining two elements of the toothbrush product system, Soladey has created a streamlined system with the potential for significantly reduced environmental impact.[2]

gDiapers

According to the EPA, in 2005 approximately 3.5 million tons of diaper waste, representing about 20 billion disposable diapers, were dumped in U.S. landfills, where they will take an estimated 500 years to decompose.[3] Two concerned parents invented the gDiaper, capitalizing on new materials and a systems-oriented product view to invent a radically new alternative.

Conventional disposable diapers are composed of an inner diaper made from wood pulp and an outer lining made of plastic, both of which are thrown away with every diaper change. The gDiaper's advantage is that the inner and outer components are detachable, so that the outer lining can be washed and reused while the inner diaper can be flushed down the toilet. This ensures that the bacteria-laden human waste winds up in the sewage treatment system where it belongs, rather than in a landfill where it can leach into the underground water.[4] Representing a feasible and convenient alternative to both cloth and disposable diapers with a measurably reduced environmental and material impact, the gDiaper is poised to take significant market share from conventional disposables.

Dematerialize

Reconceive a product so that it requires significantly fewer material inputs (and, consequently, outputs). Ask: can a product perform the same function by using only a fraction of its original materials? In many cases, the answer is yes.

Tricycle's SIM simulated carpet sample

One company that is taking a swipe at the estimated 1 million pounds of carpet samples that end up in American landfills each year[5] is Tricycle, a Chattanooga, Tennessee-based design firm. Most carpet swatches used by designers and showrooms are discarded after a single use – and since an average order of carpet samples uses more than seven gallons of oil, the environmental and financial impacts of these swatches can really add up.[6]

Thinking outside the box, Tricycle devised SIM, which relies on an inventive technology that prints images on swatch-sized pieces of paper that simulate the exact colors and textures of a particular section of carpet, but with 95% less water and energy and 100% less oil than conventional swatches. Add to that, traditionally produced swatches may take days or weeks to be delivered from carpet factories, but SIM reduces the wait time to less than 24 hours.[7]

In 2005, SIM clients were shipped about 34,000 paper samples[8] – saving manufacturers 70% of the costs associated with samples, or about $5 million per year. [9] For its efforts, Tricycle won a Gold IDEA from the Industrial Designers Society of America for 2006.

E-readers

Suddenly they are everywhere. Amazon's Kindle, Barnes & Noble's Nook, Sony's Reader, and Apple's iPad. People are fast abandoning newspapers and books and turning to these and other exciting new e-readers – handheld devices that electronically deliver the content of printed books but with many additional features. With a screen about the size of a paperback book and wireless connectivity that allows users to read their favorite newspapers, magazines, and blogs within moments of publication, users can wirelessly purchase new releases at a significant discount from hardcovers. Books take less than 60 seconds to download, and more than 1,500 titles can be stored at a time, making an e-reader an attractive option whether traveling, commuting, or at home. And the environmental benefits of using e-readers to read electronic books (ebooks) are compelling: the Cleantech Group projects that in 2012, 5.27 billion kilograms of carbon dioxide emissions will be prevented due by ebooks.[10]

Create a new system

Sometimes the most effective way to cut down on eco-impacts is to abandon a product concept altogether and create an entirely new system. This requires a business to learn from the larger environment in which its products function. It takes the efforts of cross-functional product development and marketing teams that can interpret information from the full range of product life-cycle phases and synthesize new ideas.

Holistic to the core, systems thinking holds that every employee and citizen has something significant to contribute. It may also entail cooperating with manufacturers of complementary products, reaching out beyond one's corporate borders to stakeholders in the local community, and even bringing perspectives as diverse as those of children into the process. But the rewards are potentially the most significant because of the inherent potential to change the rules of the game.

Admittedly, the challenge of creating a new system can be daunting if stakeholders feel the ultimate eco-innovation may threaten an existing business; for these reasons, eco-innovative activity needs the full support of the CEO and others responsible for long-term strategy. It is best carried out in a "spin-off" or "incubator" mode or by a start-up with no pre-existing stake in the current system. Within established businesses, potential enemies need to be converted into allies by demonstrating how they can benefit.

Better Place recharging stations

Demand for plug-in hybrid vehicles like Chevy's Volt and Nissan's LEAF is projected to skyrocket to 600,000 vehicles by 2015. The drivers of all of those new cars will benefit from an innovation being pioneered by the start-up Better Place, based in Palo Alto, California. They have invented an entirely new system that overcomes the range limitations of electric vehicles.

Rather than making drivers of electric cars wait to recharge their batteries at home overnight, Better Place shifts the paradigm, offering multiple "fill-up" stations where drivers can either exchange their battery for a newly charged one, or opt to charge their battery within the network of charging stations, wired parking lots, and battery replacement stations that Better Place has built throughout their Israeli test market. By the end of 2010, there will be a station every 25 miles – and Better Place also sells the electric cars that can be charged at those stations.[11] The company aims to have tens of thousands of electric cars on Israel's roads by 2011. With the projected costs of battery-powered car ownership as much as 50% lower than a comparable gasoline-powered car, Better Place provides an alternative that is convenient and cost-effective – as well as environmentally sensible.

2 Develop new materials

There are currently thousands of different materials on the market for consumer, commercial, and industrial use, from the softest fibers to bulletproof plastics and metals and everything in between. Each of these materials is particularly suited to meet specific needs or functions – and each bears an environmental impact. Promising new materials are in development, leading to sustainable advances and an ever-growing opportunity for innovation. One particularly exciting material with the potential for a wide range of applications is bioplastics. Now growing in volume between 20% and 30% each year, bioplastics are derived from renewable resources such as corn or sugar cane, contain no toxins (unlike petroleum-based plastics), and are generally compostable in municipal facilities and often backyard composters. Considering that only about 5% of the 30 million tons of plastic used in the U.S. annually is recycled, biodegradable bioplastics have emerged in recent years as a viable method to reduce waste from petroleum-based plastics.[12]

Coke's PlantBottle

One exciting application for bio-plastics is Coca-Cola's "PlantBottle," made from a combination of traditional petroleum-based plastic and up to 30% plant-based materials such as sugar cane and molasses, a by-product of sugar production. A life-cycle analysis conducted by Imperial College London shows the "PlantBottle" represents up to 25% reduced carbon emissions compared with 100% petroleum-based PET. Also, unlike some other plant-based plastics, it can be recycled without contaminating traditional PET.[13]

Metabolix's Mirel bioplastic

If two big companies have their way, we'll see a lot more plant-based bottles in the future. Metabolix, a joint venture with Archer Daniels Midland called

Telles, and NatureWorks, a Cargill subsidiary, are both staking our big positions in bioplastics. As of this writing, Telles is about to start shipping its Mirel plastic pellets from a new plant in Clinton, Iowa. One of the first products is resin for a $1.25 biodegradable Paper Mate pen made by Newell Rubbermaid. Paper Mate says advance demand is strong. The pen, however, does cost more to make. Metabolix charges about $2.50 a pound for its green plastic, around twice that of traditional feedstock. The good news is that Paper Mate's pens use so little plastic that the pen maker needs to reduce its margins by only a couple of percentage points compared with its regular pens.[14]

Natureworks's Ingeo bioplastic

Natureworks's Ingeo brand of bioplastics is made from 100% polylactic acid (PLA) produced by the fermentation of corn. Ingeo's versatile functionality – like traditional, petroleum-based plastics it can be molded into a variety of forms: opaque, clear, flexible, or rigid – is already being leveraged for a variety of food packaging. Catch it keeping muffins fresh at Target, in use for food serviceware, and in the lining of the Ecotainer, a compostable paper-based cold drink cup, a joint initiative between Coca-Cola and International Paper.[15] Other sustainable brands who have incorporated Ingeo into their products include Noble Juices, for the first juice bottle and shrink sleeve label made from Ingeo, Method's compostable cleaning wipes, and Green Mountain Coffee Roasters' compostable coffee bags. Ingeo polymer can also be converted into a fiber-like polyester, which can be used as fiberfill bedding for use in pillows and comforters. Most recently, it is being used in baby diapers such as the Huggies Natural line.[16]

Like all greener products, however, Ingeo has its trade-offs. It is compostable, but will typically only readily break down in industrial composters – taking much longer in backyard compost piles if at all, and there are only about 100 such facilities in the entire United States. Also, PLA products can contaminate the recycling stream when mixed with products made from PET, a look-alike petrochemical resin, thus requiring special labeling and sorting at the PLA products' end-of-life stage and educating mainstream consumers about proper disposal techniques.[17] A collection and composting system is being developed by the Bioplastics Recycling Consortium to address these issues.[18]

3 Develop new technologies

Many people argue that most of our modern-day environmental woes are a direct result of industrialization. However, new eco-innovative technologies can mitigate the problems of the past and pave the way to a more sustainable future. Such technologies can be high-tech, expensive, and complicated, but they can also represent simple, low-tech solutions of comparable efficacy. Three particularly good opportunities exist in the areas of high-efficiency lighting, portable renewable energy, and alternative automotives.

Light-emitting diodes (LEDs)

Just as consumers are getting used to CFLs as a replacement for incandescent lamps, an even more exciting alternative is here to take its place: light-emitting diodes (LEDs). Projected to represent 46% of the $4.4 billion U.S. market for lamps in the commercial, industrial, and outdoor stationary sectors by 2020, LEDs are more efficient and last twice as long – typically 50,000 hours – as CFLs.[19] Also, in contrast to CFLs, LEDs do not need a ballast and do not contain toxic mercury, so they are safer to dispose of.

Historically, prices for these wonder bulbs were an impediment to market acceptance, but thanks to recent innovations affordable LEDs are fast making their way to retail shelves. One standout is EcoSmart LED light bulbs sold exclusively in Home Depot. Retailing for $19.97, compared to over $50 for other 40 watt incandescents, the bulb uses about 80% less energy and is expected to last more than 22 years. Also, it is dimmable, completely recyclable, and offers outstanding quality of light – and will pay back its initial investment in less than two years, accounting for energy and replacement savings.[20]

Distributed renewable energy

Demand for alternative energy is exploding, and will continue to rise along with consumer concern over climate change and other threats. Thanks to advances in technology, the cost of wind power has fallen by 80% over the past 30 years to between 4 and 6 cents per kWh,[21] making it competitive to oil (5 cents per kWh) and natural gas (3 cents per kWh).[22] In fact, wind power now provides 1% of energy in the U.S., or about enough energy to power 4.5 million homes.[23]

Solio solar-powered charger

Long confined to rooftop solar panels and windmills, renewable energy sources are ready to hit the road. They are now accessible via hip, portable consumer products such as Solio, a hand-held, solar-powered charger for small electronic devices such as cell phones, iPods, and digital cameras. Fully charged after a bath in direct sunlight for 8–10 hours, a Solio can run an MP3 player for up to 56 hours.[24] Working on the same principle, tote bags and backpacks produced by Voltaic Systems[25] and Reware[26] power small electronic devices such as cell phones and even laptops via solar panels woven onto the bags.

Swift wind turbine

Who needs the grid? Some consumers are producing clean, renewable energy themselves with the Swift Wind Turbine, designed by the UK-based company Renewable Devices, and produced in the U.S. by Cascade Engineering of Grand Rapids, Michigan. Perched on a rooftop, this small $10,000 turbine sends the 2,000 kilowatts of free electricity it generates each year directly to the consumer's electric system. Considering that the typical American household consumes between 6,500 and 10,000 kWh of electricity per year, the Swift Wind Turbine can cut a home's electrical demand from the grid by one-fifth to one-third. A $1,000 federal renewable energy tax credit can defray part of that already reduced cost.[27]

Human-powered products

A limitless and clean energy resource that is literally available at our fingertips is kinetic energy – and it's powering a growing number of products. Referred to as human-powered products, these items can be conveniently small – for example, the Ventura digital watch that is powered by the motions of the wearer's wrist[28] – and they can put the power of charging small electronic devices literally into your hands. Consider the Aladdin hand generator that charges cell phones, iPods, or even a portable DVD player with just a few squeezes of a handle.[29]

Just think about all the kinetic energy produced by bicycles and treadmills! This notion dawned on the owner of a string of gyms in Hong Kong, who rigged cycling and cross-training machines to power a gym's lights and store extra energy in batteries for later use.[30] The Human Power Trainer, made by Windstream Power LLC of North Ferrisburg, Vermont, works on the same concept. It mounts a bicycle on a frame so that the rear tire can turn a turbine that generates power, which is stored in a 12-volt battery which, in turn, powers household appliances. An average person can produce between 100 and 150 watts over the course of a typical workout[31] – enough power to run a pair of speakers, an electric hand mixer, or a small television.

Alternative automotives

Watch out, Toyota Prius! Gasoline–electric hybrids are getting the attention now, but eco-innovative electric cars with zero direct emissions are driving into town. General Motors hopes to reinvent itself behind the Chevy Volt, a plug-in hybrid electric vehicle that will be released in the U.S. for the 2011 model year.[32] With a range of 40 miles from a single charge, it can successfully navigate the average (33 mile) daily round-trip commute of most Americans – using zero gasoline and producing zero direct emissions. Unlike a conventional hybrid vehicle that has a second, gasoline-powered engine, the Volt has a gasoline-powered engine that powers a electric generator which kicks in after the battery is drained, so the car is powered exclusively by electric motor.[33] Priced at a hefty $41,000 base cost, up to $7,500 in federal tax credits are available to jumpstart the mainstream market.

What may surpass even electric cars in the long term are vehicles powered by fuel cells. Although electric cars are emission-free, they are still responsible for indirect atmospheric emissions generated by coal- and gas-fired power plants. However, cars that run on hydrogen fuel cells, such as Honda's FCX Clarity, have the potential if the hydrogen can be generated without emissions, since its production requires natural gas. (Experiments going on in Iceland are currently producing hydrogen using geothermal energy.) Hydrogen fuel cells harness the power created by a chemical reaction between hydrogen gas and the oxygen found in ambient air. The sole by-product of this reaction is pure water.[34] The biggest limitation to widespread adoption of fuel cell cars is the lack of hydrogen filling stations, so when Honda rolled out the Clarity in late 2007 it did so only in Southern California, where it had also built refueling facilities.[35] Honda has calculated the Clarity's fuel consumption to be the equivalent of 68 miles per gallon in a gasoline-powered car. With a travel range of 270 miles,[36] test drivers report that the Clarity is also a dream to drive.[37]

**Addressing
the New Rules**

Nissan's innovative drive toward sustainability

Nissan, the Japanese auto giant, is revving up a holistic approach to sustainable transportation that goes beyond cranking out greener cars. Since 1992, they have been on a mission to bring forth a "Symbiosis of People, Vehicles and Nature,"[38] and have been integrating innovative design, proactive life-cycle management, and government partnerships with the goal of keeping the environmental impact caused by their operations and their vehicles within the Earth's "natural ability to absorb that impact."[39] In attempting to reduce carbon and other emissions, and promote the 3Rs (Reduce, Reuse, Recycle), Nissan demonstrates how sustainability can drive innovation and business success.

Nissan's sustainability commitment starts by making their traditional gas-guzzling vehicles more fuel-efficient via clean-diesel engines and more resourceful catalysts. Next, attempts at bringing electric, fuel-cell, and hybrid vehicles to mainstream drivers in Japan, North America, and Europe are paying off with the X-Trail FCV (fuel cell vehicle), now available in Japan for limited lease agreements, and more fuel cell vehicles are expected.[40]

On the hybrid front, in 2007 Nissan introduced the Altima Hybrid, its first hybrid car, and the Infiniti Hybrid is in the offing.[41] Nissan's LEAF, a medium-sized hatchback introduced in 2009, is slated to be the world's first affordable electric, zero-emission car. The LEAF, an acronym for Leading, Environmentally friendly, Affordable, Family car, is on track for a full rollout in Japan, Europe and the U.S. by 2012.[42] Unlike the Prius and the Volt, which combine electric batteries and gasoline engines, albeit in different ways, the Nissan LEAF is solely powered by its electric battery. Making clear that its commitment to producing electric vehicles will continue over the long term, the company plans to build a plant in Tennessee that will produce more than 100,000 electric cars annually by 2013.[43] Helping drivers conserve fuel further, Nissan empowers Japanese drivers with CARWINGS, a GPS system that uses real-time traffic information and data from other CARWINGS users to guide them towards the fastest route.[44] Nissan also lets CARWINGS members compare fuel consumption and eco-driving rankings. To notch fuel efficiency up to 10%, Nissan crafted the "Eco-Pedal System," which monitors pressure on the accelerator and alerts the driver when the car is burning more fuel than needed.[45]

With a lofty goal of attaining a 100% recovery rate, Nissan is focusing on the three Rs of Reduce, Reuse, and Recycle throughout the vehicle life-cycle. This includes reducing the use of harmful materials, incorporating more recycled plastic parts from end-of-life cars, using recycled plastics and renewable biomaterials, and improving recyclability and dismantling efficiency. Nissan certifies dealerships in Japan as Nissan Green Shops, which ensure that end-of-life vehicles are handled properly.[46] Most admirably, as of 2006, all new Nissan models in Japan and Europe claim a recoverability rate of 95% – almost ten years ahead of Japan's Automobile Recycling Law's recoverability rate target as a result of changes in the production and development.[47]

The final component of Nissan's drive toward sustainability consists of partnerships with community groups and government agencies. In Beijing, China, Nissan works with the Beijing Transportation Information Center to relieve bumper-to-bumper traffic and improve traffic patterns. With the help of French automaker Renault, Nissan has established partnership agreements with governments in Israel, Portugal, Yohoma (Japan), and Tennessee and Oregon aimed at creating settings for the integration of electric vehicles.[48]

4 Develop new business models

Eco-innovative products and services can end up being more expensive than their conventional counterparts because they lack economy of scale, or because they use new materials or technologies. But new business models can surmount these hurdles to acceptance, creating a win–win–win situation for businesses, the environment, and consumers.

Manufacturers and retailers sell products to consumers, who usually assume responsibility for maintenance and eventual disposal. One exciting alternative business model that is currently finding favor is selling the actual service provided by a product, as opposed to simply selling the product outright. Consumers already meet many of their needs through services: they think nothing of doing laundry at a laundromat, renting a car, or borrowing DVDs from Netflix. Take a moment to look at your product through a service lens. Can it be delivered partially or completely by a service? If it can, you may have an opportunity to significantly reduce costs and environmental impacts of your product. Consumers can enjoy the benefits they seek without the need for maintenance, and are assured access to the latest and cleanest technologies. A service-based business model helps businesses retain ownership of the materials and energy that are embodied in the products they design and produce. This helps facilitate repair, reuse, and recycling, whether prompted by regulation or manufacturing economies. Keep in mind that there are trade-offs involved with providing services, like the energy it takes to power an ebook, and, more importantly, to deliver the digital content.

Services can be offered in many innovative ways: providing the product as part of a service; replacing a product, partially or completely with an electronic service; or substituting knowledge, wholly or in part, for a physical product.

Offer the product as part of a service

Zipcar car-sharing service

Consumers don't need to *own* a product per se – they just need access to the service (the functionality) that the product represents. Many car owners don't want to give up the independence afforded by driving their own car, but they would like to skip the hassle of parking and maintenance. These are the principles that underpin the largest car-sharing company in the world, Boston-based Zipcar. For as little as an annual membership fee of $50 and about $8 per hour or $77 per day – gas and insurance included – members can pick up a car, run their errands, and return it to a designated parking spot ready to go for the next member (ever try to find a parking space in Paris or Tokyo at midday?) without the worry of insurance, loans, maintenance, or filling up the tank.[49]

By promoting car sharing as a popular and hip way to avoid the hassles of car ownership, Zipcar, serving 13 cities in the U.S., Canada, and London, England, is becoming the car of choice for urban dwellers, college students, and even corporate fleets – and it has myriad environmental and social benefits, too. Projecting that they have the potential to reduce the number of cars on the road by one million, the company reports that 65% of Zipcar members give up their cars or delay the purchase of a new one.[50] Furthermore, the company estimates that each Zipcar replaces over 15 privately owned vehicles.[51] Taking cars off the road can translate to less pollution, less dependence on oil, and more green space not needed for parking. And Zipcar members save money, too. According to the company, Zipcar members save more than $500 per month over the cost of car ownership.[52] As of June 2009, the company had 300,000 members and 6,500 vehicles in urban areas and college campuses throughout 26 North American states and provinces as well as in London, England.[53]

Vélib bicycle-sharing service

Representing the biking equivalent of car sharing, in 2007 the city of Paris, France, launched Vélib, a pay-as-you-go bicycle rental program. With over 20,000 bicycles in about 1,500 self-service rental kiosks, the bicycles are a convenient, cheap, trendy, and emission-free way for locals and tourists to get around town. Bikes can be rented for pre-paid amounts of time ranging from 30 minutes up to one week, and then dropped off at any kiosk. In the first year alone, more than 27.5 million trips – an average of 120,000 trips per day – significantly reduced car congestion and earned the city more than

$31 million in revenue.[54] The concept is being emulated around the world in Barcelona, Mexico City, and London.

College textbook rentals

Product sharing isn't limited to transportation; Cengage Learning, one of the largest textbook publishers in America, has recently adopted it. In August 2009, the company announced that it would begin renting textbooks to college students, who, upon purchase, will receive immediate access electronically to the first chapter, then receive the physical book by mail. They can then either return or sell the book after a set rental period.[55] At 40% to 70% of the sale price, the option to rent textbooks promises to defer the often-bemoaned cost of college textbooks, and is environmentally sound. Through its iChapters service, Cengage is also one of a growing list of companies who will sell students downloadable PDF chapters of textbooks, for a complete digital learning experience.

Power purchase agreements

Solar power is a clean energy source that is attractive because sunlight is free – but the time it takes to recoup the initial investment prevents wider adoption among homeowners. That's where the power purchase agreement (PPA) comes in. Under a PPA, a provider installs (at its own expense or usually with the help of a third-party lender or a bank) solar panels on a residential rooftop or commercial property. The customer then purchases the resulting power at a fixed rate for the term of the contract, often at a lower rate than power generated by the local electric company.[56] Launched by California's SunEdison LLC, SunPower, and REC Solar,[57] the PPA provider is responsible for maintaining the solar panel system for a set period, usually 15 years, when the customer can purchase the system or extend the PPA.

Substitute an electronic service for a product, wholly or in part

Digital media represents untold opportunity for eco-innovation by replacing material products with electronic services with superior performance. Surface mail has quickly evolved into email, newspaper content is delivered on a BlackBerry or iPhone, and a single CD-ROM can carry 90 million phone numbers. Digital product delivery lies at the heart of Apple's iPod, one of the most successful new product introductions ever, with its iTunes database of music selections. Similarly, Netflix members rent movies online and receive DVDs through the mail, or stream movies directly from the Internet. Netflix recently signed up its tenth million member and delivered its two billionth DVD.[58]

Zonbu computer service

Is there a virtual desktop in your future? If Zonbu computer has its way, traditional computer ownership will be replaced by a subscription service. In 2007, Silicon Valley's Zonbu began selling a simplified desktop computer for $99. Users pay a monthly subscription fee of about $15 for access to Zonbu's centralized Web-based programs, operating system, storage space, and virus protection. Should you lose your laptop or the computer malfunctions, your files are safe on Zonbu's servers and accessible from another Zonbu computer, eliminating the hassles of computer maintenance tasks such as software updates and virus and spyware protection. Zonbu's desktop computer (the company launched a laptop in 2008) was the first consumer-oriented computer to earn a "Gold" rating by the Electronic Product Environment Assessment Tool (EPEAT), which evaluates electronic products in relation to 51 total environmental criteria.[59]

Substitute knowledge for a physical product, wholly or in part

Integrated pest management

Why make a product when your brain can do the job with no environmental impact at all? Take pest control. Integrated pest management (IPM) relies on information about the life-cycles of pests and their interaction with the environment, keeping the use of chemical pesticides to a minimum. Pest control companies use IPM to monitor pest populations and determine if and when pest control action must be taken. Most importantly, IPM programs help manage crops, lawns, and indoor areas to prevent pests from becoming a threat in the first place. IPM represents the opportunity for a profitable contract management business model; get paid to keep pests away, rather than simply apply costly and toxic chemicals once they appear.

5 Restore the environment

Eco-design and eco-innovation share a worthy goal: minimizing environmental impact. But what if one were to consider new products or services based on revolutionary new materials and technologies that could actually restore the social, environmental, and economic systems that sustain us?

BASF PremAir ozone catalyst

Consider all the pollution a car generates. Gasoline combustion creates ground-level ozone, the main component of smog that can aggravate respiratory problems such as asthma. Enter the BASF PremAir ozone catalyst, which, when attached to car radiators, converts to oxygen up to 80% of the ground-level ozone that comes into contact with the device.[60] The PremAir catalyst purifies the air as you drive, and is now standard in several automobiles, including all Volvo models and certain BMW, Mercedes, Mitsubishi, and Hyundai cars.[61]

PUR water purifier

Procter & Gamble's PUR brand water purifier is a small satchel filled with powder. When stirred into a bucket of dirty water and filtered out, it removes dirt, microbial cysts (such as cryptosporidium) and pollutants, and kills viruses and bacteria, leaving safe, drinkable water.[62] Distributed by 70 non-profits in developing countries where it has helped to purify more than 1.6 billion gallons of water, it has now found a new market in the United States and Canada as a camping/emergency preparedness tool.

Chapters 4 and 5 discussed several strategies for greening one's existing products (eco-design) and offered several strategies for eco-innovating – developing the next generation of products and services with the ability to significantly minimize environmental impact. With greener products and eco-innovations in hand, green marketers are prepared to develop credible impactful branding and communications, the subject of the next two chapters.

The *New Rules* Checklist

Ask the following questions to help inspire you and your team to uncover creative opportunities to innovate for sustainability.

- What policy changes do we need to prepare for? Can we get a jump on these changes by eco-innovating now?

- Where along the innovation curve is our product? How much more opportunity is there to minimize environmental impact? Might we be better off, strategically, to eco-innovate?

- What do we have to do differently to deliver our product with significantly reduced – or even zero – environmental and material impacts?

- What opportunities exist for us to eco-innovate around our product's system? Can we change individual elements within our product's system?

○ In what ways might we engage with other manufacturers to reduce the environmental impacts of the total system in which our product exists? What opportunities exist to collaborate with manufacturers of complementary products to develop new products or even systems?

○ In what ways might we dematerialize our product or service? Use electronic technology? Create a new system altogether?

○ What opportunities exist to use new materials such as bioplastics?

○ What ways exist for us to make renewable energy more affordable and portable?

○ What opportunities exist for us to use new business models to grow our business with less environmental impact? Is there an opportunity to make our greener product or service more affordable or accessible by adopting a new business model?

○ Can we offer services as a replacement for our products? Or, can we lease our product to customers? Can our products be shared?

○ Can we replace our products with smarter alternatives (knowledge or more targeted products)?

○ What business model might we need to adopt to make services affordable for consumers and profitable for our business?

○ Are there opportunities to replace our product wholly or in part with an electronic service?

○ Can we provide a knowledge-based service instead of a physical product?

○ Can we offer products that might actually restore the environment?

Communicating sustainability with impact

Hertz promised to get you out of airports faster. Tide guaranteed to get clothes whiter than white. Keds sneakers assured kids that they would run faster and jump higher. But with environmentalism now a core societal value, consumers want to see green themes in marketing messages in addition to traditional promises associated with a better life. Indeed, communicating environmental and social initiatives with authenticity and impact can help establish one's brand in the vanguard of this important trend. Indeed, such messaging can even ward off legislative threats and potentially protect one's corporate reputation when things go wrong. Also, with stakeholders of all types – employees, investors, and consumers among them – wanting to know about the sustainability of products at every phase of their life-cycles, communicating the environmental and social advantages of one's brands is now critical to running a well-managed business.

Although there are many opportunities associated with communicating one's sustainability initiatives, challenges abound – and not communicating one's environmentally and socially oriented product and corporate initiatives may be riskier still. Marketers who don't tout the sustainability achievements of their brands may find that consumers and other stakeholders assume their products and processes are not ecologically sound; this is a sure way to be replaced on the shelf by a competitor with recognized green credentials! Fail to get on the radar screens of the sustainability-aware and lose opportunities to increase market share among the growing number of influential and affluent LOHAS consumers. Address the new rules of green marketing and expect to enjoy such rewards as enhanced brand equity and a stronger emotional bond with stakeholders.

Challenges of communicating sustainability

Convinced that you need to communicate the sustainable advantages of your brand? Not sure where to begin? Begin your planning process by considering the challenges. For starters, environmental and social benefits can be indirect, intangible, or even insignificant to the consumer. Consumers can't see the emissions being reduced at the power plant when they use energy-saving appliances. (They may not even immediately notice the savings on their power bill.) Similarly, they can't see the capacity increase in the landfill when they recycle, and they have to take it on faith that you pay a fair (living) wage to your employees (and your suppliers are doing likewise).

Trade-offs are a factor, too. Although many greener products are cheaper, faster, or more convenient, some are more expensive, slower, or not as attractive. Toilet paper made from 100% recycled content may be cheaper, but it may not be as soft as virgin counterparts. Taking the bus or train or carpooling saves money over driving one's car and allows one to read, socialize, work, or snooze, but these ecologically preferable options fall short on the flexibility demanded by working parents who have to pick up the kids, a take-out dinner, and the dry-cleaning along a circuitous commute home.

Getting your sustainability-oriented campaign in front of the right people can be a challenge. Demographics-based markets such as homeowners living in the parched Southwest or new mothers with extra pennies to spend on organically grown baby food are easy to pinpoint through conventional media, but lifestyle-based targets such as wildlife lovers or the chemically sensitive, while being easier to reach these days thanks to the Internet, are still pretty hard to pin down.

Sustainable branding is complex – and can be pricey to do well. In addition to underscoring consumer benefits, the historical focus of marketing communications, today's green consumers must be educated on the benefits of new, often technically sophisticated materials, technologies, and designs. New brand names must be established. Corporate green credentials must be put forth. Such tasks can overwhelm the budgets of start-ups with big green ideas. Compounding these tasks, sought-after benefits change with the times. In the past, organic produce was favored because of its perceived health benefits, but today, a wider audience scoops it up because they think it tastes better. Some homeowners install rooftop solar panels to keep up with the technologically savvy neighbors, while others simply want to save money on their energy bill.

And then there's the question of credibility. As discussed in Chapter 2, industry is found to be far less trustworthy on environmental matters than other groups such as NGOs or government. As discussed further in Chapter 7, myriad eco-labels exist, but products are often expensive to certify to, and it is difficult to wade through the clutter. Get it wrong and a backlash can occur. Green communications that appear insignificant or insincere often invite criticism from environmentalists, bloggers, and citizen journalists who are quick to sniff out perceived "greenwashers"; and U.S. state attorneys general and the Federal Trade Commission (FTC), as well as counterpart organizations in such countries as the UK (Advertising Standards Authority), Canada (Advertising Standards Canada), and Australia (Australian Competition and Consumer Commission), can be quick to take action against marketers who make deceptive environmental claims.

Finally, consumers can tire of the same green messages and imagery. Planets, babies, and daisies eventually wear thin with skeptical consumers. "Green fatigue" is brewing due to the plethora of green campaigns in so many consumer media. How many messages have you seen asking you to "do it for Mother Earth" or because "your kids will thank you for it"?

Ottman's fundamentals of good green marketing

Sustainability-oriented marketing communications targeted to mainstream consumers work best when they address the new rules of green marketing head on. As alluded to in Chapter 2, if you want to communicate green benefits to consumers, you should keep in mind that the following conditions, fundamental to all green marketing efforts, must be met:

- Consumers are aware of and concerned about the issues your product or service professes to address.

- The consumer feels, as one person or in concert with others, that he or she can make a difference by using your product or service. This is "empowerment" and it lies at the heart of green marketing. (If consumers didn't feel they would make a difference by using a greener product, they wouldn't buy it in the first place.) This assumes that the sustainability benefits of a product or service can be clearly communicated.

- The product provides tangible, direct benefits to a meaningful number of consumers. In other words, green can't be the only (or even main) benefit a more sustainable product provides. Consumers still need to be attracted to your product or service for the primary reasons why they would buy any product in that category, e.g., getting clothes clean, providing dependable transportation.

- Your product performs equally well or better than your competitors' green or still "brown" alternative. Consumers will not give up quality or performance in order to secure a greener product. Said another way, greener products must perform their intended function first; environmental benefits are viewed as a new source of added value. What's more, often the environmental benefits actually enhance a product's ability to perform its intended function, and, as described more fully in Chapter 1, in these instances, marketers can expect to earn a premium! For example, organic produce tastes better, and Samsung's new solar-power cell phone provides the important benefits of protecting one from running out of battery power.

- Premium pricing needs to be justified through superior performance or another benefit. Keep in mind that many consumers can't afford premiums for many products, including green ones, especially in times of austerity.

- Consumers believe you. This means that your sustainability-related claims can be backed up by data or other evidence. Product-related efforts are reinforced by substantive corporate progress.

- Your products are accessible. To succeed with mainstream consumers, greener products must be available on the websites or shelves at popular supermarkets and mass merchandisers, right next to the "browner" products they are designed to replace.

Ottman's fundamentals of good green marketing

Consumers must:

- Be aware of and concerned about the issues
- Feel empowered to act
- Must know what's in it for *them*
- Afford any premiums – and feel they are worth it
- Believe you
- Find your brand easily

Source: J. Ottman Consulting, Inc.

Once you're fully aware of these fundamentals, take advantage of the following strategies being forged by sustainability leaders around the globe to overcome the challenges and take advantage of the many opportunities afforded by green communications.

Six strategies of sustainable marketing communication

Six strategies of sustainable marketing communication

1. Know your customer
2. Appeal to consumers' self-interest
3. Educate and empower
4. Reassure on performance
5. Engage the community
6. Be credible

Source: J. Ottman Consulting, Inc.

1 Know your customer

In selecting the right consumer to target, keep in mind the complexity of green consumer segments. As described in detail in Chapter 2, consumers can be segmented psychographically into the five NMI segments: LOHAS, Naturalites, Drifters, Conventionals, and Unconcerneds. They can be further segmented according to specific area of personal interest: natural resource conservation, health, animals, and the outdoors.

Just as there are many different types of green consumers, there are many different kinds of environmental and social issues of concern. Figure 1.1 on page 3 showed that water quality, hazardous waste, and pollution from cars and trucks top the list, but there are literally dozens of other issues ranging from endangered species to graffiti and noise pollution that concern even the most mainstream of consumers. Not all consumers will likely be aware of or concerned about all sustainability-related issues, so it is important to pinpoint the consumers who will be most receptive to your message, and to provide any additional education that's needed to bring consumers on board.

One marketer who learned the hard way about the need to measure consumer awareness for the issues that affected their business is Whirlpool. In the early 1990s they won a $30 million "Golden Carrot" award that was put up by the U.S. Department of Energy and a consortium of electrical utilities for being first to market with a chlorofluorocarbon (CFC)-free refrigerator. But they misjudged consumers' willingness to pay a 10% premium for a product with an environmental benefit that many did not appreciate. Likely many consumers, not even knowing what a CFC was, thought the appliance to be deficient, suggesting the need to educate consumers as part of one's marketing; many examples are provided throughout this chapter.

2 Appeal to consumers' self-interest

Many readers will approach this chapter thinking the focus will be on the best ways to highlight the ecological benefits of one's products. You may have visions of ads showcasing the now tiresome images of babies, daisies, and planets that are associated so strongly with green ads. Although the environment is important to consumers – indeed, it may have been the primary reason the product was created in the first place – they will likely *not* be the primary motivation to buy your brand in preference to that of your competitors. In other words, don't commit the fatal sin of green marketing myopia! As my colleagues, Ed Stafford and Cathy Hartman of the Huntsman Business School of Utah State, and I point out in our much-quoted article, "Avoiding Green Marketing Myopia,"[1] remember that consumers buy products to meet basic needs – not altruism. When they enter a grocery, they don their consumer caps – looking to find the products that will get their clothes clean, that will taste great, or that will make themselves look attractive to others; environmental and social benefits are best positioned as an important plus that can help sway purchase decisions, particularly between two otherwise comparable products.

Keep in mind that with environmental issues a threat to health above all else, the number one reason why consumers buy greener products is not to "save the planet" (which isn't in danger of going away anytime soon) but to protect their own health. So it is important to make sure that superior delivery of primary benefits are underscored in design and marketing. Focus too heavily on environmental benefits at the expense of primary benefits like saving money or getting the clothes clean – and expect your brand to wind up in the green graveyard, buried in good intentions.

Underscoring the primary reasons why consumers purchase your brand – sometimes referred to as "quiet green" – can broaden the appeal of your greener products and services way beyond the niche of deepest green consumers and help overcome a premium price hurdle. Demonstrate how consumers can protect their health, save money, or keep their home and community safe and clean. Show busy consumers how some environmentally inclined behaviors can save time and effort. To be clear, this does not mean focusing exclusively on such benefits – to do so would be to go back to conventional marketing altogether. Today's consumers want to know your whole story, so focus on primary benefits in context of a full story that incorporates the environment as a desirable *extra* benefit; better yet, integrate relevant environmental and social benefits within your brand's already established market positioning, and you've got the stuff for a meaningful sale.

Does your green product promise to protect or enhance health? You're in luck. Categories most closely aligned with health are growing the fastest and tend to command the highest premiums. Consider a print ad for AFM Safecoat featuring 16 buckets of paint; 15 of the buckets are painted red and bear labels such as "Gorgeous Paints," "100% Pure," "Low Odor," and "Sustainable." However, the last bucket stands out in green and announces "The Only Paint that is Doctor Recommended." While the ad highlights the health aspects of the low-VOC paint, the website delves more into the "eco" in Safecoat, stating that it is "the leading provider of environmentally responsible, sustainable and non-polluting paints, stains, wood finishes, sealers and related green building products."[2]

Does your product appeal to the style-conscious? American Apparel was created as a brand proud to be made in the United States, provides excellent working conditions for its employees, and uses organic cotton. But, in 2004, when its "sweatshop free" label did not bring in the numbers that CEO Dov Charney was hoping for, he switched to promoting a sexy, youthful image for his company – complete with racy, controversial ads featuring scantily clad girls. Three years later, the company has 180 stores and revenue around $380 million.[3] (Sounds heretical? Keep in mind that the same sustainably responsible clothing is still being sold to consumers, together with all the same benefits to society and the environment; mainstream consumers simply need to hear a message that underscores the primary reason why they buy clothes in the first place.)

Does your product save consumers money? Ads for Kenmore's HE5t steam washer state that it uses 77% less water and 81% less energy than older models. The headline grabs readers with the compelling promise, "You pay for the washer. It pays for the dryer."

Is your product quieter, too? Television commercials for Bosch appliances spotlight energy efficiency and quiet performance. In one, a gentle deer walking through a forest meanders past an operating Bosch Nexxt washer and dryer tandem and never notices the appliance. A second ad highlights an owl swooping through an orange canyon to rest on the working Bosch Evolution dishwasher. Positive environmental impacts, obliquely referenced by situating the products in a forest setting and using animals, are tertiary to the silence and energy efficiency. Among its accolades is an Excellence in ENERGY STAR Promotion Award bestowed by the EPA.

When it comes to identifying the primary consumer benefits your greener alternatives can deliver, many brands like the ones described above find that their products' green benefits neatly translate into something direct and meaningful to the customer; energy savings translating into cost savings is an excellent example. (See Fig. 1.5 on page 19 for more examples.) However, when direct consumer benefits are not readily apparent, green marketers can use what my colleagues Ed Stafford and Cathy Hartman have dubbed "bundling," i.e., adding in desirable benefits.[4] An excellent example is the award-winning and highly successful Whirlpool Duet, a front-loading washing machine and dryer that bundled a highly appealing design with energy and water savings. It may be safe to say by bundling design with the environmental benefits, Whirlpool was able to fetch a higher premium for their offering.

In choosing the combination of primary and sustainability benefits to communicate, strive to *integrate* the two in order to ensure relevance. As examples, greener benefits such as recycled content or energy saving can add fresh life to the messaging of value brands, as is the case with Elmwood Park, New Jersey-based Marcal's Small Steps campaign which positions the use of 100%-recycled-content household paper products as an easy measure to take for the environment and save money. Our client, Austria-based Lenzing, makes Modal brand fiber from reconstituted cellulose from beech trees.

The resulting fabrics are touted as "dreamy soft" by Eileen West in their legendary nightgowns heralded for quality and comfort. Forbo promises that its Marmoleum linoleum flooring "Creates better environments." Synergies can come from surprising places; the cause marketing campaign mentioned later in this chapter for Dawn's dishwashing liquid relating to Dawn's role in cleaning oil-despoiled waterfowl acts as a subtle demonstration of the product's efficacy.

Understanding the specific interests of your green consumers can also add relevance to marketing communications programs in other ways. For example, segmenting green consumers can enhance targeting and relevance. In planning your green marketing campaign, ask such questions about your consumers as: To which environmental organizations do members of our target audience belong (the Appalachian Mountain Club or Greenpeace)? Which types of vacations do they take (hiking or the beach)? Which environmental magazines and websites do they read or visit (*Sierra* or *Animal Fair*)? Which types of products do they buy? (green fashions or energy-sipping light bulbs)? Which eco-labels do they seek out (Renewable "e" Energy or Cruelty-free)?

3 Educate and empower consumers with solutions

Consumers want to line up their shopping choices with their green values, and they applaud marketers' efforts to provide the information they need to make informed purchasing decisions as well as to use and dispose of the products responsibly. Especially effective are emotion-laden messages that help consumers acquire a sense of control over their lives and their world. For advertisers that make the effort to teach, educational messages represent special opportunities to boost purchase intent, enhance imagery, and bolster credibility. So demonstrate how environmentally superior products and services can help consumers safeguard their health, preserve the environment for their grandkids, or protect the outdoors for recreation and wildlife. Make environmental benefits tangible through compelling illustrations and statistics and make consumers feel as if their choices make a difference.

In 2008 Pepsi launched an empowering Have We Met Before? recycling campaign. It featured fun fact-based messages from the National Recycling Coalition that underscored the difference recycling can make, and it encouraged consumers to make recycling a part of their daily routine. Two facts emblazoned on specially designed cans included: "Recycling could save 95% of the energy used to make this can" and "The average person has the opportunity to recycle 25,000 cans in a lifetime."[5]

Increasingly, consumers are turning to the Internet for information. Opportunities abound to provide additional information on one's own website or a third party's website, in addition to conventional places such as advertising and packaging. Yahoo!'s 18Seconds.org website, named for the time it takes a person to change a light bulb, ranks states and cities according to their CFL purchases and describes CFLs and the difference it makes to use them. Also included are facts about where energy comes from and opportunities to spread the word by emailing friends or linking to the page from one's own website.[6]

Sensing an opportunity to home in on sales of the beleaguered bottled water industry, in 2007 Brita and Nalgene teamed up to co-promote their Brita filters and Nalgene water bottles as a cheaper and greener alternative to bottled water. A special website, www.filterforgood.com, described the carbon costs of producing and shipping bottled water as well as the environmental strain associated with plastic bottle waste. Visitors were invited to "take the pledge" to reduce bottled water usage. Displaying power in numbers, a map of all the pledges made across the country depicted how many bottles were saved.[7] Appealing to the "online generation," filterforgood.com also created a Facebook application that allows users to track how many bottles they have saved, and gives them a chance to win a $100 prize pack.[8]

Dramatize environmental benefits

Make your environmental achievements tangible and compelling to your target by citing statistics and using visuals that help dramatize the potential benefits. To help them reach their goal in 2007 of selling 100 million CFL light bulbs, Wal-Mart underscored the facts that, by changing out all the bulbs in an average home, customers could save up to $350 per year, and that the environmental savings represented the equivalent of taking 700,000 cars off the road or conserving the energy needed to power 450,000 single-family homes.

Similarly, Netflix markets its DVD-rental and video-streaming service on the convenience it provides; yet on its website it also points out that, if Netflix members had to drive to video rental stores, they would consume 800,000 gallons of gasoline and release more than 2.2 million tons of carbon dioxide emissions annually.[9]

Addressing
the New Rules

HSBC empowers big change with its There's No Small Change campaign

HSBC, the global banking giant headquartered in the UK, has many reasons to be concerned about global climate change, principal among them its many office buildings and thousands of branches around the world that need to be lit, heated, cooled, and ventilated, as well as running the millions of computers, printers, copiers, and other office equipment they contain. For 20 years, the bank made steady, significant investments in what eventually became an industry-leading Carbon Management Plan which helped the company achieve carbon neutrality in 2006. In recognition of its efforts, HSBC won the EPA's Climate Protection Award in 2007; and for two years straight, in 2005 and 2006, the EPA and U.S. Department of Energy named the company "Green Power Partner of the Year."

With this strong track record of environmental achievement on an issue relevant to a broad swath of consumers, we thought HSBC was ready to make a powerful message: with 120 million customers worldwide, the bank could champion the power of small changes. Hence was born HSBC's There's No Small Change marketing campaign, which we had the pleasure to work on with them. Run in the U.S. during spring 2007, it gave consumers empowering tips for reducing their own carbon footprint through various steps including HSBC's new paperless checking and statements.

Newspaper ads, in-branch posters, and other collateral developed by our partner, the New York office of JWT, the global advertising agency with support from my firm, J. Ottman Consulting, suggested ways customers could make a difference in all aspects of their lives: for instance, "get green power," "reduce paper waste," and "bank wisely." Carbon calculators provided by a leading environmental group, handed out inside the branches and made available through a special website, helped customers measure savings from such actions as powering down computers and copiers at night. New customers were presented with "Green Living Kits" packed with such envirogoodies as CFLs, a Chicobag reusable shopping bag, coupons for organic flowers, and a free issue of *The Green Guide* magazine. For every new account opened, HSBC donated money to local environmental charities, totaling $1 million by the end of the campaign. To extend reach to small business and "premier" customers, HSBC worked with local nonprofit groups to sponsor green business seminars, an Earth Day event in Central Park, New York, and a Green Drinks networking event.

Partnering with credible organizations was critical to the campaign strategy. In the words of JWT SVP, Linda Lewi, "When we developed the creative platform for 'There's No Small Change' we knew how the brand behaved as it executed the campaign would be as important as what it said, and so we developed a grassroots communications plan that partnered with green organizations to provide the everyday sustainable solutions and outreach efforts to our target consumers."

By adopting a strategy focused on credible education and empowerment, HSBC energized its employees, earned credibility among its audience of green consumers and businesspeople, and built its business: the effort yielded 46,420 new accounts (103% of goal and for only 65% of the acquisition cost of a typical customer) – with a 50% uplift in online bill paying, higher deposit balances in both Personal and Premier accounts, with three times the standard cross-sell ratio (people who opened a checking account and bought another product).

To boot, I'm proud to report the campaign won one of the first ever Green Effie awards from the American Marketing Association, sponsored by Discovery Communications' Planet Green network, honoring effective eco-marketing.[10]

Be optimistic

In the midst of a national energy crisis in 1978, U.S. president Jimmy Carter took to the airwaves in a cardigan sweater encouraging Americans to conserve energy by turning down the thermostat to 68°. His campaign failed because of its link to deprivation (and the cardigan sweater industry is still reeling from its effects). Like the entire "back to basics" green movement of which it was a part, President Carter's well-intended initiative failed because it represented a threat to the upward mobility and prosperity that is America. While some may question the idea that "bigger is better" and "growth is necessary for a healthy economy," most Americans have not historically been willing to reverse their hard-won struggles to "have" for a future characterized by "have not."

Happily this mind-set is already changing for the better in some advanced environmentally aware countries such as Germany and in Scandinavia, and ideally will in the rest of the world. But for now businesses need to play by one of the fundamental new rules of green marketing: consumers believe that technology, coupled with cooperative efforts on the part of all key players in society, will safeguard their future. So, invite consumers' participation via simple actions and the prospect of a better future – not by leveraging fear tactics, playing to pessimism, or pressing guilt buttons. That's why we guided our client, Epson, towards an more hopeful, integrated corporate positioning, "Better Products for a Better Future," and why TV commercials for Kashi cereals showcase vignettes of healthy people and end with the tagline, "Seven Whole Grains on a Mission."

Londonderry, New Hampshire-based Stonyfield Farm, makers of organic yogurt and other popular dairy products, manages to keep its messages refreshingly upbeat and fun. A visit to their "Yogurt on a Mission"-themed website lets fans meet Gary Hirshberg, the "CE-Yo," view lighthearted videos about how they make yogurt, even "Have-A-Cow" by learning about some of the specific family farms from where it sources its ingredients.[11]

Finally, offering the opportunity to "test drive a low-car and less expensive lifestyle," the Zipcar car-sharing service, in June of 2009, playfully announced the "Low-Car Diet," asking participants from all 13 Zipcar cities in the U.S., Canada, and England to swap their personal car for a Zipcar membership, supplemented by the use of bikes, public transportation, and walking. Positioning the program as a step up in lifestyle for participants, the company asserted that the "Monthlong program gives urban residents the opportunity to experience the economic, environmental and health benefits of a low-car lifestyle."[12]

Address the underlying motivations of consumers

In line with the segmentations of green consumers outlined in Chapter 2, focus your messaging on concepts that are understood by the consumers who are most important to your business. Empower the disenfranchised. Reward those consumers who are trying to make a difference.

- Motivate the deep green LOHAS consumers by demonstrating how they can make a contribution. Reward their initiative, leadership, and commitment to high standards.

- Show Naturalites (and my Health Fanatics) that environmental benefits are consistent with healthy lifestyles. Demonstrate how natural products can benefit adults, children, and pets.

- Provide Drifters with easy, even fashionable ways to make a contribution that doesn't cost a lot. Enlist the support of celebrities and help them show off their eco-consciousness on favorite social networking sites.

- Encourage Conventionals (and my Resource Conservers) with practical, cost-effective reasons for choosing greener products and behaviors. Underscore opportunities to save money immediately or over the lifetime of a product. Communicate how long a product may last, or that it is reusable.

- Help Unconcerneds understand how all individuals can make a difference. Underscore that small actions performed by many people can make big changes.

Addressing the New Rules

Toyota Prius appeals to mainstream consumers one segment at a time

On launching its Prius sedan in 2001, Toyota opted first to target not the green-leaning drivers one might expect, but rather tech-savvy, "early adopter" consumers. Featuring a beauty shot of a shiny new car parked at a stoplight and illustrated by the provocative headline, "Ever heard the sound a stoplight makes?" an introductory print ad emphasized the hybrid car's quiet ride (and specifically the fact that the motor, switched into electric gear, did not idle at stop lights like combustion engines). Putting primary benefits first, the key visual was a big, bold beauty shot of the car itself set off against a backdrop of the Golden Gate Bridge while the body copy explained the revolutionary technology. Environmental benefits appeared at the top right corner of the ad – in mouseprint – in the form of compelling statistics about the car's fuel economy and emissions. To establish its green bona fides and get a buzz going among influential greens, a supplemental campaign, "Genius," spotlighted the car's lighter environmental touch and activist group endorsements.

Spiked gasoline prices subsequently triggered a new campaign highlighting the car's fuel efficiency, no doubt bringing price-conscious Conventionals on board. Today, its distinctive styling makes the Prius a rolling billboard of one's environmental values and forward thinking. A successful public relations campaign, including stunts like celebrities rolling up to the Academy Awards in a Prius, bestow the car with a "coolness" factor – the reason why, anecdotally, many people buy a Prius.

The potential to motivate the large mass of passive greens with the promise of fitting in cannot be overstated. That's because environmental issues are inherently social – your gas-guzzling car pollutes my air; my wastefulness clogs our landfill. Today, the "cool" people care about the environment – the influential LOHAS consumers whom many emulate and, of course, so many Hollywood celebrities. Intentionally, "cool" underpinned the most successful anti-litter campaign in history. It was created for the Texas Department of Transportation by our friends at the Austin-based GSD&M advertising agency in 1985 and is still running. When research showed that slogans like "Pitch In" were having no effect on habitual litterers (men 18–34), advertising enlisted popular Texas celebrities such as Willie Nelson, Lance Armstrong, and Jennifer Love Hewitt to demonstrate that it is "uncool" to litter.[14] The Don't Mess with Texas campaign has helped to significantly reduce visible roadside litter, from 1 billion pieces of trash tossed onto Texas roads in 2001 to 827 million pieces in 2005.[15]

4 Reassure on performance

Environmentally preferable technologies are new to consumers and often look or perform differently than their brown counterparts. Carried over from the days when CFLs sputtered and cast a green haze and when natural laundry detergents left clothes dingy, as pointed out in Figure 2.11 on page 40, "Barriers to green purchasing," greener products are still perceived by some as less effective or not having the same value as the more familiar brown alternatives. And, although these perceptions are declining, it still deters some potential customers from purchasing greener products.[16] Remove this potential barrier to purchase by addressing the issue head on.

Seventh Generation (see Chapter 4) brand dishwashing liquid, which competes with Palmolive and Dawn – brands with long-established track records for cutting grease – underscores its efficacy by stressing in print ads spotlighting an adorable youngster, "Because you don't have to choose between safety and spotless dishes," while Reynolds Wrap addresses the myth that recycled content is somehow inferior to virgin, by emphasizing its Reynolds Wrap 100% recycled aluminum foil is "100% Recycled, 100% Reynolds."[17]

5 Engage the community

As underscored earlier in this book, green consumers tend to be well educated, and quite reliant on their own research. As demonstrated in Figure 6.2, they increasingly tend to trust the recommendations of friends and family even more than traditional forms of paid media; hence the astronomical rise in importance of social media in the past few years.

Figure 6.2 **Whom do consumers trust for information?**

Consumer trust in advertising by channel (trust somewhat/completely), 2009 compared to 2007

	2009 %	2007–09 % change
Recommendations from people I know	90	+15%
Brand websites	70	+17%
Consumer opinions posted online	70	+15%
Brand sponsorships	63	+29%
Ads on TV	61	+9%
Ads in newspapers	61	−3%
Ads in magazines	59	+5%
Ads on radio	55	+2%
Emails I signed up for	55	+12%
Ads before movies	52	+37%
Ads served in search engine results	41	+21%
Online banner ads	33	+27%
Text ads on mobile phones	24	+33%

Source: The Nielsen Company, *Trust in Advertising*, October 2009
Reprinted with permission

This suggests rather than simply communicating green benefits in traditional ways, take the opportunity to use your brand to educate and engage your consumers about the issues they are concerned about: the values that guide their lives and purchasing. Acknowledge the consumer's new role as co-creator of your brand and vigorously stoke the conversation. Offer credible, in-depth information and tell meaningful stories that extend beyond paid advertisements in broadcast and print, and on pack messages, to include sponsorships and information on websites and social media. Given consumers' propensity to trust others like themselves, educate them on the details of your products and packaging and provide infrastructure and content that makes it easy for them to share information about your brand with each other.

Engage in cause-related marketing

Best known as promotional efforts in which businesses donate a portion of product revenues to popular nonprofit groups, cause-related marketing can enhance brand image while boosting sales, and allows businesses to have an impact that goes far beyond that associated with just writing a tax-deductible check (philanthropy). With cause-related marketing, everybody wins. Consumers can contribute to favorite sustainability causes with little or no added expense or inconvenience; nonprofit partners enjoy broadened publicity and the potential to attract new members and financial support; and business sponsors and their retailers and distributors can distinguish themselves in a cluttered marketplace, enhance brand equity, and build sales.

No longer viewed as a short-term promotional tactic, all signs point to cause-related marketing as a mature, long-term strategic business practice approached with increasing sophistication by organizations large and small. International Events Group (IEG) Sponsorship Report predicts that cause marketing will rise by 6.1% to $1.61 billion in 2010, up from $1.51 billion in 2009.[19]

Confirming that cause-related marketing represents the power to build one's business, the 2008 Cone Cause Evolution Study revealed record high levels of positive response from consumers to cause-related campaigns, specifically:

- 85% of Americans say they have a more positive image of a product or company when it supports a cause they care about (remains unchanged from 1993)

- 85% feel it is acceptable for companies to involve a cause in their marketing (compared to 66% in 1993)

- 79% say they would be likely to switch from one brand to another, when price and quality are about equal, if the other brand is associated with a good cause (compared to 66% in 1993)

- 38% have bought a product associated with a cause in the last 12 months (compared to 20% in 1993).[20]

Cause-marketing campaigns conducted by organizations worldwide span a range of environmental and social topics. One of the most visible in the history of cause-related marketing is Project (RED). Launched in 2006 by Bono of rock group U2 and Bobby Shriver of Debt, AIDS, Trade in Africa (DATA), multiple high-profile partners including American Express, Apple, Converse, Dell, Gap, Giorgio Armani, Hallmark, Motorola, and Starbucks raise money for the Global Fund to Fight AIDS, Tuberculosis and Malaria (the Global Fund) by donating 50% of profits from products labeled as (RED). Funds generated to date have provided more than 825,000 HIV-positive people with a year's worth of antiretroviral therapy, provided 3.2 million AIDS orphans with basic care, and supported programs that have prevented more than 3.5 millions deaths.[21]

IKEA partnered with UNICEF on a promotion to benefit children in Angola and Uganda. IKEA agreed to donate $2.00 from every sale of their BRUM teddy bears to UNICEF's "Children's Right to Play" program, which uses play-based interaction to educate and empower children in need. The promotion was called "A Bear that Gives," and between 2003 and 2005 it raised $2.2 million, which went to the education of 80,000 street children in Angola and 55,000 children in displacement camps in Uganda, put 38,000 Ugandan children in daycare centers and reunited 200 of them with their families.[22]

Opportunities exist for even small businesses to get meaningfully involved in cause-marketing. Consider 1% for the Planet, founded by the environmentally passionate Yvon Chouinard (founder of Patagonia) and Craig Mathews (owner of Blue Ribbon Flies) to connect businesses and their consumers with philanthropy. Currently, more than 700 environmentally conscious companies contribute 1% of their sales to a growing list of more than 1,500 environmental groups around the world.[23] Participating organizations, ranging from Galaxy Granola in California and our client, Modo, makers of E(arth) C(onscious) O(ptics) eyewear in New York, to Natural Technology in France, benefit from the marketing boost that accrues from being listed on the 1% for the Planet website and the ability to differentiate their businesses from their competition by using the 1% for the Planet logo on their packages and promotions.

Lastly, and perhaps with important implications for the future, some brands have made causes central to their business. Consider the enormously successful Newman's Own brand, which through the Newman's Own Foundation donates all profits to charitable causes, and TOMS One for One campaign which gives a pair of shoes to a child in need for every pair of their rubber-soled alpargatas shoes they sell.

Before embarking on your own cause-marketing effort, realize that there are some rules of the road. Consumers are attracted to causes that put them in the driver's seat, and they will turn on a misguided campaign. Examples abound. Some Sierra Club members created a stir – and some even pulled out of the organization – in response to breaking news that the Sierra Club was receiving an undisclosed amount of money for what they perceived as an endorsement of Clorox's Green Works cleaning products. Sierra Club members' objections to the partnership included the fact that Clorox manufactured chlorine and that 98% of Clorox products were still made from synthetic chemicals. (Green Works only accounted for 2% of Clorox's total sales).[24] Both organizations now disclose the financial compensation that Sierra Club receives for its support, and, likely prompted more by pending legislation than by the Sierra Club, as of late 2009, Clorox announced it would no longer make bleach out of chlorine and sodium hydroxide.[25]

Reflecting its ability to gently but effectively clean waterfowl affected by oil spills, Dawn dishwashing liquid is running a cause-related campaign with the Marine Mammal Center and the International Bird Rescue Research Center in which it will donate $1 for every specially marked package bought by consumers. However, some visitors to its Facebook page and YouTube commercial have protested at the promotion, citing that Procter & Gamble tests its products on animals, forcing the company to defend its policies and remind its detractors that it has invested more than $250 million developing alternative testing methods.[26]

Finally, Ethos Water, co-owned by Pepsi and Starbucks, donates 5 cents for every unit sold to help people in underdeveloped regions to get clean water. Environmentalists question this approach, maintaining that clean, drinkable water should be a human right and not a function of corporate profits. They also maintain that promoting bottled water for environmental benefits is inconsistent with the related impacts of plastic recycling, energy expended to transport the product, and potential depletion of natural water supplies.[27]

To reap the benefits amply demonstrated over 15 years of cause-related marketing, follow these guidelines for success suggested by Cone's 2008 Cause Evolution Study:[28]

- Allow consumers to select their own cause

- Ensure that the cause you pick is both personally relevant to consumers and makes strategic sense to your business

- Choose a trusted, established not-for-profit organization

- Provide practical incentives for involvement, such as saving money or time

- Provide emotional incentives for involvement, such as it making them feel good or alleviating shopping guilt.

Get creative

Many sustainable brand leaders including Whole Foods, Seventh Generation, Ben & Jerry's Homemade, Burt's Bees, and Stonyfield Farm, have built their reputations and continue to establish goodwill credibly and affordably through such creative publicity-generating efforts as sponsoring worthy causes, adopting local charities, protecting small dairy farmers, or donating profits to charity. They have spoken out against bovine growth hormone (in the case of Ben & Jerry's and Stonyfield Farm) or supported organic and fair trade products, organizing special events targeted at younger demographics such as Ben & Jerry's One World One Heart music festival, or Burt's Bees' Beautify Your World tour, allowing consumers to try products first-hand.

With the mainstreaming of green, larger companies are starting to get creative, too. In 2007, Philips, for example, partnered with the Alliance for Climate Protection and the global Live Earth concerts to promote the use of energy-efficient lighting via their A Simple Switch campaign to combat climate change.[29] Companies such as Sprint and Coca-Cola's Odwalla brand are sponsoring signs and trail maps at parks and ski resorts, a very direct way to reach outdoor enthusiasts.[30]

Without paid media advertising how did Stonyfield Farm become the third largest yogurt brand in the U.S.? The answer is its unconventional marketing, most of it on the pack – what founder Gary Hirshberg calls "mini billboards." Packaging and lids highlight Stonyfield Farm's environmental practices and the environmental and social causes it supports, in addition to facts that educate consumers about the benefits of adopting a sustainable lifestyle. The company even offers a "Have-a-Cow" program where consumers sponsor a dairy cow, thus bringing them closer to the farmers providing the yogurt they eat.[31]

With nearly 2 billion users worldwide – more than a quarter of the population – the Internet represents an efficient means of reaching consumers with information and advice on greener products.[32] Spending on online and mobile advertising, including search and lead generation, online classifieds, and consumer-generated ads, reached almost $30 billion in 2007, up 29% from the year before.[33]

Many environmental groups have created websites in order to share information on global environmental problems, and a few sites now have microsites where consumers can shop and/or obtain information about greener products, companies, and behavior. Some good examples include GreenHome.com and Buygreen.com.

Sustainability leaders are now devising creative ways to get closer to their consumers and generate a positive buzz about their brands via blogging and social networking sites and by creating communities through their own websites. For example, Yahoo, GM, Crest, and Eden Organic are just a few of the brands that advertise to the seven million members of the Care2.com social networking site. No Sweat Apparel uses online blogs and sponsorship to create a buzz about their clothing, which is produced in factories throughout the world where all workers are paid a living wage.[34] Consumers know that greener products and services are still relatively rare, and when they find an exciting new brand which is also sustainable, they will likely tell their friends about it, sometimes with support from the brand itself. Consumers can "friend" Method on Facebook to learn about new product offerings and leave positive testimonials, and thousands of fans of the "Seventh Generation Nation" network Facebook page leave feedback and even suggest new product ideas.

Out of the 110 million Americans (making up 60% of Internet users) who use social networking sites such as Facebook, Twitter, LinkedIn, or MySpace, 52% have "friended" or become a fan of at least one brand on a social networking site.[35] One of the biggest users of such social networking sites is Whole Foods Market. To help celebrate their one millionth Twitter follower, Whole Foods held a contest that asked followers to tweet their food philosophies in five words. The ten most creative tweets received a $50 Whole Foods gift card.[36] To engage their Facebook followers in conversation, throughout the summer of 2010, Whole Foods invited them to share some of their fondest high school tunes, how hot it was where lived, and their favorite party recipes.[37] It's time to plan for their next millionth addition; as of August 2010, Whole Foods had 1,792,404 followers on Twitter in addition to 310,638 Facebook fans.

The web and social media are creating opportunities for exciting new forms of experiential marketing including YouTube videos, product placement, mobile advertising, iPhone and BlackBerry applications, and pop-up stores – all just beginning to be explored.

785266 000297

**Addressing
the New Rules**

Tide Coldwater warms up consumers with engaging website

Procter & Gamble's Tide Coldwater is specially designed to clean clothes in cold water as effectively as the leading competitive detergent does in warm water. Tide Coldwater is a concentrated formula (reducing packaging as well as energy costs) that may save consumers up to 80% of the energy they would use per load in a traditional warm/cold cycle of a hot water top-loading machine.

To assuage doubters, P&G assures customers that its cold-water formula works just as well as traditional products to wash clothes. With both a regular and high-efficiency (HE) formula, it also works with all washing machines and traditional laundry additives such as bleach and fabric softeners.

In 2005, P&G launched Tide Coldwater by announcing the Tide Coldwater Challenge. On a special website (www.coldwaterchallenge.com), this interactive challenge incentivized mainstream consumers to test the product and share the results with friends. An interactive map charted the spread of participants throughout the U.S. – at one time showing upwards of 1 million participants. Other areas of the website underscored the product's efficacy and associated the brand with energy-efficient products and programs.

The Alliance to Save Energy, an independent not-for-profit group, actively partnered with Tide Coldwater – they have sent email promotions and offer tips on the website on ways consumers can save energy and money. Such direct marketing early on and follow-up efforts, including free samples and opportunities to inform friends through email, set the stage for a successful launch.

A later Tide Coldwater campaign dramatizes how much energy consumers can save by switching from hot and warm water washes. For example, a TV ad promises, "if everyone washed in cold water, we could save enough energy to power all the households in 1,000 towns," while a more hard-hitting value-oriented pitch claims to "save up to $10 on your energy bill with every 100 oz. bottle."[38]

This chapter discussed five of six strategies for successful sustainable brand communications: among them, empowering consumers to act on the issues they care most about, integrating sustainability messages with primary consumer benefits, and underscoring the inherent value of one's sustainable offerings. None of these objectives can be met if green marketers don't meet my sixth strategy of sustainable communications, "Be credible" – a subject so important, I devote the entire next chapter to it.

The *New Rules* Checklist

Ask the following questions to uncover opportunities to add impact to your sustainable branding and communications.

- ○ Does our customer know and care about the environmental issues our brand attempts to solve? How do we know? What types of education might be necessary?

- ○ Who is the primary purchaser of our brand? Primary influencer? What role do children play in influencing the purchase of our environmentally oriented brand?

- ○ Is our environmental technology, material, etc. legitimate?

- ○ Are we asking our customer to trade off on quality/performance, convenience, aesthetics, etc. and asking for a premium price? Are we underscoring primary benefits that our brand can deliver on?

- ○ Are we taking advantage of opportunities to target specific segments of green consumers with customized messages?

- ○ Do our customers know what's in it for them (versus just the environment, society, or economy)? Does our brand offer any direct, tangible benefits to consumers? For instance, do they help consumers save money? Save time? Protect health? Enhance self-esteem and status?

- ○ Are we tailoring our messages to the specific lifestyles and green interests of our consumers?

- ○ Are the environment-related benefits of our brand well understood by our consumers? What types of education might we need to provide? To which consumers would our brand's environmentally oriented benefits appeal most?

- ○ In what ways can our brand and marketing communications empower consumers to solve environmental problems? Does it save energy? Conserve water? Cut down on toxics? In what ways? By how much?

In what ways might we dramatize the sustainable benefits of our products to make our message more tangible and compelling?

○ Are our messages upbeat and empowering, and do they use positive imagery? Do we stay away from trite imagery and jargon?

○ Are there opportunities to engage consumers via a cause-related marketing campaign?

○ Do we need to reassure consumers about the quality/performance or our product or service?

○ In what ways can we generate a buzz among influential consumers?

○ What mix of media represents the best fit with our consumers and our message?

○ How can we use interactive Web vehicles or social media such as a customized website, Facebook, or Twitter? How might we use You-Tube, mobile advertising, iPhone and BlackBerry apps, and other kinds of experiential marketing?

Establishing credibility and avoiding greenwash

In 1990 Sam Walton promised that Wal-Mart would reward the Procter & Gambles and Unilevers of the world with special shelf talkers (the signs that appeal alongside a given product), if they could prove that their products had greener features. Respond they did, and soon Wal-Mart's shelves were emblazoned with all sorts of messages about the greener features of various products including dubious ones such as household paper towels where the cardboard core was made of recycled content but not the paper towels. Not surprisingly, environmental activists called the effort a sham, on two counts: the features had been there all along, so no real progress was being made, and the presence of one green feature didn't necessary mean a product was green overall. This example and others like it represented the very first, likely unintentional, case of greenwashing, and it set the stage for new standards of eco-communications firmly rooted in genuine progress and transparency.

Greenwash!

With green awareness now squarely mainstream, many companies cater to newly eco-aware consumers by launching products and services that may, intentionally or not, be less than legitimately "green." The popular term for such activity is "greenwashing." Coined by environmentalist Jay Westerveld to criticize hotels that encouraged guests to reuse towels for environmental reasons but made little or no effort to recycle waste, accusations of green-washing can emanate from many sources including regulators, environmentalists, the media, consumers, competitors, and the scientific community, and it can be serious, long-lasting, and hugely detrimental to a brand's reputation. With an eye toward making headlines and creating an example for everyone else to heed, advocates tend to target the most trusted and well-known companies. BP, for one, received heaps of criticism on launching its $200 million Beyond Petroleum campaign touting its commitment to renewable energy which, in fact, represented less than 1% of total global sales; and that criticism was only compounded by the oil spill in the Gulf of Mexico, an estimated 18 times the size of the epic Exxon oil spill in Prince William Sound in spring 1989.

Bill Ford Jr.'s reputation – and that of his family's venerable company – was tarnished when as chairman of the Ford Motor Company he was unable to fulfill his pledge to build greener cars and follow through on an otherwise laudable Heroes of the Planet campaign. Instead, with the company falling on hard times, he bent to the collective will of senior associates who advocated continuing to crank out gas-guzzling SUVs – and wound up paying dearly for the consequences.[1] Relatedly, in the summer of 2008 General Motors got flack from advocate bloggers for announcing plans to "reinvent the automobile" while continuing to manufacture perhaps the most environmentally unfriendly car on the planet – the soon-to-be-defunct Hummer.[2] Meanwhile, its Chevrolet division compounded the PR trouble by running ads heralding a "gas friendly" Volt electric car that was not yet in production.

Greenwashers: consumers are on to you! According to a survey conducted in December 2007 at the UN Climate Change Conference, nearly nine out of ten delegates and participants agreed with the statement, "Some companies are advertising products and services with environmental claims that would be considered false, unsubstantiated, and/or unethical."[3] In January 2007, British Telecom found only 3% of UK consumers think businesses are honest about their actions to become more environmentally or socially responsible, with 33% believing businesses exaggerate what they are doing.[4]

The risks of backlash are high. Using resources and energy and forever creating waste, no company and no product can ever be 100% green. Corporate efforts hinting at aspirations to be green often attract critics. And warm-hearted depictions of furry animals that strike emotional chords with consumers may simultaneously incite the wrath of environmentalists (another reason to lead with primary benefits!). Among other credibility hurdles, consumers perceive that it is not in industry's interest to promote environmental conservation. After all, industry has a track record of unfettered pollution, and consumers think planned obsolescence was invented by industry to ensure growth; in fact, many people accuse marketers of creating ads that make consumers buy what they do not need.

Advocates often maintain that heavy polluters have no right to tout green initiatives, however admirable. So if you are in the petroleum, chemical, or mining industries, your green attempts, no matter how sincere, may not be viewed as such. Consider the case of the Washington Nationals' new ballpark. It opened for the 2008 season as the first major baseball stadium to earn LEED certification from the U.S. Green Building Council. This was great news for the team and their fans, but not so for the sponsor ExxonMobil. When environmentalists were quick to object to prominent Exxon billboards throughout the park, Alan Jeffers, a spokesperson for Exxon lamented, "We get criticized for not doing enough for the environment, and then get criticized when we do run an environmental campaign."[5]

To complicate matters, there are no clear-cut guidelines for environmental marketing. The U.S. Federal Trade Commission (FTC) issued "Green Guides" in 1992; however, since they were last updated in 1996, new terms such as "carbon footprint" and "carbon offsets," and "sustainable," have come into the picture. These Guides are in the process of being updated; meanwhile, without fresh guidelines even the best-intentioned green marketers risk making erroneous claims in these and other unaddressed areas.

A word of caution. The Internet is making the stakes higher now than ever before. According to the new rules, media attention to greenwashing has grown with the launch of environmental news websites such as Grist.org, Treehugger.com, Worldchanging.com – and thousands of 24/7 green bloggers and tweeters. Greenwashing even has its own website, greenwashingindex. com. Founded in 2007 by the EnviroMedia agency in collaboration with the University of Oregon, greenwashingindex.com lets visitors rate the authenticity of green marketing claims using "Greenwashing Index Scoring Criteria." Consumers can read greenwashing news and submit ads to be evaluated by others. Recent marketing campaigns spotlighted on the site include easy-Jet, who claimed that flying their airline generates less carbon dioxide than a typical airline or even driving a passenger car; Monsanto, the giant producer of genetically modified seeds, who pledged to practice sustainable agriculture; and Fiji bottled water claiming that "every drop is green," despite the fact that water is shipped thousands of miles across the sea compared to tap water which is readily available.

Tired of hearing the term "green fatigue"? It's a new phrase being used to describe consumers who feel inundated by green marketing buzzwords and a dizzying array of all things green. As a result, they have trouble separating genuine progress from just another green gimmick. The risk of greenwashing and green fatigue from the deluge of advertising claims and green PR pitches is that it can unintentionally create skeptical consumers out of a general public short on facts, and this directly impacts even the best-intentioned organizations, tangibly and intangibly. Being perceived as a greenwasher can represent a direct hit on corporate trust and credibility and ultimately hit the bottom line, either from reduced revenues or depressed market share when disillusioned customers shift their purchases to more trustworthy competitors.

Much can be done, however, to avert the risks from greenwashing. Start with well-crafted sustainable branding and marketing plans that reflect an understanding of the target audience's needs. Make sure your products and services are greened via a life-cycle approach (see Chapter 4). And engage and educate potential users to consume responsibly. Thankfully, powerful strategies exist to establish credibility and minimize the potential for backlash. The place to begin is inside one's own organization.

Five strategies for establishing credibility for sustainable branding and marketing

Follow the strategies discussed below to establish credibility for your green marketing campaign and minimize the chance of it being dubbed "greenwash."

> **Five strategies for establishing credibility for sustainable branding and marketing**
>
> 1. Walk your talk
> 2. Be transparent
> 3. Don't mislead
> 4. Enlist the support of third parties
> 5. Promote responsible consumption

1 Walk your talk

Companies that are strongly committed to sound environmental policies need not apologize for failure to achieve perfection. Consumers understand that the greenest of cars will still pollute, the simplest of packaging eventually needs to be thrown away, and the most energy-efficient light bulbs will consume their share of coal, gas, or nuclear energy at the power plant. Thwart the most discriminating of critics by visibly making progress toward measurable and worthy goals, communicating transparently, and responding to the public's concerns and expectations. Companies that are in the vanguard of corporate greening have many of the following attributes in place, and are consequently the most able to take advantage of the many opportunities of environmental consumerism.

A visible and committed CEO

To successfully develop and market environmentally sound products and services, one must adopt a thorough approach to greening that reaches deep into corporate culture. With consumers scrutinizing products at every phase of the life-cycle, corporate greening must extend to every department – manufacturing, marketing, research and development, consumer and public affairs, and even to suppliers who provide the raw materials, components, and packaging. Only a committed chief executive with a clear vision for his or her company can add the necessary weight to the message that environmental soundness is a priority.

The need to start with – and communicate the commitment of – the CEO cannot be overstated. CEOs can forge an emotional link between a company and its customers, acting as a symbolic watchdog who supervises corporate operations and ensures environmental compliance. That's why CEOs of such environmental standouts as Interface, Patagonia, Seventh Generation, Timberland, and Tom's of Maine all maintain high profiles; Tom and Kate Chappell historically included a signed message to consumers on each their natural personal-care products. Jeffrey Hollender maintains a blog on Seventh Generation's website entitled "The Inspired Protagonist." By projecting a personal commitment to the environment, CEOs win their stakeholders' trust. Such leaders are especially believable because they are perceived as having a personal stake in the outcome.

CEOs who are not seen as watching the shop run the risk of derision by corporate watchdogs. Taking Apple to task for not doing as much as competitors to green their products and company, Greenpeace created a special "Green My Apple" campaign and website, encouraging Apple customers to voice their concerns. In May 2007, Steve Jobs, CEO of Apple, responded with a letter entitled, "A Greener Apple." In it, he detailed his company's efforts to remove toxic chemicals from its products and expand post-consumer recycling. He apologized for keeping consumers and investors in the dark regarding Apple's plans to become even greener and promised to communicate such efforts to the public in the future.[6]

Empower employees

The best-intentioned CEOs will only be as effective as their employees. Only when employees are on top of the issues and given the authority to make changes will greener products be launched and sustainable practices be put into place. Employees have many reasons to get concerned about green issues. Relying on secure jobs for their livelihoods, they have a direct stake in their company's success.

However, just like consumers, employees need to be educated about environmental issues in general, and of course about the specifics of their company's processes and brands. Many companies regularly enlist outside speakers to bring employees up to speed about trends in demographics, technology, and the economy; now, speakers, like myself, devoted to environmental specialties meet the demand for talks on climate change, clean technology, and green consumer behavior. Some companies have set up intra-company blogs or wikis to help employees identify ways to get involved, locate other colleagues with similar interests, and make a difference in their communities. Burt's Bees gives employees money to offset home energy use and Bank of America subsidizes employee purchases of hybrid vehicles.

Be proactive

Most big businesses adhere to the International Organization for Standardization (ISO)'s ISO 14001, a voluntary international framework for a holistic strategic approach to an organization's environmental policy, plans, and actions that helps an organization to (1) identify and control the environmental impact of its activities, products, or services, (2) continuously improve its environmental performance, and (3) implement a systematic approach to setting environmental targets and understanding how these will be achieved and measured. And they likely have their audits certified by an independent third party and voluntarily report results to the EPA and the public.

But the companies that project credibility go beyond what is expected from regulators and other stakeholders. So, proactively, and publicly, com-

mit to doing your share to solve emerging environmental and social problems such as protection of rainforests or elimination of sweatshops – and
discover competitive advantage in the process. Being proactive projects
leadership and sends a message to investors that risks are minimized. Regulators are less likely to impose restrictions on companies whose actions tran-
scend minimum standards. Being proactive also allows companies to help
define the standards by which they will be judged and affords the greatest
opportunities to find cost-effective solutions to environmental ills while
beating competitors in meeting regulations and consumer expectations.
Finally, proactive companies are better prepared to withstand the scrutiny
that overtly "green" companies often face. In 2005 our client, HSBC, became
the first major bank and member of the FTSE 100 to address climate change
by becoming carbon-neutral. Its carbon management program consisted of
four key steps: (1) measuring its carbon footprint, (2) reducing energy consumption through an aggressive program of energy efficiency upgrades in
corporate offices and bank branches, (3) buying renewable forms of electricity to power whatever energy it could not reduce through efficiencies, and (4)
offsetting whatever carbon it could not reduce via efficiency and offsets. By
shooting for carbon neutrality and by initiating an industry-leading Carbon
Management Plan, HSBC gained the needed credibility to launch its Effie-
award-winning "There's No Small Change" U.S. retail marketing program in
spring 2007, described in Chapter 6.

Be thorough

Green marketing practices have their environmental impacts, too. So look
for opportunities to be environmentally efficient with marketing materials.
Look for opportunities where the Internet or electronic media could work to
reduce the use of paper. Be sure to use recycled paper from sustainably harvested trees and soy-based inks for printed marketing communications.

2 Be transparent

Provide the information consumers seek to evaluate your brands. These
days, consumers crave even more information than most businesses are
willing to disclose. Almost four out of five (79.6%) respondents in an April
2008 online survey used the Internet to conduct research on green initiatives
and products, yet almost half (48%) of them found the availability of corporate information on green and environmentally safe products and services to
be lacking – rating the information as fair or poor.[7] To be perceived as credible in the eyes of the consumer, provide access to the details of products and

corporate practices and actively report on progress. So the public can feel good about purchasing your products, include anecdotes about exemplary community outreach efforts – digging a well, tilling a farm, or helping out at a local school.

In the future, disclosure of brand-related environmental impacts and processes may be required by law. Get a jump on competitors and regulators – and score some points with consumers – by voluntarily disclosing as much as possible about your products. In the hotly contested green cleaning-aids industry, competitors Seventh Generation, Method, and SC Johnson now disclose the ingredients (but understandably not the exact formulas) of their products. Seventh Generation even lets consumers ask "Science Man" specific questions.

Be accessible and accountable. Report the good – and the bad – about your company. Consistency in reporting such data is critical to stakeholders' ability to track progress and make comparisons. The Global Reporting Initiative (GRI) is a spin-off of the Boston-based Ceres, founders of the Ceres Principles of good corporate environmental conduct, in partnership with the United Nations Environment Programme (UNEP). It is a voluntary global standard and framework for organizations to measure, benchmark, and report on economic, environmental, and social performance. More than 1,500 companies including BP, Coca-Cola, GM, IBM, Novartis, Philips, and Unilever have adopted this de facto standard for reporting. Ben & Jerry's has gone one step further by also using a reporting standard called the Global Warming Social Footprint (GWSF), developed by the Vermont-based nonprofit Center for Sustainable Innovation, to understand if it is contributing its "proportionate share" (as measured against the performance of similar-sized companies) toward returning greenhouse gas concentrations to safer levels.

One thousand conscientious companies in 54 industries have also taken the step of joining the fast-growing ranks of B Corps (described in Chapter 3), denoting that the nonprofit B Lab has certified their companies to strict sustainable business standards, or they have benchmarked their performance to the organization's free B Impact Rating System.[8]

It's one thing to report on the good, but what about the bad? Under the new rules of green marketing, leaders communicate with "radical transparency." One pathfinder is Patagonia, the Ventura, California-based outdoor equipment manufacturer. Its Footprint Chronicles microsite at patagonia.com lets visitors trace the environmental impacts of ten Patagonia products from design through delivery, including components and where they come from, innovations used to reduce impacts on the environment, and what the company thinks it can improve on. Patagonia encourages customer comments – a move that builds loyalty – and is not hesitant to critique itself; as the company learns more, it applies this knowledge to its broad spectrum of offerings. For example, despite its reputation for using recycled fibers, Patagonia is not afraid to reveal on its site that it still uses 36% virgin polyester to make its Capilene 3 Midweight Bottoms, carefully explaining that it is needed to achieve the desired performance and durability.[9] In 2008, the Footprint Chronicles won high accolades as the People's Voice winner in the Corporate Communications category at the Webby Awards (aka "the Oscars of the Internet").[10]

Don't hide behind bad news! SIGG, the makers of popular and eco-trendy reusable aluminum bottles, learned this lesson the hard way. Thought to be BPA-free by consumers and the media, SIGG came under fire when an open letter to customers from CEO Steve Wasik in August 2009 disclosed that bottles produced prior to August 2008 contained trace amounts of BPA in the bottle's inner epoxy liner – and that the company had known about it since 2006. Although SIGG was quick to use public outreach to address consumer and retailer concerns, the damage was done. Customer trust was compromised: articles and blog posts quickly sprang up entitled "How SIGG Lost My Trust" and "Et Tu, SIGG?" written by SIGG customers who felt betrayed by the company's lack of transparency. Competitor brands such as CamelBak and Klean Kanteen were quick to capitalize on the situation by reassuring shoppers that their products were BPA-free.[11]

3 Don't mislead

Consumers may claim to know what commonly used terms such as "recyclable" and "biodegradable" mean but they can be easily mistaken, – creating risk for unsuspecting sustainable marketers. For example, products or packaging made from recycled content can be crafted from 10% recycled content or 100% recycled content. Counterintuitively, 100% recycled content is not necessarily environmentally superior to 10% if, for example, the recycled content must be shipped from far away. A package made from cornstarch may be compostable in theory, but may not break down in backyard composters; industrial composting facilities where such packages do decompose are currently limited to only about 110 communities in the United States and even these facilities may not be convenient (e.g., the closest one to San Francisco is 25 minutes away in the city of Richmond).

What about terms such as "carbon footprint," "carbon neutral," and "sustainable" which have recently come into the picture? Does a carbon footprint encompass only the emissions of a manufacturer in making a specific product or all of the organizations in the manufacturer's supply chain for that same product? Opinions abound about the best way to trace claims related to "carbon offsets" and Renewable Energy Certificates (RECs). For example, advertisers sometimes sell products for which the greenhouse gas emitted during their production and/or use is offset by funding projects such as wind farms, tree planting, or methane capture facilities that may have happened already. Advertisers also may promise that a product was produced with RECs – tradable commodities representing proof that a certain amount of electricity used in production was generated from an eligible renewal energy source, again not under their domain, so the sources may not be verifiable.

Inconsistent guidelines are further complicating the carbon-offset debate. There are currently four proposed U.S. regional greenhouse gas cap-and-trade programs, nearly 30 mandatory state regional energy portfolio standards, and voluntary REC and carbon-offset markets – all with varying, and sometimes conflicting, requirements. The FTC believes use of the term "carbon offsets" in advertising can be inherently misleading if the ad does not specify the particular manner in which reductions in carbon emissions have been obtained.[12]

Two things are clear in this debate: adopting specific standards for disclosure will indeed be tricky, and setting standards for what is a "carbon offset" and a REC will most likely take years. Since not all carbon-offset partners are legitimate, advertisers are advised to properly vet partners prior to communicating their participation. Examples of some of the most respected include *Native*Energy and TerraPass. More detail about carbon footprint labeling is included below.

Carbon labeling issues aside, the best advice for green marketers looking to stay out of trouble is to simply follow the FTC (or other appropriate government guidelines) as best you can and, if possible, to consult with lawyers who specifically address green claims. Broad guidance based on extracts from the current FTC guides can be summarized as follows:

Be specific and prominent

Marketers are liable for what consumers may incorrectly interpret as well as what they correctly take away. Prevent unintended deception with the use of simple, crystal-clear language. For example, be sure to distinguish between the packaging of a product and the product itself, like the label on the Wheaties box on your breakfast table. Emblazoned on the lid is the familiar "chasing arrows" Möbius loop symbol with the descriptive claim, "Carton made from 100 percent recycled paperboard. Minimum 35 percent post-consumer content." This claim is specific and, because it qualifies the exact amount of recycled materials, it prevents consumers from thinking the box is made of 100% materials collected at curbside, or is fully recyclable. Precision can pay off in credibility with consumers. For example, according to the 2008 Green Gap Survey conducted by Cone LLC and the Boston College Center for Corporate Citizenship, 36% of respondents found the message "environmentally friendly" credible when describing a paper product, but 60% found the message "made with 80% post-consumer recycled paper" credible.[13]

Don't play games with type size or proximity of the claim to its qualifiers. A Lexus ad in the UK made a headline claim of "High Performance. Low Emissions. No Guilt." The UK Advertising Standards Authority (ASA) deemed this to be misleading since the text of the ad clarifying the claim was not prominent enough. Plus, the claim "No Guilt" implied the car caused little or no harm to the environment.[14]

Provide complete information

Consider a product's entire life-cycle when making claims about one particular characteristic or part of the item. A washing machine advertised as "green" because of its low energy and water consumption may not have been manufactured or distributed in a green way. Advertising the washer specifically as "energy-efficient" or "water-efficient" with substantiation from, or a comparison to, existing benchmarks could help to avoid misleading customers.

In the UK, an ad for Renault unfairly compared the CO_2 emissions of a brand sold in the UK compared to one in France, with its significantly lower emissions levels due to a high percentage of nuclear in the energy mix. The ad was criticized by the ASA for misleading consumers. Accordingly, when comparing your own product's sustainability benefits to those of a competitor or a previous model, provide enough information so that consumers can stack them up fairly. Make sure the basis for comparison is sufficiently clear and is substantiated by scientific test results. A claim such as "This water bottle is 30% lighter than our previous package" is preferable to the more ambiguous "This water bottle is 30% lighter."

Do not overstate

Avoid vague, trivial, or irrelevant claims that can create a false impression of a product's or package's environmental soundness. The Colorado-based

BIOTA brand of spring water claimed to be the first company to use a bio-degradable water bottle made from corn-based bioplastic. That may be true in theory, but the average consumer does not know that decomposition can take at least 75 days and only when exposed to the continuous heat and humidity found in municipal composting facilities – conditions that do not exist in backyard composters and certainly not in landfills.[15] So the company now touts itself as being "the world's first bottled water/beverage packaged in a commercially compostable plastic bottle."[16]

In August 2009, the FTC sued four manufacturers of bamboo textiles, claiming they mislabeled their products as "natural," "biodegradable," and "antimicrobial." The product, akin to rayon, is not natural and uses toxic chemicals to manufacture. In addition, the biodegradable and antibacterial properties do not make it past the manufacturing process. The companies squeaked by without a penalty but will need to label their fabrics as "vis-cose" or "rayon" and do away with claims of biodegradability and antimicro-bial.[17] In a case very similar to the Hefty photodegradable trash bag debacle of 1990 the FTC also charged Kmart, Tender Corp, and Dyna-E International, for falsely claiming that their paper plates, wipes, and dry towels were "bio-degradable" when most of these products simply wind up in landfills where they will not degrade.[18]

Broad statements such as "environmentally safe," "Earth friendly," and "eco friendly," if used at all, should be qualified so as to prevent consumer deception about the specific nature of the environmental benefit of the product asserted. Preferable alternatives include: "This wrapper is environ-mentally friendly because it was not bleached with chlorine, a process which has been shown to create harmful substances." Always be sure to substan-tiate and qualify terms such as "carbon neutral," "renewable," "recyclable," and "compostable." Answer questions such as: How have the claims been determined? For how long? By whom? Where? Compared to what?

Similar rules apply for corporate advertising. Overstating the environ-mental benefits of one's efforts – wrapping one's company in a green cloak – creates skepticism and invites backlash. In November 2007, the ASA in the UK ruled that a Royal Dutch Shell ad that showed an oil refinery (with envi-ronmentally preferable practices) sprouting flowers was likely to be mislead-ing, given the environmental impacts of even the cleanest of refineries, and ordered the ad off TV. Less than a year later, the ASA ruled against another Shell ad claiming the oil sands in Canada were a "sustainable" energy source. The Canadian oil sands projects have proven controversial, as they require more energy and water than traditional extraction and refining. The ASA ruled that the ad was misleading since the claim of "sustainable" was an ambiguous term and that Shell had not shown how it was effectively managing the oil sands projects' carbon emissions.[19] Shell was not alone. In March 2008, the ASA banned a campaign by the Cotton Council International, a group committed to increasing the export of U.S. cotton, which referred to cotton as "sustainable." The ASA disagreed, maintaining that cotton is a pesticide- and energy-intensive crop that depletes groundwater.[20]

Avoid generalities or sweeping statements such as "We care about the environment" with no connection to projects you have undertaken. Quantify plans, progress, and results. For example, if you claim your company prevents pollution, explain what kind of pollution and how much. Explain the specific emissions-reduction steps taken both internally and for specific products consumers can buy. In 2005, GE launched its Ecomagination campaign which, despite GE's history of significant environmental transgressions, met with very little backlash. Why? The company was upfront about their belief that financial and environmental performance can work together. The initiative was built on ten products representing tangible investments and promising new technologies, and was supported by a pledge by GE Corporate to reduce its own carbon footprint. Finally, ecomagination.com helps businesses and consumers learn more about GE's commitment, specific goals, and how customers can reduce their own "footprint."

Tell the whole story

Decide for yourself: should advertising conducted by the U.S. Council on Energy Awareness touting the clean air benefits of nuclear energy mention the radioactive waste it generates? Should the Chevrolet Division of General Motors have run ads for cars (e.g., the Chevy electric Volt) that weren't in production yet? Does a household paper product made from partial recycled content and bleached by a chlorine-containing compound deserved to be called "Scott Naturals"? To be certain your marketing and environmental communications do not confuse or mislead the consumer, test all green messages among your audience – and in your conscience.

4 Enlist the support of third parties

As depicted in Figure 2.7 on page 34, manufacturers and retailers have lower credibility than NGOs and government when communicating on environmental matters. Fortunately, there are many ways that businesses can bolster their own credibility, among them: let stakeholders in on the steps the organization is taking, educate the public on what they can do, and, importantly, align positively with third parties that perform independent life-cycle inventories and certify claims and award eco-seals. Once having shunned relationships with industry, many nonprofit organizations now welcome associations with industry as a way to work positively toward market-based solutions. This extends their influence within society, and helps to raise money for their groups. Third-party support can take many forms. Cause-related marketing, awards, and endorsements are all possibilities. When launching the Prius, Toyota proudly touted in supplemental ads targeted at deep-green drivers the fact that the Sierra Club, the National Wildlife Federation, and the United Nations had each bestowed some type of award or endorsement on the car.

Logos, trademarks, and symbols for greener product labels and certifications seem to be everywhere: on product packaging, marketing, and advertising communications, on websites, and at trade shows. In fact, more than 400 different eco-labels or green certification systems have been found in over 207 countries. These span the gamut of industries, but are predominant in consumer products such as paper and packaging, forest products, food, cleaning products, and household appliances. Some are government-run or -sponsored, while others are run by private corporations, trade associations, or NGOs. The labels vary in the level of rigor applied to the criteria and the rules around verification; some require independent third-party certification and stakeholder review, while others allow manufacturers to self-verify. At last count, 27 countries around the globe, including China and the European Union, have active multi-attribute eco-labeling programs that require third-party certification (see Fig. 7.1).[21] More certifications and labels are expected as governments, environmental groups, NGOs, trade associations, retailers, and even manufacturers create labels and advertising symbols for products that promise environmental and social benefits.

Independent seals of approval have much to recommend them, but they are not without risk. They can lend credibility to environmental messages, – 28% of consumers look to certification seals or labels on product packaging to tell whether a product is or does what it claims[22] – and they can open the door to conversations with distributors and retailers. Markets that are especially receptive to eco-seals and independent claim certification include government agencies and their contractors looking to procure environmentally conscious goods, and retailers who are anxious to stock green goods but lack the ability to screen for "green" existing product lines and a constant stream of new product introductions. However, despite their apparent proliferation, eco-labels do not exist for all product categories or environmental or social attributes. For example, there is no label for mattresses or flatware. And, as seen in Figure 7.2, only a handful of eco-labels – the chasing arrows recycled logo (Möbius loop) (93%), ENERGY STAR (93%), and USDA's Certi-

Figure 7.1 **Worldwide eco-labels**

fied Organic (75%) among them – have broken through the clutter to gain awareness and, more importantly, purchase influence.

Also, labels and certifications can be expensive. Many seal programs require manufacturers to test their products via third parties, and some independent organizations, such as the GreenGuard seal for indoor air quality or the C2C (Cradle to Cradle) logo, require manufacturers to pay what can amount to hefty licensing fees. What's more, international governments will often require that a product be tested in one of their own country's labs, creating redundancy and exorbitant extra costs for multinational marketers.

What type of criteria should be used in selecting an eco-label? It varies. Some eco-labels focus on a single product attribute (e.g., recycled content), which keeps things simple, but can potentially mislead consumers into thinking the product is greener overall. Other labels look at several characteristics of a product, or even a product's entire life-cycle; such multi-attribute

Figure 7.2 **Which eco-labels work best?**
% U.S. adults

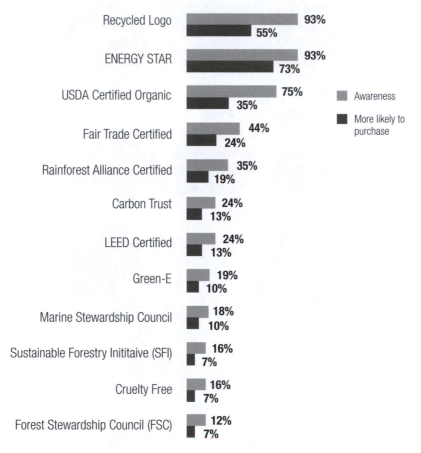

Source: © Natural Marketing Institute (NMI), 2009 LOHAS Consumer Trends Database®
All Rights Reserved

certifications may raise questions about the credibility of a single-attribute certified product while also preventing easy comparisons.

Be prepared for dueling logos that fight for your consumer's attention and your pocketbook. In the forest products industry, for instance, the FSC label denoting sustainable wood harvesting, the product of a consortium of environmental advocates, progressive timber companies, and groups that support indigenous and workers' rights interests, competes with SFI-certified, the product of a not-for-profit spin-off of the American Forest and Paper Association and Canada's Forest Products Association with standards that are perceived as less strenuous.[23]

Are there too many eco-labels? Which ones are better at helping consumers decide if a product is really "greener" than another? Should more than one label exist in a product category? Should eco-labels be single- or multi-attribute? These are all questions that are on green marketers' minds, but may not be fully addressed even when the FTC releases their anticipated Green Guide updates. For businesses that can navigate the thicket of such challenges, enlisting a third party to attest to a product's green bona fides provides a powerful indicator of business integrity.

Finally, for businesses for whom third-party certification does not work, the opportunity exists to create one's own eco-label, or "self-declaration." Independent claims and standards setting and verification exists as another alternative. Consider the following as you choose the certifications that will provide the most value to your own sustainable branding efforts:

Single-attribute labels

These labels focus on a single environmental issue, e.g., energy efficiency or sustainable wood harvesting. Before certification, an independent third-party auditor provides validation that the product meets a publicly available standard. As suggested by Figure 7.2, there are many single-attribute seals available. Many of these are sponsored by industry associations looking to defend or capture new markets, or by environmental groups or other NGOs that want to protect a natural resource or further a cause.

Two single-attribute labels with a global presence include the FSC label (used for this book) and Fair Trade Certified. The FSC label ensures the sustainable harvesting of wood and paper sources. The Fair Trade Certified label, a service of Fairtrade Labelling Organizations, a global not-for-profit group, works with local bodies such as TransFair USA to guarantee strict economic, social, and environmental criteria were met in the production and trade of a range of mostly agricultural products including coffee, tea, chocolate, herbs, fresh fruit, flowers, sugar, rice, and vanilla.

Multi-attribute labels

As their name suggests, multi-attribute labels examine two or more environmental impacts through the entire product life-cycle. Wal-Mart's Sustainability Consortium promises to eventually deliver multi-attribute guidance in the form of a Sustainable Product Index, and several multi-attribute labels exist, primarily for specific categories such as EPEAT in electronics, and Global Organic Textile Standards, among them. Others address specific areas of concern: for instance, the Carbon Trust's Carbon Reduction label, and the C2C label with its emphasis on material chemistry.

Figure 7.3 **FSC and Fair Trade labels**

Reprinted with permission from the Forest Stewardship Council and TransFair

One of the oldest and most credible multi-attribute labels in the U.S. is the Washington DC-based Green Seal (Greenseal.org), founded in 1989 by a coalition of environmentalists and other interested parties. They provide a seal of approval for products that meet specific criteria within categories where they have created standards. Companies pay a fee to have their products evaluated and annually monitored. Products that meet or exceed the standards are authorized to display the Green Seal certification mark on the product and promotional material. All products or services in a category are eligible to apply for the Green Seal. The group has finalized standards spanning a wide range of commercial and consumer products and services including cleaners and cleaning services, floor-care products, food-service packaging, lodging properties, paints and coatings, papers and newsprints, and windows and doors. Wausau Paper, Anderson Windows, Clorox, Kimberly Clark, Hilton, and Service Master Cleaning franchises are just a few of the organizations whose products now bear the Green Seal certification mark – a blue globe with a snappy green check.

A de facto multi-attribute label, the Carbon Reduction label ensures that a product's carbon footprint has been measured and is being reduced.

Figure 7.4 **Green Seal certification mark**

Reprinted with permission from Green Seal

The intention is that in a low-carbon economy, global climate-change-related information will ultimately become as important and visible on product labels as price and nutritional content. Introduced in 2007 by the Carbon Trust, a UK-based not-for-profit company, the label has already been adopted by more than 65 leading brands and can be found on over 3,500 individual products with annual sales worth £2.9 billion (around $4.4 billion in mid-2010).

In April 2008, UK-based retailer Tesco commenced a test of the label on its own brand of orange juice, potatoes, energy-efficient light bulbs, and laundry detergent. Working with the Carbon Trust, Tesco seeks to accurately measure the amount of CO_2 equivalent put into the atmosphere by each product's raw materials, production, manufacture, distribution, use and eventual disposal. The label features a carbon footprint logo. Brands can also choose to indicate the amount of life-cycle-based CO_2 and other greenhouse gases on its labels.

The Carbon Reduction label is expanding its global presence. Since 2007, Tesco has opened 125 Fresh and Easy stores in Southern California, Las Vegas, and Phoenix, so it is possible their carbon-labeled products may be making an appearance soon in the U.S. Working with Planet Ark; products bearing the Carbon Reduction Label were introduced into Australia in 2010.[24]

Figure 7.5 **The Carbon Reduction label**

Voluntary government labels

Unlike some countries, including Canada, Japan, and Korea, the U.S. government has opted for voluntary single-attribute, rather than multi-attribute labels. (The private sector and not-for-profit groups hold sway in the area of multi-attribute eco-labeling.) Outside of those associated with independent testing, the government-backed labels don't require any fees.

The most visible voluntary labeling program is ENERGY STAR (whom we at J. Ottman Consulting were proud to advise over many years). Launched in 1992, this joint program of the EPA and the U.S. Department of Energy identifies and promotes energy efficiency in more than 60 product categories including major appliances, lighting, and electronics used within homes and offices, and commercial buildings and homes. Nearly 3,000 product manufacturers now feature the ENERGY STAR label on their products. According to the Natural Marketing Institute, by 2009, 93% of the American public claimed to recognize the ENERGY STAR label, and 73% said it influenced their purchase (see Fig. 7.1).

Other EPA labels include WaterSense, to identify water-efficient toilets, faucets, showerheads, and other products and practices; Design for Environment (DfE), to acknowledge safer chemical formulations in cleaning products; and SmartWay, for fuel-efficient and low-emission passenger cars and

Figure 7.6 **Voluntary labels of the U.S. Environmental Protection Agency**

light trucks, as well as heavy-duty tractors and trailers and other forms of transportation used in distribution and delivery operations.

Labels or standards signifying that food and non-food products are organically grown exist throughout the globe, for example, in Europe (EU 834/2007), Japan (Japan Agricultural Standards), and Canada (Canada Organic Regime) and in the U.S. (USDA National Organic Program). Launched in 2002, the USDA Organic label now appears on a wide range of over 25,000 products from 10,000 companies including food, T-shirts, and shampoo. Stonyfield Farm, Earthbound Farm, and Horizon Organic are just a few of the popular consumer brands that bear the USDA organic seal on packages, advertisements, and other marketing communications, signifying that their products do not contain or were not processed with synthetic fertilizers, pesticides, radiation, antibiotics, hormones, or GMOs (genetically modified organisms); and they monitor other long-term processes such as soil management and animal conditions.[25]

Figure 7.7 **USDA Organic label**

Reprinted with permission from the USDA

Since 2002, the USDA has been running the BioPreferred program encouraging federal procurement officials to give preferential treatment to a list of 5,000 products in 50 product categories, and growing. Sensing mainstream consumer demand for biobased products – defined by the USDA as non-edible consumer and commercial products that are based on agricultural, marine, or forestry-based raw materials – Congress has authorized the USDA to ready a new label to help consumers identify biobased products. Expected to be launched in 2011, the new label (with which we at J. Ottman Consulting are pleased to be assisting), will appear on products and packaging ranging from compostable gardening bags made from cornstarch, to lip balms made from soybeans, even towels and bed sheets made with eucalyptus fiber.

Self-certification programs

Issued by manufacturers to denote their own environmental and social achievements, self-certification programs do not carry endorsements or the credibility of an impartial third party. However, they do provide distinct advantages in controlling costs and providing flexibility in the types and amounts of information that is provided to consumers. Some self-certification systems showcase government or third-party labeling.

Several large companies have attempted to put forth their own self-certifications; examples include: SC Johnson (GreenList), NEC (Eco Products), Sony Ericsson (GreenHeart), GE (Ecomagination), Timberland's Green Index, to be discussed in Chapter 9, and Hewlett-Packard (HP). Building from a history of environmental focus, HP's Eco Highlights label, introduced in 2008, spotlights key environmental attributes and certifications on the packages of select HP products. The easy-to-read rectangular label (see Fig. 7.8), which now appears on more than 160 HP products, allows consumers who purchase selected printing, computing, and server products to learn more about features such as power consumption compared to previous models, ENERGY STAR compliance, and percentage of recycled material used in the product. It also includes specifics on the recyclability of the packaging and the product, and updates on HP's overall recycling goals.[26]

Figure 7.8 **HP Eco Highlights label**

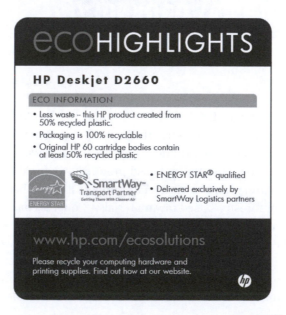

Independent claim verification

Independent for-profit organizations, including Scientific Certification Systems of Oakland, California and UL Environment of Northbrook, Illinois, will, for a fee, verify specific claims and develop standards in industries where none exists. They will also certify products against standards developed by other organizations. For example, they will certify commercial furniture to the new BIFMA (Business and Institutional Furniture Manufacturers Association) e3 multi-attribute, life-cycle-based standard (levelcertified.org) which was developed in line with the American National Standards Institute (ANSI) standards development protocols.

Environmental product declaration

ISO standards describe three types of eco-label, two of which are described above: Type I: Environmental Labels, Type II: Environmental Claims and Self Declarations, and Type III: Environmental Product Declarations (EPDs). More often used in Europe and Asia than the U.S., EPDs provide detailed explanations of the full life-cycle impacts of a given product. An excellent example is the EPD issued per ISO 14025 by Steelcase for its Think Chair, designed to fit the needs of consumers around the world. Displayed at the company's website, Steelcase.com, the EPD shares the results of three life-cycle assessments (needed to accurately assess impacts in North America, Europe, and Asia), and describes the various certifications it has received from different countries around the globe.

Considering an eco-seal endorsement or independent claim certification for your brand? Maximize its potential value and avoid backlash by sticking to these four rules of thumb:

Choose wisely

Ensure that the organization behind the seal and its methodologies are credible. Look in particular to see that their standards have been developed in accordance with such standards-writing organizations as ISO and local bodies such as the American National Standards Institute or the British Standards Institute. Labels should be consistent with expected amendments to the FTC Green Guides as well as other appropriate national environmental guidelines.

Be relevant

With so many available, it is possible that your brand may qualify for more than one eco-label, and for more than one product attribute, e.g., ingredients, packaging, manufacturing, etc. Therefore, aim to certify those attributes that are most relevant to your brand. Also, integrate your eco-labels into existing brand platforms. GE's Ecomagination (and more recent Healthy Imagination) designations extend from the company's longstanding "Imagination at Work" brand platform.

Educate

Let consumers know about the specific criteria upon which your eco-seal is based. With single-attribute labels, take care to communicate that only the specific product attribute is being certified and do not imply that the entire product is "greener" as a result. For credibility's sake, if appropriate, communicate attempts to extend the greening process to other product attributes. Products bearing self-declarations are advised to identify their label as having been issued by their own organization to avoid misleading consumers otherwise. For added credibility, products with self-declarations can consider third-party certification. Share additional details on a corporate website.

Promote your eco-label

Considering that many eco-labels are not widely recognized, help to create demand for your eco-label via marketing communications consistent with your seal's own guidelines. The ENERGY STAR label enjoys strong awareness thanks largely to the promotional efforts of the many manufacturers whose products bear the label, coupled with pro bono advertising. Be sure to look for opportunities to distinguish your commitment to your selected eco-label from competitors using the same label. Earning and promoting ENERGY STAR "Partner of the Year" status is one good route.

5 Promote responsible consumption

Are Frito's SunChips's bags truly "compostable" if consumers drop them in the trash rather than a composting bin? Is an ENERGY STAR-rated light bulb really green if it remains on after everyone leaves the room? It is one thing to design a product (and its system) to be greener, but impacts throughout the total product life-cycle cannot be minimized unless people use (and dispose) of it more responsibly. "Responsible consumption" – what I consider to be the high road of green marketing and product development – is about conserving resources associated with using products, including encouraging consumers to use only what is needed, and consciously reduce waste. Sustainability leaders are striving for the ideal goals of zero waste and zero energy, but we will never get to zero until consumers learn to responsibly consume and properly dispose of the products they buy.

As discussed in Chapter 4, consumer usage can represent a significant portion of a product's total environmental impacts, especially when it comes to those that consume resources such as energy or water. Products can be designed to make it easier for consumers to minimize resource use, like a duplex printing feature on a printer, or a dual-flush toilet. Real-time information, like Toyota's dashboard and the new crop of energy meters and monitoring services help, too.

Representing what is now an unwritten rule of green marketing – but one that will undoubtedly be writ large in the not-too-distant future – enlisting consumer support for responsible consumption is a sure-fire way to build credibility and reduce risk. Consumers intuitively understand that it is not possible to spend our way out of the environmental crisis. At the micro level, simply switching one supermarket cartful of "brown" products with "green" ones will not cure environmental ills. Creating a sustainable society requires, among other things, that every one of us use only what we need and that we help to recapture resources for successive uses through recycling and composting. When markets fail to address environmental ills, governments are sure to intervene. (Witness mandated shifts to energy-, fuel- and water-efficient appliances, light bulbs, and cars. Will cold-water laundry detergents, organic cotton, and leather-free shoes be next?) Another issue industry needs to be mindful of "the rebound effect" – whereby consumers will buy or use more of a product if it costs less to use due to enhanced efficiency. The classic case is fuel-efficient cars that are driven more miles than less-efficient vehicles.

As we learned when advising HSBC, a key to the credibility of their There's No Small Change campaign was empowering individuals and businesses to reduce their carbon footprint, in line with the bank's own efforts. In other words, we weren't asking HSBC's customers to do anything the bank hadn't already done itself. Cognizant of the risk associated with promoting a compostable bag that might only get thrown away, Frito-Lay emblazons a "compostable" message on its SunChips bags and supports additional education through a television campaign and website. Below are examples of ways that businesses are winning their stakeholders' respect by communicating the need to consume responsibly especially in the area of energy use.

HP earned the #1 spot on *Newsweek*'s list of the top green companies of 2009 by pledging to reduce product emissions and energy usage 40% from 2005 levels by 2011. Realizing it needs to partner with consumers to reach that goal, the company has launched its Power to Change campaign, encouraging users to turn off their computers and printers when they do not need them. Users can download software that reminds them to turn off their computers at night and tracks actions to calculate energy and carbon impact.

Levi Strauss and Co. has teamed up with Goodwill to educate consumers on how to lower the life-cycle impacts of blue jeans. The company's A Care Tag For The Planet campaign uses online and in-store messaging and a new care tag on jeans to encourage owners to wash in cold water, line dry when possible and, at the end of their useful life, to donate their jeans to Goodwill thrift stores. The company estimates that such steps taken by responsible consumers can reduce the life-cycle climate-change impacts by 50%. Relatedly, in Europe, Procter & Gamble's Ariel runs a Turn to 30 (degrees centigrade) campaign to encourage consumers to wash at lower temperatures, and spurred by the threat of regulation, the laundry detergent industry as a whole has united to promote responsible washing. And an industry-wide Washright campaign (washright.com), launched in 1998 by the Brussels-based International Association for Soaps, Detergents and Maintenance Products (AISE), reached 70% of European households with tips on how to wash laundry in environmentally preferable ways.[27]

A final example: the Sacramento Municipal Utility District now knows that peer pressure is an excellent strategy for promoting responsible consumption – and may be even more motivating than saving money. In a test that began in April 2008, 35,000 randomly selected customers were told via "happy" or "sad" faces printed on their monthly utility bills how their energy use compared with their neighbors' and with that of the most efficient energy users in the district. Customers who received the information cut their electricity use by 2% compared to flat usage by counterparts who did not receive messages. The utility expanded the program to 50,000 households in August 2009.[28]

Operating by the new rules of green marketing requires new strategies for engagement with the vast panoply of stakeholders who are motivated to help businesses green their products, develop effective communications, and engage consumers in exciting new ways – the subject of the next chapter.

As we go to press . . . The FTC issued proposed revisions for their Green Guides, which were last revised in 1996. The proposed Guides can be located at ftc. gov/opa/2010/10/greenguide.shtm. After the requisite rule-making process including comment period, the revised guides will be finalized, likely in the spring of 2011. The content of the proposed revisions are consistent with much of the guidance in this book. Please visit the author's website, www. greenmarketing.com, for continuing updates and her analysis.

The *New Rules* Checklist

Ask the following questions to help ensure credibility for your green marketing claims and communications.

- Are we walking our talk? Does our CEO openly support sustainability? Do our stakeholders know it?

- Are our green marketing claims consistent with our corporate actions? (i.e., are we making claims that are true?)

- Are we following official guidelines for environmental marketing claims? Are we keeping up with the dialogue on the use of newer environmental marketing terms? Does our state and/or our company's legal department have its own guidelines for the use of environmental marketing claims?

- Have we thoroughly considered all that can go wrong so as to minimize the chances of backlash from greenwash and enjoy the full benefits of positive publicity? Do we have a process for monitoring our online reputation?

- Are our brand-related sustainability claims meaningful, specific, complete, and without exaggeration? Have we tested their believability among consumers?

- Are we being transparent about the pollution our products represent as well as their environmental benefits?

- Are we being environmentally efficient with our marketing materials? Have we identified where the Internet or electronic media could work to reduce our use of paper? Are we using recycled and/or sustainably harvested paper and vegetable-based inks for our marketing communications?

- Are we taking advantage of third parties to underscore credibility? Are we considering our own self-declaration or the use of third-party verifiers?

- Do consumers know how to use and dispose of our products responsibly? In what ways might we make it easier for consumers to practice responsible consumption of our products and packages?

Partnering for success

Historically, the only groups with a direct interest in a company's products or operations were investors, employees, customers and end consumers, suppliers, and the press. However, with increased awareness of industry's impact on our water, land, and air, new eyes from practically every corner of society now scrutinize a firm's environmental and social impact, writing new rules for the ways business is conducted and brands are marketed. Today, a host of new corporate environmental and social stakeholders are now on the list, including the general public, citizen journalists and bloggers, educators, environmental and social activists, government bodies, community groups, church leaders and other religious groups, and even children and future generations who will feel the effects of today's corporate activities in decades to come (see Fig. 8.1).

With potential influence on such diverse activities as how businesses procure raw materials, design their products, and produce and promote them, some groups monitor corporate polluters: boycotting, conducting negative media campaigns, and lobbying for stiff new laws are tools in their arsenal. Other groups engage companies one-on-one in positive efforts, and there is much to gain from collaborating with them. Representing a myriad of capabilities and resources that can help solve complex environmental and social problems, diverse stakeholder groups can help improve understanding of how your company is perceived in the world at large. They can help identify issues to address and evaluate stakeholder satisfaction.

Figure 8.1 **The new corporate environmental and social stakeholders**

Traditional stakeholders	New stakeholders
Retailers and end consumers	General public
Employees	Children and future generations
Plant neighbors	Educators
The press	Environmental and social activists
Suppliers	Civic and religious leaders
Financial institutions	Citizen journalists
Regulators	Other government groups

Source: J. Ottman Consulting, Inc.

Forming constructive partnerships or coalitions with various stake-holders provides many advantages, including uncovering ways to cut costs, improving the value of existing products and creating new products, bolstering credibility for greener products and communications, and enhancing public image. In order to drive sustainable progress and capitalize on valuable green marketing opportunities, marketers need to follow new rules. Characterized by transparency and cooperations, these new rules call for engaging with stakeholders in frank, open discussion. They also involve the need to disclose once closely held information on product ingredients and how products are produced and workers are treated, so listen carefully to the stakeholders who take a broad view of your industry.

The general public

The power of the general public – defined as consumers and those who influence them – is on the rise. As described in Chapter 2, consumers' perceptions of the environmental impacts of products and companies now factor into their decisions of what, where, and how often they purchase. Fueled by the many opinions now broadcast over the Internet, newly uncovered learning (correct or incorrect) can upend an industry, seemingly overnight. The draft report released in 2008 from a small study on the chemical compound BPA, forcing Nalge Nunc International to quickly reformulate its polycarbonate bottles in order to prevent a complete collapse in demand for its products, is just one example.[1]

Bottlers of water are still reeling from the numerous environmental offenses being heaped on the industry – some deserved, some not. First, there's the perception of mountains of unrecyclable and unrecycled plastic bottles that clog landfills, and contribute to the Great Pacific Garbage Patch. That's compounded by the environmental impact of the millions of barrels of oil used to make the bottles, the multiple pints of water needed to fill each bottle, and the greenhouse gases associated with shipping all this water from Evian, France, and islands as far away as Fiji.[2] Finally, there's water sourcing, a favorite of the press. Nestlé Waters (Poland Spring, Perrier) and other bottlers are being accused by local residents of draining precious water supplies, while others such as Coke (Dasani) and Pepsi (Aquafina) are being condemned for simply filtering municipal supplies and failing to label it as such. (Pepsi has since come around but, as of this writing, Coke has not, preferring the more euphemistic water-process descriptors of "Pure, Fresh Taste" and "Reverse Osmosis.") Once considered hip, bottled water is now banned from government offices from Fayetteville, Arkansas to Seattle, Washington. New York City is testing a program of using filtered tap water in water coolers and it is encouraging city workers to use their own reusable water bottles.[3] Aided by nascent green marketing efforts by Nalgene and Brita (Chapter 6), consumers are increasingly turning to tap water and new, trendy reusable bottles.

The bottled water industry is especially vulnerable with its strategy of bottling water that is comparable in many instances to what's available from the kitchen tap. But it need not be in such a pickle – many consumers prefer the taste of bottled waters, and some fear chlorine in municipal water supplies. The industry could have done a better job of protecting its business and reputation: for instance, by first taking a life-cycle approach to its products – using recycled and recyclable packaging, promoting refills of its own water, tapping into local as opposed to foreign water supplies, and better ensuring the sustainability of its water sources. They also could have educated the public about the health and refreshment (beyond the convenience) benefits of their products, and publicized efforts to reduce (or offset) their environment impacts, not to mention underscoring legitimate health claims.

Strategy for educating the general public

Conduct media campaigns that can engage the general public in relevant environmental issues

The beleaguered bottled-water industry and individual players are now mobilizing to help clarify misguided criticism and reduce risks going forward. In the summer of 2007, the International Bottled Water Association (IBWA) launched a fact-based campaign consisting of full-page advertisements in key media outlets and in the *New York Times* and the *San Francisco Chronicle*. The goal: to demonstrate the industry's commitment to environmental stewardship and underscore its support of recycling and bottled water regulation and safety, especially in targeted markets. Realizing that bottled water was taking the heat while soft drinks slipped under the radar, the campaign also noted the benefits of water compared to other more widely consumed beverages in plastic bottles.[4]

Leading the charge was Coca-Cola, Nestlé Waters, and PepsiCo, which make up the bulk of bottled water sales. Each has made strides to reduce its own environmental footprint, primarily via the use of "eco-shape" bottles that helped Coke reduced the weight of its Dasani bottles by 30% and PepsiCo reduce the weight of its Aquafina bottles nearly 40%.[5] Nestlé also went so far as to reduce the size of the paper labels on Poland Spring, Deer Park, and Arrowhead water bottles by 30%.[6] Recognizing the need to engage his company's entire supply chain to take more meaningful step, in 2008 in a keynote speech to a sustainable business conference, Kim Jeffrey, CEO of Nestlé Waters North America, acknowledged the negative impact the electronic media can have on one's business and challenged corporations to put sustainability at the core of their businesses. Among other steps, he reached out to suppliers and other stakeholders to increase the percentage of recycled PET in their bottles to 25% and to work to increase recycling rates of PET containers to 60% by 2013.[7]

Children

In their learning years from preschool through college, young people find their identity, develop their values, and discover their passions. Slowly but surely, children become empowered to act on environmental issues through their own purchasing and consumption habits, suggesting a key opportunity to shape their consciousness while their sustainability-related values are forming.

Children and young adults are important industry stakeholders because of their own buying power and their ability to influence the purchases of their family – especially when it comes to a topic they are ardent about: the environment. In fact, more than half of kids between the ages of six and eight are reported to encourage their parents to buy greener products.[8] Armed with simple environmental slogans such as "Reduce, Reuse, and Recycle" (which all too often translates to "recycle, recycle, recycle"), four-foot-tall "eco-cops" can dictate behavior at home that can be misguided. Meanwhile, their college-bound elder brothers and sisters – the bright minds and future leaders of the next generation – are forming their own brand preferences for such products as laundry detergents, snacks, cars, and clothing that will often stick with them for life.

Strategies for educating children

Empower educators to teach the facts about environmental issues and how to consume responsibly

Environmental topics fit well with the full range of curricula, from science and math to the arts and social studies. For teachers, the environment and ecology are topics with a "hands-on" appeal that can liven up an otherwise dry math class or civics lesson. Teachers and administrators are willing partners when they sense an opportunity to impart legitimate information that educates students – and helps to extend tight budgets.

Supply educators with fact-based teaching materials and curriculum. Partner with a not-for-profit for added impact and credibility. During the 2004 back-to-school shopping season, the Staples Foundation for Learning, a nonprofit division of Staples, the stationery products giant, partnered with Earth Force (an international education program that involves young people in hands-on education, conservation, and restoration projects) to outfit schools with environmental educational curriculum and program materials. Representing a win–win for both organizations, the Staples Foundation has donated $1 million annually since 2004, helping Earth Force to equip more than 20,000 students each year with the skills, knowledge, and hands-on opportunity to better understand the causes and impacts of many environmental issues and do something about it![9] Taking the program up a notch, in 2007, the partnership launched the Staples Earth Force Award to recognize local student groups' environmental achievements. Award recipient Robinson Elementary School in Tampa, Florida, worked to eliminate invasive species and reintroduce native species in a local area nature preserve,[10] while the Holland Middle School students in Pennsylvania focused on the energy and cost savings that resulted from instituting a 'dark school' day when the whole community reduced their lighting and air conditioning usage.[11]

A cautionary note: when developing industry-sponsored eco-efforts for schools, be careful to avoid suggestions of bias, self-promotion, or anything that hints of greenwashing. This can backfire and mar your organization's reputation.

Find hands-on ways to engage youth in reducing their own and their family's impacts

Organize collection programs that involve students in recycling or reuse of otherwise valuable waste items. TerraCycle, the New Jersey company founded by Princeton University dropout Tom Szaky, first made headlines in 2006 by selling fertilizer made from worm poop to the Home Depot and other major retailers. They now put non-recyclable items such as food wrappers to work as raw material for tote bags and other fashion items. "Brigades" enlisted within hundreds of schools collect packaging of sponsors including Capri Sun, Kool-Aid, Oreo cookies, and Stonyfield Farm yogurt. Each used pack collected earns the school a one- or two-cent rebate to help build a garden or buy school supplies. And educators jump at the opportunity to encourage kids to recycle, to earn extra money for schools, and to repurpose what would otherwise be "trash" into new products. The Islesboro Central School in Maine lost no time in putting the monies raised by their students to work at building composting bins and supporting the Rainforest Network's efforts to buy rainforest land for restoration.[12]

Sponsor eco-oriented programming for children, teens, and families

In partnership with Boys & Girls Clubs of America, the Natural Resources Defense Council, the National Wildlife Federation (NWF), the NFL (National Football League), the NEA Foundation (National Education Association, a public entity that supports public education), and the Girl Scouts of America, the popular cable network Nickelodeon launched a section on its website entitled, "The Big Green Help," giving more than two million kids practical tips on how to be greener through online games and opportunities to participate in local activities. Nickelodeon also founded the Big Green Help Public Education Grants program,[13] awarding $200,000 in grants to support sustainability projects in schools, furthering their effort to empower kids to improve the environment.[14]

Encourage college students, faculty, and staff to collaborate on exciting educational initiatives

Beyond simply funding projects, consider ways to extend your sponsorship dollars by providing access to your products and employees. Biannually since 2002, BP Solar (part of BP's alternative energy business) has partnered with the U.S. Green Building Council and the U.S. Department of Energy to sponsor the Solar Decathlon, an international biennial competition where teams from 20 universities work together over two years to design and build solar-powered homes. In addition to funding, BP equips the teams with discounted solar materials and technical advice. The resulting homes are exhibited on the National Mall in Washington, DC. According to a 2007 winner, "The house is a wonderful example of how energy efficiency, energy generation, and good design can all work together to create spaces for living. I hope more sustainable projects take a cue from this project."[15]

The NWF runs an annual Chill Out program to raise awareness and seek practical solutions for global warming by reaching out to colleges and universities. Students and faculty from universities across the United States submit projects that help solve or mitigate the impact of global warming associated with their campuses. The schools that implement the most creative solutions are featured in a video webcast posted on the NWF website.[16] Since 2006 the Chill Out contest has engaged students on over 500 campuses and recognized the efforts of more than 20 schools.[17] Sponsors of the Chill Out program include brands with an incentive to deepen their connection with this key student target and tap their brainpower to find innovative solutions to climate change: Stonyfield Farm, ClimateCounts.org (a nonprofit organization funded by Stonyfield), Kaplan Test Prep and Admissions, and Discovery Channel's Planet Green.

Finally, DoSomething.org, a nonprofit based in New York City that inspires and empowers teenagers to get involved in topics including health, poverty, and the environment, organized a nationwide Increase Your Green competition in the fall of 2008. Open to all middle and high school students in the United States, the competition called on participants to carry out eight-week projects that reduced the environmental impact of their school and involved and/or impacted as many people as possible. All projects were designed and led by the students, whether as a class, extracurricular club, or even an entire school. Projects were judged by a panel at DoSomething.org and an outside panel of green experts, who looked at the number of hours of energy saved, the number of people involved and/or impacted, and the amount of waste recycled.

Two winners received a $1,500 grant for their school, funded by the National Grid Foundation; one winning team from Scituate High School, Massachusetts, built a biodiesel production tank. Overall, 75,000 students participated in the competition, with projects ranging from starting recycling programs and composting projects to planting community gardens.[18]

The *New Rules* Checklist

Ask the following questions to uncover opportunities for enlisting the support of the general public and youth for your company's environment-related initiatives.

- How sensitive to and knowledgeable are our consumers about the environmental issues that affect our industry, company, and products?

- Which types of messages do we need to be getting to consumers about the issues?

- What do consumers need to know in order to safely and responsibly use, recycle, and dispose of our products and packaging?

- What role do children and teens play in influencing the purchase of our brands?

- What opportunities exist to develop environmental education programs or curricula?

- What types of programs and events might we sponsor to reach the next generation with our messages? Community projects? Environmental clubs? Children's media? Teen initiatives? College and university programs?

- In what ways might we leverage social media – texting, Facebook, Twitter, etc. – to reach youth?

- Who might be appropriate and willing partners in helping us to extend our reach, enhance credibility, and share costs?

Employees

Employees wear many stakeholder hats. Relying on secure jobs, they have a direct stake in their company's success. They also have a personal stake in their employer's reputation – who wants to tell their kids they are working for a polluter that lacks a social or environmental conscience? Educated employees can recommend ways to green up the workplace, brainstorm ideas for new eco-sensitive products, build bridges to their brand's consumers, and enhance their company's image. The 2008 Society for Human Resource Management *Green Workplace Survey* found that employee morale (44%) is a top benefit in implementing environmental responsibility programs. In companies that have not already launched sustainability plans, nearly three out of four employees say they want their employers to "go green."[19] Potentially ardent consumers of a firm's products or services, workers can be a crucial link in forging good relations and building trust between the organization and the communities in which they live, as well as between their brands and consumers.

Strategy for empowering employees

Create initiatives that encourage employees to make a positive impact on their communities and brands
Many businesses now have programs for employees and even their children on Earth Day, but the environment needs to be an *everyday* priority. Eco-programs that create internal awareness and celebrate successes should be ongoing for greatest impact and credibility.

Since 2006, Alcoa has declared October as a "Month of Service," highlighting the company's dedication to sustainability and its employees' commitment to community service. Alcoa staffers around the world are encouraged to volunteer with local community groups to plant trees, rehabilitate local parks and rivers, recycle, and find solutions to climate change. In 2007, Alcoa employees clocked 634,000 hours of voluntary service aiding 187 schools, delivering over 2,300 meals, building Habitat for Humanity homes, planting 12,000 trees, and saving over 1,700 tons of CO_2.[20]

Before attempting to green its operations, Wal-Mart opted to green the people who could make it happen. Starting in 2007, the 1.3 million employees of Wal-Mart and Sam's Club were encouraged to take on a Personal Sustainability Project (PSP) aimed at achieving an attainable goal related to improving their personal health or the welfare of their family, community, or planet. Whatever worked for them made the grade, whether eating healthy meals and shedding pounds, using eco-friendly household cleaning products, recycling at home, or carpooling or riding bicycles to work. Wal-Mart claims this award-winning effort made its employees healthier, increased work satisfaction and productivity, and reduced turnover, increasing revenue and decreasing costs. It also sent a message that personal and environmental sustainability can be achieved by all workers – even those with hectic schedules, long working hours, and stretched family budgets.[21]

The Home Depot's employees know a lot about building things, and this can come in handy in the many communities in which they live and work. In January 2009, the Home Depot teamed up with KaBOOM!, a national non-profit organization committed to building playgrounds within walking distance of every child in America. In addition to financial support, tools, and raw material provided by the Home Depot, more than 100,000 Home Depot employees have volunteered their time to build or refurbish more than 1,000 play spaces. Looking to minimize the environmental impact of each playground and to maximize the opportunity to educate the community, KaBOOM! seeks to reuse and recycle materials at each site and has introduced composting bins, tree planting, and rainwater collection systems. The Home Depot employees benefit from this partnership as well: according to one employee in the Midwest, "The partnership . . . allows us to demonstrate our core value of giving back to the community and we feel great after every build when a couple days later the kids come back and play on the new playground. It's just a great experience."[22] No doubt these efforts resulted in more aware salespeople, able to guide customers to greener purchases once inside the stores.

The *New Rules* Checklist

Ask the following questions to assess opportunities for enlisting employees in your company's environment-related initiatives.

- ○ Are our employees aware of our environmental and social commitments?

- ○ What environmental and social issues are of most concern to our employees?

- ○ What do employees know about the environmental issues that affect our business? What gaps in education need filling in?

- ○ Are employees engaged in reducing their own environmental impacts and those of the organization?

- ○ In what ways might we educate employees and their families to live more sustainable lives overall?

- ○ What opportunities exist to engage our employees in our local communities?

Retailers

Fueled by health concerns, pesticide-free foods and organically grown cotton now top many a "Naturalist's" or "Health Fanatic's" shopping list. However, the environmental benefits of such products are not always so clear. For instance, many people believe that organically grown cotton clothing is healthier to wear, but do not actually know that organic growing methods are significantly less hazardous to soil and farm workers than those for traditionally grown cotton, which is extremely pesticide-intensive. Retailers can help shoppers see the links between your products and a more sustainable lifestyle.

With unique opportunities to educate the public at the point of sale, retailers are a key ally in the effort to enlighten shoppers. Often queried by the millions of now ardent green consumers about the environmental aspects of the products they stock, they need credible, cost-effective ways of responding to their customers about eco issues in general, as well as the specifics about the products they stock. Despite their desire to fill their shelves with the greener alternatives today's consumers seek, retailers fall short verifying vendor options as "green."

With IKEA, Trader Joe's, Wal-Mart, and Whole Foods Market in the lead in the U.S. and Marks & Spencer and Tesco in the UK, many retail chains have created their own lines of eco-branded products. Some are promoting the use of specific labels storewide; examples include Home Depot's Eco Options program, and Tesco's support for the Carbon Trust's Carbon Reduction Label, discussed in Chapter 7. Sensing opportunities to lead the way to all things green, Best Buy electronics retailer launched a Greener Together program to teach its 165,000 employees how to help customers make smarter shopping decisions. Their focus: how to use electronics more efficiently to save energy, and how to recycle, reuse, or trade in products at the end of their useful lives.[23]

In 2009, Wal-Mart announced a multi-stakeholder Sustainability Consortium tasked with creating a supplier index or score that will first measure the sustainability performance of suppliers, and eventually, the impacts of individual consumer products. Ratings that will likely influence which products make it to Wal-Mart's shelves, and in what quantities, will take into consideration such things as carbon footprint, material efficiency, use of natural resources, and social issues. Its goal is to influence the next generation of sustainable products, materials, and technologies. To do the job correctly Wal-Mart has enlisted the support of leading manufacturers, NGOs, government regulators, and academia. Partnering with eco-minded retailers is not just enticing; with the market quickly skewing toward greener goods, it is essential.

Strategy for partnering with retailers

Help retailers train staff, promote more sustainable products, or conduct special media outreach

Companies that partner with retailers can strengthen vendor relations and secure increased merchandising support for their brands in weekly circulars and newspaper ads, enhanced in-store signage, couponing, and sampling.

Responding to Wal-Mart's interest in greener goods, in 2005 Sun Products created a triple win for consumers, retailers, and the environment when they launched "All small & mighty," the triple-strength laundry detergent concentrate mentioned in Chapter 4. Representing myriad benefits for consumers and the environment, for retailers it could optimize space on their shelves, reduce shelf-stocking costs, and reduce customer disappointment from out-of-stock products. No wonder All small & mighty became a poster child of then Wal-Mart CEO Lee Scott with all the resulting PR benefits for the All brand.

**Addressing
the New Rules**

Partnering with ENERGY STAR

Since its inception in 1992, the U.S. Environmental Protection Agency has leveraged retail partnerships to promote its ENERGY STAR brand and to assist both its manufacturer and retail partners to sell more energy-efficient products. Today, more than ever, with the increased demand for greener products among consumers, Jill Vohr, Marketing Manager for ENERGY STAR Products Labeling, recognizes the corresponding increase in opportunities to partner with retailers on promoting ENERGY STAR qualified products ranging from electronics to lighting, to appliances. According to Ms. Vohr, the key to leveraging these trends successfully through retail partnerships depends on where your retail customers sit on this issue. Here are three examples she provides:

1. If your retail customers have taken the initiative to develop consumer-facing platforms promoting green to their consumers, such as the Home Depot's Eco Options label, then the best course of action for you as the manufacturer is to do your homework and find out how the retailer identifies products for its green line – for the Home Depot it would be Scientific Certification Systems (SCS) – and demonstrate that your product meets these criteria.

The ENERGY STAR program supports the Home Depot by providing not just products, but also educational content and, of course, government-backed credibility to the energy-efficient pillar of the Home Depot's Eco Options. The result: ENERGY STAR is not only a feature in many of the Home Depot's Eco Options promotional activities, but manufacturer partners reap the rewards of favorable positioning for Home Depot product line reviews.

In addition to the Home Depot, there are a number of other retailers that have developed environmental marketing platforms, such as Ace Hardware's Helpful Earth Choices, Staples' EcoEasy, and JCPenney's Simply Green. Many more have programs in the works to meet consumer demand for more sustainable alternatives.

2. If the retailer has internal programs supporting greener initiatives, such as Best Buy's Greener Together platform and Wal-Mart's work with the Sustainability Consortium, manufacturers of green products should get to know others at the organization – beyond their respective merchants – who manage these programs (more often than not, the director of sustainability or environmental affairs) and identify shared interests in promoting green brands to consumers. Being proactive and taking the initiative may translate into a first-mover advantage for your brand and priority placements featuring effective environmental messages.

ENERGY STAR works with both Wal-Mart and the Sustainability Consortium to help them define and implement optimal energy-efficiency criteria for their products. For Best Buy, the ENERGY STAR program not only provides general support for promoting ENERGY STAR-labeled products within their stores, it also provides strategic guidance for where they take Greener Together and forms the basis for the energy-saving component of the Greener Together platform.

3. A final set of retailers are those that characterize their consumers as less interested in green or are taking a wait-and-see approach to green marketing and thus have held off on green marketing initiatives. These retailers are still more likely than not to be keen on green. This is simply because for retailers, even those with "browner" consumers, playing a role in the green movement adds value to their image, and this image value corresponds with enhanced loyalty and increased sales overall. Moreover, few consum-

ers would view effective green marketing negatively. If anything, they shop based on other criteria, but still recognize that the retailer cares and that counts for a lot.

So for retailers that do not seem to be engaged at all, it still might be strategically advantageous for manufacturers to educate them about the green consumer and encourage them to consider how carrying green products might be a good first step towards doing the right thing. This, in turn, may lead to an ongoing relationship with a retailer that translates into an eventual flagship role for your brand in a new green marketing effort.

For ENERGY STAR, not all retailers are gung ho about green marketing. For those retail partners that shy away from the green marketing movement for whatever reason, Ms. Vohr finds that there are still opportunities to increase ENERGY STAR penetration both for products and messaging simply because the retailers appreciate guidance they can get from partners: in this case, EPA. Similarly, manufacturers who have a handle on what's green and the benefits of green can leverage partnerships with hold-out retailers to help them navigate this new space, thus increasing the likelihood of brand favorability in the future.[24]

The *New Rules* Checklist

Ask the following questions to assess opportunities for enlisting retailer support for your company's environment-related initiatives.

○ What are the most important environmental issues facing our key retailers in their trading areas?

○ To what extent are our retailers aware of our environmental initiatives and the environmentally sound attributes of our products and packaging?

○ What types of education and training do buyers and sales personnel require about environmental issues for our brand/category?

○ Which retailers have in-store eco-labeling programs and other eco-initiatives that we have an opportunity to get involved with?

○ What are the opportunities for our brand to get enhanced sales by building in-store support among less aware retailers?

Suppliers

Today's complex global supply chains often cloud visibility into raw material sourcing and product manufacturing and shipping as products wend their way over increased distances and circuitous routes. With heightened interest in sustainability specifics throughout a product's entire life-cycle, suppliers, with their intimate knowledge of their own materials, components, or technologies can offer critical support in reducing environmental impacts and bringing new product and service innovations on board.

Wal-Mart's manufacturer vendors have a big incentive to work with their own suppliers to go green. In 2006, as part of their global effort to meet consumer environmental demand and likely to help shore up an image tarnished by labor issues, Wal-Mart introduced a green rating system designed to push their 60,000 worldwide manufacturer vendors to reduce the amount of packaging they use by 5%, to use more renewable materials, and to slash energy use. Requiring unprecedented knowledge of their suppliers' own operations, Wal-Mart's vendors are being asked such questions as: What are your corporate greenhouse emissions? What is total water use of the facilities that produce for Wal-Mart? What is the location of all the facilities that supply your products? Companies that achieve high rankings are named "preferred suppliers," while those with low rankings risk losing coveted real estate on Wal-Mart's shelves.[25]

Working with suppliers to meet consumer and retailer environmental and social demands is challenging. First, many suppliers are loath to disclose trade secrets. Your supply chain can consist of several entities, stretched out long distances around the globe. Some suppliers are way upstream and are unknown to manufacturers of finished products. Suppliers may be new to environmental and social management, so may not be prepared to answer your tough questions, much less pay hefty fees for sophisticated analyses of their materials, ingredients, and processes. Taking the time to educate and work with suppliers while protecting their trade secrets can result in new products and packaging and greened-up life-cycles that can establish competitive advantage.

Strategies for partnering with suppliers

Identify chemicals in your products to ensure they are safe
SC Johnson's GreenList system, which it licenses to other manufacturers, evaluates and rates chemicals in its products. HP is collecting data from suppliers of 240 chemicals of "emerging concern," while Nike maintains a

restricted substances list in an effort to identify and evaluate chemicals contained in their products.

Work with suppliers on innovative materials

Squeezed by rising energy costs and looking to reduce waste, in summer 2009 KLM, the national Dutch airline turned to its supplier, Moonen Packaging, for a new idea in on-board coffee and tea cups. Working with Nature-Works, Moonen created a paper cup coated with Ingeo brand plastic made from cornstarch. KLM's new Bio-Cups not only provide environmental benefits, they are also lighter and they pack and store better than the traditional foam cups used in-flight.[26]

Encourage suppliers to provide solutions to packaging and waste challenges

Guided by the Environmental Defense Fund, a leading environmental group, in 1990 McDonald's worked with James River Corp. to replace foam clamshells with source-reduced "quiltwraps" as an alternative to recycling polystyrene clamshells. This groundbreaking alliance was the exception then, but today it's the rule for suppliers of all stripes to actively work with retailers and manufacturers to reformulate products and packaging with green in mind, because nearly 20 years later packaging is still on the hot seat.

A number of packaging-related coalitions have since sprung up to deal with the many challenges of reducing packaging while protecting contents until they fulfill their intended purpose. The Sustainable Packaging Coalition of Charlottesville, Virginia, brings together end-product manufacturers with packaging suppliers to share best practices and designs, support innovation, and provide education, resources, and tools that can lead to environmentally and economically robust packaging. The Paperboard Packaging Alliance and the Corrugated Packaging Alliance have teamed up to raise awareness for the benefits of using renewable raw materials and for recycling at high rates through a Responsible Packaging Campaign. One of the 2009 Greener Package Awards went to Green Toys and its packaging supplier, Unisource, for using 100% recyclable corrugated box packaging for its tea sets, sandbox play sets and other toys made from recycled plastics.[27]

Encourage suppliers to provide innovative solutions to energy and carbon challenges

With the cost of a barrel of crude oil steadily increasing during 2007 (before hitting all-time highs during the summer of 2008) and the prospect of government restrictions on carbon emissions looming in the not-too-distant future,

Continental Airlines is just one of many airlines looking to tread lightly in the skies. In March 2008, they announced their intention to work with General Electric and Boeing to identify and test more sustainable fuel sources.

The *New Rules* Checklist

Ask the following questions to assess opportunities for enlisting the support of suppliers for your company's sustainable product and packaging initiatives.

- ○ Do we know the sources of all of our product ingredients?
- ○ Do our suppliers understand our environmental goals?
- ○ How much do we know about our suppliers' environmental commitments and initiatives?
- ○ How can we partner with our manufacturing suppliers to "green" our entire supply chain?
- ○ Do we have a forum for regular and ongoing communication with our suppliers about green issues?
- ○ Do we have a supplier scorecard to effectively assess and measure each supplier's eco-credentials?
- ○ Do we know the new materials and technologies our suppliers are testing and developing that we can incorporate into our own new product and packaging design?

Government

Governments have a direct stake in eliminating and preventing the pollution created by consumer products and services. Federal, state, and local governments develop environmental policy, laws, and regulations that can impact directly or indirectly on the products and services of suppliers and end-product manufacturers. Government has the power to subsidize, tax, regulate, or otherwise heavily influence industry processes and product design based on their sustainability or their external cost to the environment. But not all government officials have a background in business, much less the technical aspects of product design and service delivery, and this can result in misguided policies that can unnecessarily hurt industry. Working *with* lawmakers instead of *against* them can help corporations prepare for and reduce the risks associated with legal challenges such as bans on chemicals with a negative perception or laws that might add costs to an already expensive process. By working together with government representatives, industry can take part in the dialogue to ensure new regulations are well informed and that new laws are balanced.

Government also has the ability to allocate financial support to projects and businesses that can stimulate the economy; of late, financial stimulus money has been earmarked in large measure to green businesses and technologies. So it behooves green marketers to check out available funding.

Strategies for partnering with the government

Participate in voluntary programs

Since the early 1990s, federal, state, and local governments have discovered that working with industry can yield better results than wielding the traditional "command and control" sledgehammer. So they have crafted a number of voluntary programs that benefit both industry and the environment.

These voluntary programs can extend an unbeatable package of incentives for businesses looking to control their environmental destinies. Business partners enjoy increased flexibility in meeting existing laws and regulations and can gain access to expertise and technical resources that can lead to competitive advantage, new marketing opportunities, and enhanced credibility and public recognition for their efforts. By participating in these programs, chances of being caught off guard when new regulatory laws go into effect are minimized. Voluntary participation is recognized by the government and this can lend credibility to member companies. Labeling programs such as ENERGY STAR and the USDA's Organic seal have been discussed earlier in this book. Other voluntary programs help businesses make environmental improvements cost-effectively. Examples include the EPA's WasteWise and WaterWise programs that help businesses to reduce and recycle municipal solid waste or conserve water. Many of these programs have awards components that can build recognition for one's participation and achievements. ENERGY STAR Partner of the Year is a good example.

Lobby for stricter regulations

Sometimes businesses can gain competitive advantage by lobbying for strict government regulations they are prepared to accommodate, reflectively positively on an organization and its brands. For instance, in 2006 Philips, the global lighting and consumer products giant, was struggling to get people to pay the hefty premiums required for its Halogena-IR energy-sipping light bulbs that last approximately four times longer than traditional incandescents. So Philips initiated a lobbying effort to increase light bulb efficiency standards and was rewarded when Congress passed a new energy bill, the Energy Independence and Security Act of 2007 (set to take effect in 2012) which will increase energy efficiency standards enough to eventually phase out traditional incandescent light bulbs. It is slated to save the United States an estimated $18 billion per year in energy costs – and guarantees Philips a future market for its energy-efficient bulbs without attracting the negative attention that usually comes with lobbying for self-serving regulations.[28] GE's CEO Jeffrey Immelt is now imploring government to regulate greenhouse gas emissions. His motivation? The certainty that companies need to make multi-billion-dollar bets on the types of cleaner energy technologies that his company stands ready to sell.

Partner on new product ideas

Do you have a new product idea and need the seed money to get it from bench to market? Partner with government agencies that can provide a ready source of new product technologies, funding, and expertise for meeting your goals. Numerous government organizations provide financial and technical support for environmental innovations, among them, the U.S. Department of Housing and Urban Development's Sustainable Housing and Communities Program, which offers local communities technical and financial support for sustainability projects including green commercial buildings, water-conservation initiatives, and local public transportation initiatives.[29]

The U.S. Department of Agriculture is looking to support the development of biobased products as a way to help boost the farm economy and reduce carbon emissions. Among many companies that have received support, Metabolix of Cambridge, Massachusetts received a $350,000 grant to develop biobased, biodegradable resins suitable for blow-molding into bottles. According to the American Plastics Council, more than two million tons of high-density polyethylene (HDPE) plastics are used annually for blow-molded bottles, containers, and other types of packaging, so shifting to biobased resins could make a big difference.[30]

In addition to awarding the DfE eco-label described in Chapter 7, the EPA's Design for the Environment (DfE) Partnership for Safer Chemistry works with industry to help develop safer alternatives to a wide range of products including automotive refinishing, chemical formulators, detergents, furniture and printed circuit board flame retardancy, nail polish, and wire and cable.

The *New Rules* Checklist

Ask the following questions to assess opportunities for enlisting the support of government stakeholders.

o What legislation is in effect or under way at the federal, state, and local levels that will affect our brands and company?

o What steps can we take to promote self-regulation and avoid mandatory regulations?

o What opportunities might exist to gain competitive advantage by lobbying for stiff regulations?

o What voluntary programs being conducted by governments can we join to help to preempt legislation, gain recognition and advantage, and set standards in our industry?

Environmental groups

Everyone's heard of the National Audubon Society and the Nature Conservancy, but there are actually more than 12,000 environmental organizations in the U.S. alone,[31] and of many different kinds. Some address a specific cause such as lobbying for pure air, cleaning up the Great Lakes, protecting spotted owls, or expanding their city's municipal recycling program. Others conduct research, influence policy, provide technical support, raise awareness, or meet a short-term goal. Ranging from local organizations of two or more people to global groups with 10,000-plus members, environmental groups are typically membership-based nonprofit organizations relying on fundraising and financial contributions from members and donors to achieve their mission.

Once scorned as extremists, the mainstreaming of green has made it acceptable practice for environmental groups to help businesses and governments improve their environmental sustainability. Many environmental groups now realize that, since business and government control many of the resources and yield much of the power in a market-based economy, joining together in a market-focused approach is the most effective way to clean up the environment and pave the way for a more sustainable society. While some extremist groups still adopt an antagonistic approach to working with industry, and may even be the first to encourage a boycott of products, a growing number of environmental groups actively cooperate with business leaders to effect change by acting as a sounding board, helping them improve their environmental policies and practices, and even assisting in the development and promotion of their brands.

Strategies for partnering with environmental groups

In working with environmental groups, one naturally thinks of cause-related marketing as discussed in Chapter 6. But other constructive partnership opportunities exist, starting with leveraging special expertise, working positively to protect supplies of new materials and create markets for worthy products, and strategic corporate philanthropy.

Leverage the special expertise of specific environmental groups

For-profit companies, expert in creating economic value, have much to learn from nonprofits that excel in creating and measuring environmental and social value. Happily, under the new rules, many environmental groups are now willing to share their unique expertise with well-intentioned businesses. Some nonprofits, for example, know how to best protect endangered species or nurture the forests and this can translate into innovative ways to improve a company's sustainability performance. Constructive partnerships can add credibility to a brand's image and provide businesses with important protection from environmental groups with opposing perspectives and media attacks that can mar a company's reputation.

In 2002, McDonald's, the world's largest food-service retailer, enlisted Conservation International (CI) as a partner to help develop ways to incorporate sustainability into their massive supply chain. CI developed an "environmental scorecard" for the international suppliers of McDonald's to measure and rate their use of water and energy, solid waste, and air emissions.[32]

Sometimes even former environmental foes can turn into allies. In August 2009, Kimberly-Clark, the makers of Cottonelle, Kleenex, and Scott, announced a partnership with Greenpeace to meet a lofty goal to obtain 100% of the company's wood fiber for tissue products from environmentally responsible sources. Officially ending their longstanding Kleercut campaign against the company, Greenpeace will assist Kimberly-Clark in promoting forest conservation and sourcing sustainably harvested and recycled FSC-certified fibers for its beloved brands. In the words of Scott Paul, Green-peace's USA Forest Campaign Director, "These revised standards are proof that when responsible companies and Greenpeace come together, the results can be good for business and great for the planet. Kimberly-Clark's efforts are a challenge to competitors. I hope other companies pay close attention."[33]

Protect supplies of raw materials and create new markets for sustainable products

Former owners of the Gorton's brands, Unilever, who saw the stocks of many of its most popular fish species in decline, partnered with the World Wildlife Fund (WWF, now its name outside North America) in 1995 to create the Marine Stewardship Council (MSC) and help develop sustainable fishing practices. An increasing number of grocery stores in both the U.S. (A&P, Lunds & Byerly's, Target, Wal-Mart, Wegmans, Whole Foods Market, and more) and the UK (Marks & Spencer, Sainsbury's, Waitrose, and others) now use the blue MSC eco-label on fish products to help customers identify seafood from fisheries that meet their strict environmental standards. The MSC also operates Chain of Custody certification that ensures that every company in a particular supply chain that takes ownership of MSC-certified fish, from the dock onward, does not mix certified with uncertified fish. In late 2008, the University of Notre Dame in Indiana became the first U.S. university to obtain Chain of Custody certification for all fish served in on-campus dining facilities.[34]

For the most part, publishers print books on paper that is largely composed of virgin forest fibers because paper containing recycled content is not widely available in either book grade or bulk quantity. In 2001, sensing an opportunity to create a new market by meeting the needs of the industry, Canopy, a Canadian nonprofit dedicated to protecting forests by working with businesses to create sustainable supply chains, collaborated with San Francisco-based New Leaf Paper company to develop environmentally sustainable paper stock for book publishing. In 2001, author Alice Munro became the first "big name" author to use New Leaf Paper's 100% post-consumer recycled, chlorine-free paper for the Canadian edition of her book *Hateship, Friendship, Courtship, Loveship, Marriage*. The Canadian edition of J.K. Rowling's bestselling *Harry Potter and the Order of the Phoenix* also used this new environmentally sustainable paper, proving to the publishing industry that high-quality recycled paper stock could be both mass-produced and reliably developed while remaining cost-effective. Since then, New Leaf Paper and Canopy have worked together to shift the paper-hungry book, magazine, and newspaper publishing sectors in Canada and the U.S. away

from endangered forests and chlorine-bleached paper to focus on incorporating forest protection and sustainability into the paper supply chain.[35]

Leverage corporate philanthropy strategically on behalf of the environment

Corporate philanthropy, consisting of deductible gifts made through a foundation arm or at least noted as such by a corporation in IRS filings, has historically been an effective marketing and public relations tool. Donations to
charities and the arts, for example, have long helped such major corporations as ExxonMobil, IBM, and Altria (formally Philip Morris) burnish their
leadership images and make friends with society's influentials. Although it
can be criticized as a form of propaganda, environmental giving can help
companies strategically, by contributing to solution finding on issues that
affect their businesses while creating more favorable impressions for a
company overall – with employees, financial institutions, and consumers.
According to the IEG Sponsorship Report, almost all Fortune 500 companies make charitable donations, with 25% of these committing to community service and social betterment in their mission statements. In 2005, U.S.
corporations donated more than $12 billion to nonprofits, and invested $1.6
billion in cause-related marketing programs with nonprofits.[36] These donations provide not only a tax deduction, but also an opportunity to strategically align with environmental and social causes based on employee and
customer interests. And, even with the expected decrease of funding in the
aftermath of the 2008–2010 recession, corporate commitment to sustainability and environmental sponsorship is expected to remain a part of these
organizations' core values.

One example of strategic corporate philanthropy is Bank of America's
sponsorship of the Climate Change exhibit at the American Museum of
Natural History in New York City in 2008,[37] which reinforces the bank's overall initiatives to reduce the impacts of climate change associated with their
massive real estate holdings around the world. (Buildings create more global
warming emissions than cars.) Cargill's financial support of the Nature Conservancy, Wildlife Conservation Society, Conservation International, and
World Wildlife Fund, among others[38] – all credible groups that can help protect the environment where their grain grows – supports preservation of biodiversity in addition to initiatives that create bioplastics out of corn.

Representing another example, in 2002 the Home Depot, the world's
largest seller of wood products, announced it would donate $1 million over
five years to the Nature Conservancy to assist in the fight against illegal logging and promotion of sustainable timber programs in Indonesia. The dona-

tion was part of the retailer's push to identify the sources of all wood products sold on its shelves. The Nature Conservancy used these funds to launch a pilot sustainable forestry and timber certification program. Since announcing its donation to the Nature Conservancy, the Home Depot has reduced its imports of Indonesian wood products by 70%, and now less than 1% of the wood sold in its stores is from Indonesia.[39]

This chapter concludes our discussion of the new ways that today's consumer demands are changing the rules of green marketing, and the seven strategies for successful green marketing laid out in Chapter 3. While it may seem a tall order to address all the new rules successfully, some companies are doing a most laudable job of integrating green into the life-cycles of their products, instilling a green culture into their companies, and communicating their sustainable brands with credibility and impact. Two such sustainable brand leaders, Starbucks and Timberland, are profiled in depth in the next chapter.

The *New Rules* Checklist

Use the following checklist to assess opportunities for enlisting the support of environmental group stakeholders.

- ○ Which environmental groups can lead us to sustainable approaches to running our business? Help underscore our credibility? Protect supplies? Help foster new markets for sustainable products?

- ○ Which environmental groups have special expertise that can help us develop or refine products with minimal eco-impact?

- ○ What opportunities exist to conduct strategic corporate philanthropy with environmental groups?

785266 000297

Two sustainability leaders that superbly address the new rules

The new rules for addressing the demands of today's sustainability-minded consumers not only represent a seismic shift in communication strategy but also now require a thorough, life-cycle approach to product development and the ability to forge constructive coalitions with a wide array of new corporate stakeholders. While most businesses are still learning the new rules and trying to adapt accordingly, some business are leading the way, pioneering new strategies, and enjoying the myriad benefits. While many companies, large and small, fit into this category, two have been chosen to be profiled in depth in this chapter: Starbucks and Timberland.

Of course, no company can be considered 100% sustainable – and these companies have their eco-shortcomings, too – but I believe that the progress made by these two firms can represent a model for others who follow in their steps and, I hope, a platform from which to build on even these leaders' efforts. Consumer loyalty to these companies and their offerings proves that new sustainable branding strategies can form the basis of an enduring business and provide leverage in the face of formidable competition. They superbly demonstrate how new strategies of green marketing can create jobs, build brand loyalty, and return hefty profits, all the while contributing to a more sustainable society.

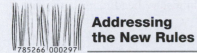

**Addressing
the New Rules**

The Timberland Company

In 2009, Timberland had over $1.3 billion in sales, more than 200 stores in 15 countries – and an environmental consciousness that reflects the aspirations of customers who appreciate the high quality of the company's footwear and apparel. And it all starts with CEO Jeffrey Swartz. Now leading the company his grandfather acquired in 1952, Swartz actively and strategically imprints his environmental and social values on the company. Passionate and visible within the environmental business community, his position on the environment is perhaps best summed up in the philosophy behind Timberland's Mountain Athletics® shoe line: "Enjoying the outdoors to the fullest, and leaving it the way you found it." Swartz believes that he has a responsibility to be proactive in minimizing his company's environmental impact and maximizing its benefit to the community. So Timberland does the right thing in order that its customers (who have good reason to care about the environment and their communities) will be educated accordingly – and will reward Swartz by choosing his company's products over those of his competitors.

Swartz's philosophy that "doing well and doing good are inextricably linked" demonstrates that Timberland is about more than just profit and exemplifies his company's strategy at a time when consumer purchases and trust in business are low. He believes that the current economic recession will strengthen his company and provide an opportunity for the brand to reinforce its status as an environmental leader in its industry.

An emphasis on cutting carbon

From its offices to its manufacturing plants to its retail stores, all of Timberland's operations are conducted with an eye toward minimizing environmental impact, along with the goal of achieving carbon neutrality in Timberland facilities and employee travel by 2010. The company uses multiple, leading-edge strategies to reduce its overall carbon footprint.

First, Timberland aims to reduce overall energy demand (which in turn yields savings). At their Stratham, New Hampshire global headquarters and the European distribution center in the Netherlands, activities such as installing skylights and replacing the outdated lighting system with energy-efficient alternatives saved 460,000 kWh of energy in its first year. An innovative new roof was installed at the New Hampshire headquarters to make it easier and cheaper to cool the building.

Second, Timberland has been able to transfer over 12% of its energy to renewable sources. Wind and other renewable sources provide 100% of the electricity needed to run Timberland's European distribution center. A $3.5 million, 400 kW solar array at Timberland's distribution center in Ontario, California provides about half of the facility's electricity – with the added bonus of preventing hundreds of thousands of pounds of greenhouse gas. In a 2006 press release announcing the Ontario solar array project Jeffrey Swartz said, "We are fully committed to reducing our environmental impact and decreasing dependency on non-renewable resources by finding alternative ways to produce energy."

Timberland enlisted the support of the Business for Social Responsibility (BSR) Clean Cargo initiative to develop tools for tracking carbon emissions. Timberland applies these tools to evaluate carrier and transportation choices for transporting products from factories to its distribution centers. These efforts to reduce its own carbon footprint have led Timberland to consider the footprint of its employees, specifically emissions associated with employee commuting. Timberland created prime reserved parking spaces at its corporate headquarters for employees who drive fuel-efficient vehicles or carpool. To further assist in the reduction of the carbon footprint associated with its employees' activities, in 2008 the New Hampshire headquarters began a "Victory Garden" from which employees purchase vegetables. Employees are able to get fresh produce without the food miles and all proceeds from the sale go to a local food bank.

Timberland's industry-leading carbon reduction strategies have not only significantly reduced its environmental impact (between 2006 and 2009 emissions reduced by 36%) but have also returned hefty financial savings; combined energy savings and reductions in business travel are helping the company save over a million dollars per year.

A social conscience, too

Timberland's environmental activities are complemented by a strong social conscience, embodied in numerous programs that engage its youthful target audience while providing opportunities for employees to develop their leadership skills and appreciate the natural environment.

First, as a global brand and a global citizen, Timberland recognizes that they have a responsibility to ensure that their products are produced in an ethical way. Their Code of Conduct helps them ensure fair, safe and non-discriminatory workplaces for their 175,000 workers in 290+ factories in 35 countries, and they aim to create positive change in communities where their products are made.

For more than 20 years, Timberland employees have been given paid time off and "service sabbaticals" to perform community service, usually associated with the outdoors. Community service "challenges [the] employees' potential, builds strong teams and galvanizes [the] company's greatest resource as a united force for change."[1] Employee volunteer time has benefited over 200 community organizations in 30 countries. By the end of 2009, more than 600,000 hours of meaningful change had been "clocked" by Timberland employees in the service of local communities and the environment.

Timberland's programs support a wide variety of social and environmental initiatives, creating goodwill in local communities and reflecting positively on the brand. For example, since 1989 Timberland has supported City Year, a Boston-based nonprofit that unites young people of all backgrounds for a year of full-time service, giving them skills and opportunities to change the world. Jeff Swartz served as chair of the group's board of trustees between 1994 and 2002, and for 20 years Timberland has provided uniforms for City Year's corps members.

The majority of Timberland's cash and product donations currently reinforces the company's Earthkeeping agenda. Current partners include Yele Haiti and Trees for the Future, which create and maintain sustainable fruit tree nurseries in the outskirts of Gonaives as part of a broader effort to reforest Haiti. Timberland also works with World Wildlife Fund's tree planting program in Nepal and Green Net, a Japan-based NGO focused on stopping the desertification of China's Horqin Desert. Since 2005, Timberland has supported Green Net and has sent volunteers to China to help plant trees and restore the formerly rich grasslands in that area.

Other company-wide programs serve as morale-boosters and leadership opportunities for employees. For example, Serv-a-palooza is an annual daylong service event that takes place at Timberland locations around the globe and focuses on improving community green spaces. Over a hundred projects get carried out in upwards of 20 countries, and include cleaning up public spaces in Lawrence, Massachusetts, to planting trees in an urban forest in Bangkok, Thailand. Outreach programs such as these not only signify positive social change, but also translate into happy employees; Timberland is consistently listed by magazines such as *Fortune* and *Working Mother* as one of the best places in America to work.

Products with minimal impact

Timberland's products combine an outdoor aesthetic, quality, and functionality characterized by their durability and ability to withstand the elements, and are made with the environment in mind.

Timberland seeks to reduce its environmental impact at different stages of its products' life-cycle, starting with concerted efforts to reduce the impact of leather – a key ingredient in the company's signature boots. That's why, in 2005, Timberland banded together with the UK-based BLC Leather Technology Centre to convene a cross-brand organization called the Leather Working Group (LWG), whose members work together toward the common goal of better environmental performance of tanneries. Timberland's Earthkeepers™ product line is specially designed to represent its environmental values in actions. The products feature organic, recycled, and renewable materials. Starting in the fall of 2009, Earthkeepers outsoles incorporate Green Rubber™, a recycled, devulcanized rubber made from waste material by Malaysia-based Green Rubber Inc., using a new proprietary technology. Timberland estimates that the fall 2009 Earthkeepers collection will use 50 tons of Green Rubber material – cutting down on the need to use some 42 tons of virgin rubber. The company launched a Design for Disassembly boot and boat shoe that can be returned to any Timberland store for recycling at the end of their life.

Aside from shoes and boots, the Earthkeepers line-up includes clothing, outerwear, hats, and bags – some of which incorporate organic, recycled, and/or renewable materials. Recycled PET plastic is used to create the nylon for Earthkeepers backpacks and messenger bags, as well as the majority of Earthkeepers knit scarves and hats. Organic cotton is used in the scarves, knitted hats, T-shirts, and baseball caps; the wool jackets incorporate 50% recycled wool; and the belt even uses small recycled leather panels.

Although Timberland products have in the past transcended the boundaries of their traditional market and emerged prominently in the "hip hop" fashion realm, Timberland's marketing strategy is aimed at a loyal base of 16–35-year-old consumers who appreciate its functional products and the company's values. Timberland recognizes two types of customers: the genuine outdoorsy types and working-class people who appreciate the functionality of their products – and those who wish they were, or simply want to look the part.

Timberland's retail stores (the newest of which are LEED-certified) have an outdoorsy feel – think exposed timber and earth tones. The use of virgin products and toxic materials is creatively minimized: existing concrete floors are polished, wood fixturing is made from recycled or FSC lumber, and wall paints and floor finishes contain very low or no volatile organic compounds.

Store décor is customized to their locality: a New York City store, for instance, sports an entire wall devoted to depicting green spaces in the five boroughs.

Communicating green

Timberland's Earthkeeper advertising campaign capitalizes on its target clientele's outdoorsy yet fashionable aspirations, while challenging them to take responsibility for the environment. The company's ad campaign, launched in 2008, draws in consumers with emotional, visual representations of Timberland's slogan, "Take it all on™." Ads promoting new Earthkeepers products underscore the connection with nature with such promises as: "Wear new Earthkeepers™ [footwear] made with recycled materials or nature might get you back" and "Wear new Earthkeepers™ [footwear] made with recycled materials and nature might return the favor."

In addition to having an informative website, Timberland uses the younger generation's connectivity through a corporate presence in every social media arena, from Facebook pages to YouTube channels, to spread messages of social change. 2,400 customers now follow Jeff Swartz on Twitter. The company's environment blog covers topics such as green book reviews, green legislation, and updates on how Timberland is becoming greener. Entries are written by various members of the Timberland team, including CEO Jeff Swartz.

Cause-related marketing is an important part of Timberland's strategy, too. In one partnership, Timberland teamed up with actor Don Cheadle (of *Hotel Rwanda* fame) to create limited-edition boots, boot tags, and shirts with "Not on My Watch" and "Save Darfur" messages to raise awareness and inspire action to help stop genocide in Sudan, with profits going to AmeriCares.

Transparency

Timberland is a pioneer in transparent communications, setting standards that have become a model for others inside and outside the industry. Most notably, in the fall of 2006, Timberland pioneered the use of nutrition-type environmental labels, placing them on over 30 million shoeboxes. In the spring of 2007, to supplement the "nutrition" label, it rolled out its Green Index® rating system for select footwear, which calculates product-specific environmental impacts for each pair of Timberland shoes (see Fig. 9.1).

OUR FOOTPRINT *NOTRE EMPREINTE*

Climate Impact *Incidences sur le climat*
Use of renewable energy
Utilisation d'énergie renouvelable   11.63%
Chemicals Used *Produits chimiques utilisés*
PVC-free   *Sans PVC*   85.5%
Resource Consumption *Consommation de ressources*
Eco-conscious materials
Matériaux écologiques   26.5%
Recycled content of shoebox
Contenu en matières recyclées de la boîte de chaussures   100%
Trees planted through 2009
Nombre d'arbres plantés en 2009   1,118,538

PRODUCT FOOTPRINT
EMPREINTE DU PRODUIT

Green Index® Rating   *Classification de L'Indice vert*^MD
Lower Impact   Higher Impact
Peu d'Impact   Impact élevé

0   **6**   10

For more information visit www.timberland.com/footprint
Pour plus d'information : www. timberland.com/footprint

TIM-NGI6

Figure 9.1 **Timberland's Green Index® label**

Reprinted with permission of Timberland

The label comprises two sections: "Our Footprint" delineates corporate-related impacts including climate impact (denoted by the amount of renewable energy used by Timberland footwear overall); chemicals used (the percentage of Timberland footwear that is PVC-free); resource consumption (the percentage of Timberland footwear that uses "eco-conscious materials," as well as the percentage of recycled content of the shoebox itself); and the number of trees Timberland has planted to date. The second section, "Product Footprint," provides product specific environmental information including, where available, the Green Index® rating.

The company plans to expand the use of the Green Index rating to all of its footwear in 2012, and to adapt these labels for use on its apparel and other products in the future, with the goal of increasing transparency on the environmental impacts of its products. It is also partnering with the Outdoor Industry Association to develop standard environmental metrics for outdoor industry products.

Results

Timberland's attention to quality, passion for the environment and society, and transparency has earned it a strong customer following willing to pay its premiums, even through the current economic recession, and allow it to be poised for continued long-term growth. The company has also reaped benefits in terms of its positive reputation and goodwill in the communities where employees work and serve through their volunteer projects. For instance, according to Michael Brown, the CEO and founder of City Year, a national service organization which engages young people as tutors and mentors, and long-time Timberland partner:

> Every one of the 1,550 diverse young people in service with City Year across America annually is a testament to Timberland's sup-

port for City Year. Timberland provides each young leader with a signature red jacket and a pair of boots that are a symbol of hope and help to tens of thousands of urban students in high-poverty schools, and to communities nationwide. Timberland has been essential to building every aspect of City Year for 20 years. Its people have joined us in service around the globe, our partnership has been highlighted by the Harvard Business School and we seek to redefine what a company and nonprofit can do to change the world together.[2]

Timberland has also received numerous awards and recognitions. In 2009 the Cause Marketing Forum granted Timberland a Golden Halo award for its goal of being carbon-neutral by 2010 and its policy of encouraging employee volunteerism. *Fortune* magazine rated Timberland number 78 of the "100 Best Companies to Work For" in 2007, and it has been in the top 100 ever since the list's inception in 1998. Timberland was also a 2007 recipient of the EPA's Green Power Leadership Award for its voluntary use of green power. And, in 2010, Timberland was named one of *Outside* magazine's "Best Places to Work."

Perhaps the greatest indicator of success comes straight from Jeffrey Swartz, who says,

With passion, innovation and a sense of purpose, Timberland has sought to improve our communities, our environment and the condition of those beside whom we live and work. We have improved as a company and as a community of individuals through the wisdom, humility and strong sense of justice we have gained . . . and continue to gain every step in our journey.[3]

Addressing
the New Rules

Starbucks

Starbucks proves that a global company can turn a proactive approach to sustainability into a strategic and profitable part of its brand. Key to its successful strategy is to actively listen to, interact with, and act on the expectations of its customers, who possess a strong environmental and social conscience, and to constantly demonstrate reductions in the environmental footprint of its operations. In the words of Ben Packard, Vice President, Global Sustainability, at Starbucks:

> Consumer brands, while they may not be heavily regulated or political, are on the front lines. We see over 50,000,000 customers in our stores each week, and interact with even more of them online. They give us great ideas about what we should be doing to reduce our environmental impact. We need to take that passion and mobilize it, because consumers are increasingly committed to spending their money with companies that support the global issues that they care about.

Starbucks is that medium and that company. Here's their sustainability story.

With over 16,000 stores in over 50 countries on six continents, Starbucks has many reasons to be oriented toward sustainability. Volume-wise, coffee is the second most traded commodity in the world (behind oil) and living conditions for coffee workers tend to be below par. Starbucks consumes millions of disposable cups, coffee grounds, and packaging each day along with the water used in making coffee, not to mention the 37 gallons of water embedded in the production of each cup of coffee (52.83 gallons for each latte) and in their operations. It all adds up to a significant environmental footprint, and all because of an innocuous-looking little cup of coffee!

Company: Addressing environmental and social considerations

Starbucks' history of environmental and corporate social responsibility (CSR) stretches a long way. Acknowledging a need to contribute to the communities where their coffee is produced, in 1991 Starbucks began contributing to CARE, an international development and relief organization that supports coffee-producing communities. By 1995 Starbucks became one of CARE's largest donors, and they are still in partnership today.

In 1992 Starbucks wrote an environmental mission statement and created an environmental affairs department that was charged with developing environmentally responsible corporate policies and minimizing the company's footprint. The department was also active in educating partners through the company's Green Team initiatives and using environmental purchasing guidelines. One of the department's first initiatives consisted of using recycled paper sleeves instead of double cupping. In 1999 Starbucks named its first senior vice president of its newly created CSR department, which grew from one person to fourteen in its first two years.

In 2008, the company launched its Starbucks™ Shared Planet™ initiative, integrating its social and environmental commitments to doing things that are good for the people and the planet. From the way it purchases coffee, to minimizing the company's environmental footprint, to being involved in local communities, it is a recommitment to core values, about using its global size for good, and getting its consumers and employees educated, involved, and excited about giving back. Starbucks' Shared Planet platform divides its environmental and social initiatives into three categories with specific measurable goals within each area: (1) ethical sourcing, (2) environmental stewardship, and (3) community involvement.

Environment

Since Starbucks relies on agricultural products for most of its raw materials and supplies, it makes good business sense for them to steward the environment. Under the environmental section of its Shared Planet platform, Starbucks includes products, operations, and buildings. In 2008, Starbucks outlined a series of environmental targets it is committed to reaching by 2015. Its goals are outlined as follows:

Products

- 100% of cups will be reusable or recyclable by 2015
- A 100%-recyclable cup will be developed by 2012.

Operations

- 25% of cups in its stores will be reusable
- Recycling will be available in all of its stores
- 50% of the energy used in company-owned stores will be derived from renewable resources by 2010.

- Greenhouse gas emissions will be reduced by making company-owned stores 25% more energy-efficient by 2010

- It will accomplish a significant reduction in water usage

- It will champion tropical rainforest protection as a solution to climate change.

Buildings

- All new construction will be LEED-certified and locally sourced by 2010.

Social

Starbucks is pioneering the way toward ethically sourced coffee. There may be smaller brands in the marketplace with higher percentages of fair trade coffee within their portfolios, but no company has bought more ethically sourced coffee or done more to help promote it than Starbucks.

One of Starbucks' core beliefs is that a better cup of coffee is one that also helps create a better future for farmers and a more stable climate for the planet. In this spirit, Starbucks began purchasing fair trade coffee in 2000 and became the largest buyer in 2009 when it doubled its purchases to 40 million pounds of certified coffee. At the same time, Starbucks continued to build on its own Coffee and Farmer Equity (C.A.F.E.) Practices, developed with Conservation International, the global environmental group, in 2003. C.A.F.E. Practices is a set of stringent guidelines to ensure that Starbucks' coffee purchases are ethically sourced by monitoring hiring practices. These include ensuring biological pest and disease control, and protecting water sources and minimizing water consumption of coffee suppliers, among other things.

Starbucks bought 385 million pounds of coffee in 2008, 77% of which was sourced through C.A.F.E. Practices. Starbucks' goal is to have 100% of its coffee responsibly grown and ethically traded by 2015. Its other goals in this area are:

- To invest in a better future for farmers and their communities by increasing loans to farmers by 60%, from $12.5 to $20 million

- To combat climate change by offering farmers incentives to prevent deforestation, starting with pilot programs in Sumatra, Indonesia, and Chiapas, Mexico.

To help ensure long-term supplies of its products, Starbucks has also committed to improving the lives of people in coffee-growing communities. Accordingly, it has set up the Small Farmer Sustainability Initiative (SFSI) by partnering with the Fairtrade Labelling Organizations (FLO) and TransFair USA to create a small-scale coffee farmer loan program. These loans help farmers survive the current global economic crisis and emerge as stronger business partners. Starbucks has already invested $12.5 million which small-scale coffee farmers have access to, but it has pledged to expand the fund to $20 million by 2015.

Starbucks has also developed Farmer Support Centers in Latin American and Africa. There are currently two support centers: one opened in Costa Rica in 2004, and a second in Rwanda in 2009. The Farmer Support Centers provide a team of experts in soil management and field-crop production to enhance the quality of coffee and improve farmer yields. Through the centers Starbucks has also committed to support women coffee growers (and help reduce extreme poverty) through continued training and professional development.

Empowered employees

Employees have always been at the center of Starbucks' commitment to sustainability; founder Howard Schultz's philosophy is to "treat people like family, and they will be loyal and give their all." Among its many industry-leading employee initiatives is a generous benefits package for both full- and part-time employees. Eligible employees, or "partners," receive full health benefits and a share in the company's growth through the "Bean Stock" stock option plan that allows them to buy shares of Starbucks common stock at 85% of the market value.

Starbucks also makes an effort to include its employees in its CSR initiatives. For example, two years after Hurricane Katrina hit New Orleans, when public and media attention on the city had long since dissipated, Starbucks flew 10,000 partners into the area and committed 50,000 hours, the largest amount committed by any single company. Later it was in front of the same group that Howard Schultz announced Starbucks' Shared Planet targets and new initiatives.

Sustainably innovative products

In order to keep up with its Shared Planet commitments and to stay ahead of the curve, Starbucks sells its ethically sourced drinks in containers meant to be as environmentally responsible as possible. In 2004, Starbucks put itself on the recycling scene by launching the first-ever hot cup approved by the U.S. Food and Drug Administration (FDA). The hot cup is made with 10% recycled material. Although 10% sounds small, the numbers add up quickly with volume as high as Starbucks: this cup eliminates 5 million pounds of solid waste, 11,300 tons of wood, 58 billion British Thermal Units (BTUs) of energy, and 47 million gallons of waste-water a year.

To help plan for the 100% recyclable cup scheduled to launch in 2012, in May 2009, Starbucks convened a Cup Summit, attended by 30 cup, cup-stock, and coating manufacturers, recyclers, and waste managers and an equal number of Starbucks partners. In September 2009, the company launched a pilot program in seven New York stores which examined the possibility of collecting and recycling coffee cups in the same waste stream as corrugated cardboard; its goal is to enable the recycling of all sorts of other paper food packaging, making Starbucks the leader and standard-setter in this industry.

Starbucks is also looking to make the plastic cups in which they sell more than one billion cold beverages per year more environmentally sound. In 2008, Starbucks commissioned a group of life-cycle-analysis scientists to study the environmental impact of the plastic cups. They found that changing the cups from polyethylene terephthalate (PET) to polypropylene (PP) would use 15% less plastic overall and emit 45% less greenhouse gases in production, so in 2008, Starbucks began the changeover to PP with the launch of its new Vivanno smoothie cups.

With an eye to reducing waste in its stores, Starbucks is relaunching an aggressive campaign to get customers to bring in reusable cups by providing a 10-cent discount off their drink. The company is also restocking reusable mugs. With Starbucks' new iPhone application, which customers can use to pay for drinks by scanning a digital barcode, the company gets one step closer to eliminating plastic in its stores altogether. And Starbucks has also found a way to reduce the 7 million tons of coffee grounds headed for landfills each year by creating the Grounds for your Garden program which offers customers and others spent coffee grounds for use in their gardens.

Green marketing and communications focused on consumers and transparency

Starbucks' marketing integrates sustainability initiatives with communications that specifically focus on interacting with consumers and transparency, in line with the needs of its Millennial and Generation X customers and partner (employee) expectations that the businesses they patronize and work for embrace sustainability and social responsibility. Starbucks' response is embodied in a website and two high-profile campaigns directed at its very global, very mainstream audiences.

Starbucks makes customers feel a part of the brand through a highly informative and interactive website where they can learn about and participate in five CSR efforts. The (Product) RED page explains what Starbucks is doing to support people living with AIDS in Africa. A separate Shared Planet site details Starbucks' commitments to ethical sourcing, environmental stewardship, and community involvement, with informative videos and opportunities to get involved. There is also a link to a report on progress of Starbucks' Shared Planet initiative,[4] written in line with guidelines provided by the Global Reporting Initiative. Finally, a My Starbucks Idea site, allows customers and partners to give suggestions about what they would like to see done in a variety of areas such as products and CSR. Starbucks responds on its Ideas in Action page, where it reports the ideas it has launched or is currently considering.

In addition, a high-profile media campaign consisting of traditional paid and social media highlights the brand's values and overall quality and value. With the tagline "You and Starbucks: It's Bigger Than Coffee," it draws a clear connection between consumers and Starbucks' CSR activities and communicates what "responsibly grown and ethically traded" means, a fundamental part of Starbucks' core brand. This connection to something larger than just the product it sells helps to increase brand loyalty by making consumers feel a stronger relationship with the company, as well as augment the impact of Starbucks CSR programs. The campaign includes such messages as "How can you help create a better future for farmers? You already are."

The campaign also redefines value as something that isn't about what is cheapest but about what is best for consumers, their families, and the world around them. In an economic time when there is less money to spend and Starbucks is facing increased competition from competitors such as McDonald's and Dunkin' Donuts, the campaign tells Starbucks' story by underscoring quality, value, and Starbucks' social and environmental values. The campaign validates for consumers, and for employees, that they are making the right choice and being conscientious consumers by choosing Starbucks.

Teaming up with stakeholders

Making all of these initiatives possible are Starbucks' partnerships with stakeholders. Starbucks enriches its social and environmental efforts and ensures their credibility and visibility by teaming up with a myriad of stakeholders who lend their expertise, credibility, and reach. They work with some of the best experts in coffee and international development on the planet.

To help them achieve their ambitious goals, Starbucks partners with Conservation International, with whom it has been working since 1998 to develop socially and environmentally responsible guidelines for coffee purchases through C.A.F.E. Practices; the African Wildlife Foundation, with whom it has worked since 2005 to protect wildlife and conserve natural resources in Africa and promote high-quality coffee, while improving farmer livelihoods; and, of course, fair trade.

It has also partnered with Earthwatch, with whom it has worked since 2001 to help partners and customers participate in expeditions to replant rainforests and learn about sustainable farming practices, and the U.S. Green Building Council which has been helping Starbucks since 2000 to design LEED-certified retail stores, plants, and offices.

Results

Starbucks is an excellent example of a company that has been able to turn sustainability and social initiatives into quantifiable returns on investment, whether they are in the form of growth and profits, brand loyalty, reputation, or employee attraction and retention.

Starting with six Seattle-based stores in 1987, Starbucks has over 16,000 units and currently commands 52% of the coffeehouse sales in the United States. Long a fixture on *Fortune*'s top 500 companies, Starbucks counts among its numerous accolades and awards for its sustainability and corporate social responsibility work being named on both *Fortune*'s "Twenty Most Admired Companies in America" and *Fortune*'s "100 Best Companies to Work For" lists. They have also been counted among the *Financial Times*' "World's Most Respected Companies," "Most Admired for HR" company by *Human Resources Magazine*, one of *Business Ethics Magazine*'s "100 Best Corporate Citizens" every year since 2000, and *First Magazine*'s "International Award for Responsible Capitalism." In 2009, Starbucks was also named one of the ten "Greenest Big Companies in America" by *Newsweek* and "Most Ethical Coffee Company in Europe" by Allegra Strategies.[5]

785266 000297

Conclusion

The maturing of greening as a consumer phenomenon, and its decided shift from the fringe into the mainstream, changes the rules of green marketing. A new green marketing paradigm now exists. It is characterized by a keen sensitivity for the total person who constitutes one's consumer and his or her new needs for brands that balance age-old benefits of performance, afford-ability, and convenience with minimal environmental and social impacts, and engage their consumers in meaningful dialogue. Manufacturers, retail-ers, and marketers looking to sustain their businesses long into the future must heed these new rules with communications that empower their con-sumers to act on pressing issues backed up by a proactive and demonstrated corporate commitment to conducting business in a sustainable way.

Meeting today's consumer needs won't be easy. Many challenges are associated with sustainable branding and green marketing – and many nota-ble attempts, inadvertent or deliberate, of "greenwashing" abound.

But consumers want worthy businesses to succeed. As evidenced by growing participation on corporate-sponsored websites, Facebook pages, and the like, consumers are willing partners with favorite brands in the quest for innovative new ideas. In addition, much support is available from a plethora of new corporate stakeholders, among them voluntary government programs, environmental advocates willing to share expertise and partner in positive relationships, retailers looking for greener offerings, and even edu-cators of our youth.

The marketplace will become greener and more socially aware in the years and decades ahead. Consumers' understanding of all things "green" and "sustainable" will grow, and with it their demands for more information about the eco and social performance of the products and services they buy. Businesses looking to build authentic, sustainable brands will start to ask the many questions outlined on the checklists provided throughout this book; businesses that are already leading the way will use those questions to refine their offerings and make their brands even more credible and relevant.

For further information

Web resources

Information, news, and commentary

AIGA Center for Sustainable Design
Provides graphic designers with case studies, interviews, resources, and discourse on sustainable business practice.
sustainability.aiga.org

Carbon Neutral Digest
Provides an up-to-date rating of U.S.-based organizations that offer solutions to help reduce or offset carbon footprints, and descriptions of their practices.
carbonneutraldigest.com

Circle of Blue Waternews
Daily go-to source for global water news and data.
www.circleofblue.org/waternews/waterviews

Clean Edge
A resource for companies, investors, governments, and nonprofits in the clean-technology sector. Market research reports, stock indexes benchmarking, cleantech events, free cleantech newsletter, and connecting cleantech job seekers, employers, and recruiters.
www.cleanedge.com

Climate Change
U.S. Environmental Protection Agency resource site with comprehensive and accessible information on climate change.
www.epa.gov/climatechange

Earthtweet
Social networking site. When twitter users put "#earthtweet" before a tweet, their environmentally related post is automatically posted to this site.
earthtweet.com

Eco Voice
Australia's environmental news website.
www.ecovoice.com.au

Ecolect
Tools and resources on sustainable materials.
ecolect.net

EcoWorld
Comprehensive information source on wide range of environmental information and opinion covering topics from animals and wildlife, to businesses and services, to water, oceans and ice. Latest headlines and photos.
www.ecoworld.com

ENDS Europe
Europe's environmental news and information source.
www.endseurope.com

Environment for Europeans
A European Commission sponsored website featuring environmental news, reports, and events.
ec.europa.eu/environment/news/efe/index_en.htm

Environmental Leader
News for environmental and sustainability executives.
www.environmentalleader.com

Global Oneness Project
Web-based film project that documents "our growing understanding of what it means to be part of one interconnected, interdependent world." Short films and interviews featuring people around the world working in sustainability, conflict resolution, spirituality, art, agriculture, economics, indigenous culture, social justice, and politics can be viewed and downloaded for free and used as an educational resource in schools and communities.
www.globalonenessproject.org

Green Energy TV
Online channel featuring videos on alternative/renewable/clean energy.
greenenergytv.com

Green Maven
Search engine and directory just for green and sustainability sites.
www.greenmaven.com

GreenBiz
Environmental information, tools and data for the mainstream business community. Includes Greenbuzz, a free weekly update, and the State of Green Business annual report.
www.greenbiz.com

The Greenwashing Index
A website produced by EnviroMedia Social Marketing and the University of Oregon, helps consumers evaluate environmental claims and rate ads.
www.greenwashingindex.com

The Green Power Network
News and information on green power markets operated and maintained by the National Renewable Energy Laboratory of the U.S. Department of Energy.
apps3.eere.energy.gov/greenpower

Grist
Environmental news and green living tips from an esteemed and wry voice in environmental journalism.
www.grist.org

Information/Inspiration
Eco-design resource created to support the design of environmentally and socially responsible products.
www.informationinspiration.org.uk

Institute for Sustainable Communication
Non profit organization dedicated to greening marketing communications. Addresses issues of digital and print media supply chains.
www.sustainablecommunication.org

Justmeans
Social media site for socially responsible businesses.
www.justmeans.com

LCA Information Hub
Information source maintained by the European Commission on life-cycle-related databases, tools, services, developers, and providers.
lca.jrc.ec.europa.eu/lcainfohub/index.vm

LCAccess
Resource site developed and maintained by the U.S. Environmental Protection Agency to educate people about life-cycle assessment (LCA) while "serving as a focal point for LCA practitioners and decision-makers to stay current with the field of LCA."
www.epa.gov/nrmrl/lcaccess

Learning About Renewable Energy
Run by the National Renewable Energy Lab, provides information and educational resources on energy efficiency and various applications of renewable energy.
www.nrel.gov/learning

LOHAS Online
Provides information and resources for businesses looking to appeal to LOHAS consumers.
www.lohas.com

Planetsave

One of many blogs produced by Green Options Media, encourages people to take environmental action and provides a place for visitors to share commentary, ideas, and solutions related to environmental challenges.
planetsave.com

Raymond Communications

Subscription, news, and reference information on recycling and environmental legislation in the United States and around the world.
www.raymond.com

RealClimate

Commentary by working climate scientists writing in their spare time for the interested public and journalists. Restricted to scientific topics, not involved in political or economic implications of the science.
www.realclimate.org

Sierra Club Compass

One of many blogs written by the Sierra Club, provides twice-monthly news, green living tips, and ways to take action on energy issues.
www.sierraclub.typepad.com/compass

Sustainable Life Media

Produces live and virtual sustainable business conferences and educational events (including the industry-leading Sustainable Brands conference) and offers targeted e-newsletters on eco-strategy, sustainable business, sustainable brands, green design, and an online community.
www.sustainablelifemedia.com

Sustainable Materials

Site of the Centre for Design at Royal Melbourne Institute of Technology with resources on sustainable materials, projects, tools, publications, training, and links.
www.cfd.rmit.edu.au/programs/sustainable_materials

SustainableBusiness.com

Targeted to new green ventures, includes daily news, reportage of sustainable stocks, and the SB newswire where businesses can post their press releases. Features links for green investing, sustainable job services, and business networking.
www.sustainablebusiness.com

Sustainablog.org

Provides information on environmental and economic sustainability, green and sustainable business, and environmental politics. Regularly features environmental leaders and experts in alternative energy and green technology.
www.sustainablog.org

Wal-Mart Canada ShareGreen

A platform which allows the public to browse and discuss the sustainable business practices of Canadian industries. Contains case studies that focus on waste, water, and energy management, sustainable solutions, and employee engagement. Initial case studies from Pepsi, Nike, and Stonyfield Farm.

sharegreen.ca

Worldchanging

This nonprofit online magazine, written by a global network of independent journalists, designers, and thinkers, features tools, models, and ideas for addressing environmental concerns related to building, transportation, communications, and quality of life.

www.worldchanging.com

Consumer-oriented and social networking websites

Amazon Green

Special section of Amazon.com's website, highlighting consumer-selected greener products.

www.amazon.com/green

Animal Fair

Lifestyle magazine for animal lovers and pet owners.

www.animalfair.com

Buygreen.com

A shopping site for consumer products ranging from bamboo clothing to solar-powered lights.

www.buygreen.com

Carbonrally.com

Assists consumers in reducing their carbon footprint.

www.carbonrally.com

Care2

Powered by Care2, a for-profit business, one of the largest online communities of people making a difference in healthy and green living, human rights and animal welfare. Includes free email, as well as shopping at the Eco-Superstore, healthy tips, eco news, petitions and alerts. Accepts advertising.

www.care2.com

Celsias.com

Helps consumers combat climate change. Users can read articles, join conversations, ask questions, commit to actions to reduce their carbon footprint, and create, join, and rate climate change projects. Companies can post information on what they are doing to reduce climate impact.

www.celsias.com

Change.org

Raises awareness about global warming, homelessness, women's rights, human trafficking, healthcare, and criminal justice. Provides information about how to take action with leading nonprofit organizations.
www.change.org

ClimateCounts.org

With the goal of bringing consumers and companies together to fight global climate change, this website rates the world's leading companies on climate impact and posts the resulting scores on the website's scorecard.
climatecounts.org

TheDailyGreen.com

Billing itself as "the consumer's guide to the green revolution," this lifestyle site owned by Hearst Communications provides news, information, and a community about going green. Accepts advertising.
www.thedailygreen.com

Do Something

Not-for-profit organization that promotes voluntarism among teens.
www.dosomething.org

Dwell

Magazine focusing on eco home design, products, and comfortable living.
www.dwell.com

E – The Environmental Magazine

Information, news, and resources for consumers concerned about the environment. Available both online and in print.
www.emagazine.com

Gaiam

Founded in Boulder, Colorado in 1988, Gaiam is a provider of information, goods, and services for people who value the environment, a sustainable economy, healthy lifestyles, alternative healthcare, and personal development.
www.gaiam.com

Global Green USA

The American arm of Green Cross International created by President Mikhail S. Gorbachev, focuses on stemming global climate change by creating green buildings and cities. The Green Building Resources center features building strategies and products that mitigate any adverse effects on the environment.
www.globalgreen.org

GoodGuide

Assigns 70,000 food, toys, personal care, and household consumer products a rating, combining health, environmental, and social performance, on a 1–10 scale. Also features articles about current environmental issues, such as buying organic and local.
www.goodguide.com

The Green Guide
A product of *National Geographic Magazine*. Comprehensive source of lifestyle greening, complete with green buying guides of products ranging from food and personal care, home and garden, to travel. Accepts advertising.
www.thegreenguide.com

GreenerChoices
A website of *Consumer Reports*, informs consumers of products and green ratings, hot topics, and solutions. The website features a "Toolkit" section including several different calculators and a section on toxic chemicals found in consumer products.
www.greenerchoices.org

GreenHome.com
Comprehensive online shopping site for greener products. Offers advice and information on greening one's life.
www.greenhome.com

HealthyStuff.org
Shopping tool listing test results on the chemical composition of more than 5,000 consumer products.
www.healthystuff.org

IGive.com
Up to 26% of each purchase made at this online store goes to shoppers' favorite causes. Among the 700+ stores in the network are Gap, Staples, Nordstrom, and Best Buy.
www.igive.com

Ideal Bite
Now owned by Disney, provides daily "Go Green" eco-living tips aimed at helping "light green" consumers take simple steps towards change.
family.go.com

MakeMeSustainable
Individuals, families, and businesses can join this online community to calculate their carbon footprint and learn about ways to reduce it.
makemesustainable.com

Natural Awakenings
A magazine with 2.5 million readers promoting a holistic orientation to nutrition, fitness, creative expression, personal growth, and sustainable living
www.naturalawakeningsmag.com

Natural Health Group
Commercial website providing information on vegetarian, vegan, and raw diets.
www.naturalhealthgroup.org

Natural Life Magazine
Website of magazine founded in 1976. Serves "thinking people around the world who want positive alternatives to high cost, high consumption lifestyles for themselves and their families."
www.naturallifemagazine.com

Organic Authority

Commercial website selling organic products and offering information promoting organic lifestyle.

www.organicauthority.com

Planet Green

One of Discovery's multi-platform channels of sustainable living ideas, energy conservation tips, freecycle information, green shopping, and more. Accepts advertising.

planetgreen.discovery.com

Skin Deep Cosmetic Safety Database

Database produced by the Environmental Working Group. Provides chemical composition and safety scores for over 50,000 cosmetic products.

www.cosmeticsdatabase.com

The Story of Stuff

Official website for this highly popular 20-minute animation of the consumerist society. Includes footnoted script, credits, blog, and resources.

www.storyofstuff.com

Treehugger.com

A Discovery Company website that allows users to get informed, interact, and take action. Features include information about green design and living, pop quizzes, and a sustainability-related job board.

www.treehugger.com

WorldCoolers

An online grassroots initiative that aims to raise public awareness of global warming. Website features a free downloadable Web browser add-on that gives updates on global warming topics.

www.worldcoolers.org

Yahoo! Green

Advertiser-sponsored mega-site for shopping and news, blogs, and tools for living green.

green.yahoo.com

Organizations

Business, government agencies, trade groups, environmental advocacy

1% for the Planet

A not-for-profit that facilitates businesses in donating at least 1% of their annual revenues to environmental organizations worldwide.

www.onepercentfortheplanet.org

Advertising Standards Authority
UK's independent regulator investigates complaints and monitors advertisements for false, offensive, or misleading information.
www.asa.org.uk

Advertising Standards Canada
Canada's independent self-regulatory nonprofit body that handles complaints on false, misleading, and harmful advertising campaigns.
www.adstandards.com

Alliance to Save Energy
Nonprofit coalition of business, government, and consumer leaders supporting energy efficiency and policies that minimize energy costs and lessen greenhouse gas emissions. The organization does research, conducts educational programs, advocates policies, designs and implements energy-efficient projects, and promotes technology development.
ase.org

American Center for Life Cycle Assessment (ACLCA)
Nonprofit membership organization, and part of the Institute for Environmental Research and Education (IERE), created to build capacity and knowledge of life-cycle assessment among industry, government, and NGOs. Developed and manages the Life Cycle Assessment Certified Professional (LCACP) Certification.
www.lcacenter.org

American Council for an Energy Efficient Economy (ACEEE)
Nonprofit organization dedicated to advancing energy efficiency as a means of promoting both economic prosperity and environmental protection. Contains extensive consumer resources on appliances, cars, lighting, etc.
www.aceee.org

American Hiking Society
A recreation-based nonprofit organization that champions conservation issues, builds partnerships between public and private stakeholders, and provides critical resources to plan, fund, and develop foot trails.
www.americanhiking.org

American Rivers
With 65,000 members, protects and restores rivers for the benefit of people, wildlife, and nature.
www.americanrivers.org

Australian Competition and Consumer Commission (ACCC)
As part of its primary responsibility to ensure that individuals and businesses comply with the Commonwealth competition, fair trading, and consumer protection laws, the ACCC publishes the Green Marketing and the Trade Practices Act which assists manufacturers, suppliers, advertisers, and others to assess the strength of any environmental claims they make and to improve the accuracy and usefulness to consumers of their labeling, packaging, and advertising.
www.accc.gov.au

B Lab Corporation
A nonprofit organization that bestows B Corporation certification ratings for businesses that meet comprehensive and transparent social and environmental standards and institutionalize stakeholder interests.
www.bcorporation.net

Beyond Pesticides
Formerly National Coalition against the Misuse of Pesticides, it seeks to eradicate pesticide use via identifying risks and promoting non-chemical and least hazardous alternatives.
www.beyondpesticides.org

Biodegradable Products Institute
A nonprofit association of key individuals and groups from government, industry, and academia that educates manufacturers, legislators, and consumers about the importance of biodegradable materials. The association also promotes the use and recovery of compostable materials through municipal and backyard composting.
www.bpiworld.org

Biomimicry Institute
Nonprofit organization that promotes the study and imitation of nature's designs.
www.biomimicryinstitute.org

Canopy
Based in Palo Alto, California, this nonprofit organization advocates for the urban forest and works to educate, inspire, and engage the community as stewards of young and mature trees.
www.canopy.org

Carbon Disclosure Project
Nonprofit organization holding the largest database of primary corporate climate change information in the world to support financial and policy decision-making. Represents institutional investors and 60 businesses including Cadbury, PepsiCo, and Wal-Mart.
www.cdproject.net

Carbon Trust
Set up by the British government, this London-based nonprofit company offers products and services geared towards saving energy, managing carbon management, and developing low-carbon technology. Featured support services include energy-efficiency loans, carbon surveys, an action plan tool, a carbon footprint calculator, and applied research grants. Offers the Carbon Reduction Label for use on consumer products.
www.carbontrust.co.uk

Center for a New American Dream
With the goal of helping Americans consume responsibly, enhance quality of life and promote social justice, this nonprofit group offers an action network, campaigns and program information, a community action guide, publications available for download, as well as sections for kids and teens.
www.newdream.org

Centre for Sustainable Design

Led by sustainability expert Martin Charter, and established in 1995 within the Faculty of Design, The Surrey Institute of Art & Design, University College, UK, this organization facilitates discussion and research on eco-design and environmental, economic, ethical, and social considerations in product and service development and design. Featured services and resources include research and training projects, an annual Sustainable Innovation conference, workshops, consultancy, and publications. The Centre also acts as an information clearinghouse and a focus for innovative thinking on sustainable products and services.

www.cfsd.org.uk

Ceres

A North American network of investors, environmental organizations, and other public interest groups working with companies and investors to address sustainability issues such as global climate change.

www.ceres.org

Choice

Formerly known as the Australian Consumer's Association, focuses on testing and ranking various consumer products in addition to reporting on false advertising.

www.choice.com.au

Conservation International

Using science, policy and fieldwork to protect our planet's resources.

www.conservation.org

Defenders of Wildlife

Founded in 1947, a nonprofit organization dedicated to protecting native plants and animals.

www.defenders.org

Department for Environment, Food and Rural Affairs (Defra)

The UK government body responsible for policy and regulations. Its priorities are to support British farming and encourage sustainable food production, help to enhance the environment and biodiversity, and support a strong and sustainable green economy, resilient to climate change.

www.defra.gov.uk

Earth Day Network

Educates the public and organizes global activism for a cleaner planet.

www.earthday.net/

Earthjustice

Formerly the Sierra Club Legal Defense Fund, this national nonprofit law firm lobbies for environmental legislation and takes legal action to stop environmental offenses by industries in the areas of climate and energy, wildlife and places, health and toxics.

www.earthjustice.org

Ecolabel Index
The largest global database of eco-labels, tracking 328 eco-labels in 207 countries and 40 industry sectors as of 2010
www.ecolabelindex.com

The Economics of Ecosystems and Biodiversity (TEEB)
International initiative created to draw attention to the global economic benefits of biodiversity and the growing costs of biodiversity loss and ecosystem degradation. It brings together expertise from the fields of science, economics, and policy.
www.teebweb.org

Electronics TakeBack Coalition
Promotes green design and responsible recycling in the electronics industry to protect the health and well-being of electronics users, workers, and the communities where electronics are produced and discarded. It urges consumer electronics manufacturers and brand owners to take full responsibility for the life-cycle of their products, through public policy requirements or enforceable agreements.
www.electronicstakeback.com

Environmental Defense Fund
A nonprofit environmental advocacy group that partners with Fortune 500 businesses, governments, and communities to advocate market-based solutions to environmental problems. Website features publications and resource tools for businesses to reduce their environmental footprint.
www.edf.org

Environmental Media Association
Mobilizes the entertainment industry to educate and inspire the public to act on environmental issues.
www.ema-online.org

Environmental Protection UK
Nonprofit organization based in the UK that focuses on environmental policy, campaigns, and innovation. Brings together industry leaders, academics, policy makers, and the public to bring about environmental change.
www.environmental-protection.org.uk

Environmental Working Group
A nonprofit environmental and consumer advocacy group providing information and promoting legislation on the human health and environmental impacts of consumer products.
www.ewg.org

European Advertising Standards Alliance
A nonprofit organization that brings together self-regulatory advertising organizations in Europe and also Australia, Brazil, Canada, Chile, India, New Zealand, and South Africa to promote ethical standards in advertising through self-regulation.
www.easa-alliance.org

European Environmental Bureau

Federation of European environmental citizens' organizations. Website has news, environmental articles, events, policy. It also lists active environmental organizations in Europe.

www.eeb.org

Federal Trade Commission

Publishes "Green Guides," Guides for the Use of Environmental Marketing Claims, general principles, and specific examples

www.ftc.gov/bcp/grnrule/guides980427.htm

Friends of the Earth

Environmental nonprofit organization with a network of grassroots organizations in 77 countries that focuses on global warming, toxic technologies, and promoting smarter, low-pollution transportation alternatives.

www.foe.org

Global Environmental Declaration Network (GEDnet)

An international nonprofit organization of Type III environmental declaration organizations and practitioners, organizing and allowing an open exchange of information on the various Type III environmental product declaration programs.

www.gednet.org

Global Footprint Network

International think-tank working to advance sustainability through use of the Ecological Footprint, a resource accounting tool and data-driven metric that allows the calculation of human pressure on the planet.

www.footprintnetwork.org

Global Reporting Initiative

Network-based organization that has developed the world's most widely used sustainability reporting framework involving business, civil society, labor, and professional institutions.

www.globalreporting.org

Green America

Formerly known as Co-op America, this national not-for-profit organization promotes sustainability and social and economic justice through strategic efforts aimed towards individuals, businesses, and communities. Resources include National Green Pages, a directory listing of thousands of businesses that have made commitments to sustainable, socially just principles, Green Business Network, an education system for environmentally responsible consumption and investing, and Green Festivals in major U.S. cities.

www.greenamericatoday.org

Green Design Institute, Carnegie Mellon University

Offers green design courses and provides a space for companies, foundations, and government agencies to discuss issues of environmental quality and economic development.

www.ce.cmu.edu/GreenDesign

GreenerChoices

Website for consumers run by Consumers Union, the nonprofit publisher of Consumer Reports. Provides in-depth information on green consumer products and practices.

www.greenerchoices.org

Greenhouse Gas Protocol Initiative

Partnership between the World Resources Institute and the World Business Council for Sustainable Development working with businesses, governments, and environmental groups worldwide "to build a new generation of credible and effective programs for tackling climate change." Developed the most widely used international accounting tool for government and business leaders to understand, quantify, and manage greenhouse gas emissions.

www.ghgprotocol.org

Greenpeace

A global campaigning organization that acts to change attitudes and behavior, to protect and conserve the environment by addressing such issues as energy, oceans, ancient forests, toxics, and sustainable agriculture. Campaigns have featured "Greening the Apple" (Apple Inc.) and "Kleercut" (Kimberly-Clark).

www.greenpeace.org

IEG

Provides consulting, valuation, measurement, research and training to the global sponsorship industry. Develops ways for companies and brands to partner with sports, arts, events, entertainment, nonprofit, and causes.

www.sponsorship.com

Impact Reporting and Investment Standards

Initiative developed by the Rockefeller Foundation, Acumen Fund, and B Lab to create a common framework for defining, tracking, and reporting the performance of impact capital that will allow comparison and communication across organizations that have social or environmental impact as a primary driver.

iris.thegiin.org

Industrial Designers Society of America

Annual IDEA awards feature environmental criteria. Resources in eco-design provided by eco-design special interest group.

www.idsa.org

International Association for Soaps, Detergents and Maintenance Products (AISE)

Dedicated to the sustainable improvement of products for hygiene, detergents and household and industrial maintenance products. Manages the Washright campaign in the European Union to promote responsible laundry care.

www.aise.eu

J. Ottman Consulting, Inc.

Founded in 1989 by green marketing expert and author Jacquelyn Ottman, advises Fortune 500, entrepreneurial firms, and government agencies on strategies for green marketing and sustainable product innovation. Ottman is the author of *The New Rules of Green Marketing*.

www.greenmarketing.com

Japan Environment Association

Founded in 1977, the JEA is concerned with Japan's environmental conservation activities. Their main areas of focus are: global warming, promoting the green marketplace, and environmental education.

www.jeas.or.jp

Japan Environmental Management Association for Industry

Established in 1962, this public organization with 1,100 member companies focuses on environmental assessments, air and water pollution, and global environmental issues. JEMAI controls the Eco-Leaf Product Environmental Aspects Declaration program.

www.jemai.or.jp

KaBOOM!

A nonprofit dedicated to create play spaces for children in the U.S.

kaboom.org

Life Cycle Initiative

International life-cycle partnership launched by the United Nations Environment Programme and the Society for Environmental Toxicology and Chemistry to put life-cycle thinking into practice and improve supporting tools through better data and indicators.

lcinitiative.unep.fr

Material Connexion

Member-based global materials consultancy and library of innovative and sustainable materials.

materialconnexion.com

National Advertising Division, Council of Better Business Bureaus

Reviews advertising for truthfulness and accuracy and makes its findings available to the public.

www.nadreview.org

National Audubon Society

A national network of community-based nature centers and chapters. Conserves and restores natural bird ecosystems.

www.audubon.org

National Geographic Society

Nonprofit scientific and educational organization that promotes the globalization of geographic knowledge while conserving the world's cultural, historical, and natural resources.

www.nationalgeographic.com

National Institute for Environmental Studies
Japanese environmental organization that focuses on environmental research. Areas of interest include health, chemicals, waste, and recycling.
www.nies.go.jp

National Wildlife Federation
Nonprofit organization with more than 4 million members, geared toward protecting wildlife and confronting global warming.
www.nwf.org

Natural Marketing Institute
Consulting, market research, and business development company specializing in the health and wellness marketplace. Authors of the *LOHAS Consumer Report.*
www.nmisolutions.com

Natural Resources Defense Council
With 1.3 million members and online activists, an environmental action group combining grassroots with scientists and other professionals aimed at safeguarding the Earth's people, plants, animals, and natural systems.
www.nrdc.org

The Natural Step
Not-for-profit organization that promotes a science-based model to help communities and businesses better understand and integrate environmental, social, and economic considerations. Working with companies, municipalities, academic institutions, and not-for-profit organizations.
www.naturalstep.org

The Nature Conservancy
Nonprofit conservation organization working to protect ecologically important lands and waters.
www.nature.org

O$_2$ Global Network
Members of this global network organize lectures, projects, workshops, and distribute newsletters and other material to promote, teach, and implement sustainable design. The O$_2$ site includes resources on sustainable design and a global listserv.
www.o2.org

Open MIC
Nonprofit using market feedback to make corporate management practices of the media industry more open and responsible.
www.openmic.org

Organic Consumers Association
Online and grassroots nonprofit dealing with issues of food safety, industrial agriculture, genetic engineering, children's health, environmental sustainability, and fair trade.
www.organicconsumers.org

Organic Exchange
A membership organization focused on increasing the production and use of organically grown fibers.
www.organicexchange.org

People for the Ethical Treatment of Animals
Nonprofit group that promotes animal rights via campaigns including ending fur and leather use, meat and dairy consumption, factory farming, circuses, and bull fighting.
www.peta.org

Planet Ark
Nonprofit organization based in Australia that aims to teach both individuals and businesses simple ways in which they can make substantial reductions to their environmental impact.
planetark.org

Project (RED)
Businesses donate 50% of the profits of (RED) products to help buy and distribute antiretroviral medicine for those dying of AIDS in Africa.
www.joinred.com

Rocky Mountain Institute
Independent, entrepreneurial nonprofit think-tank of a group of industry experts, thought leaders, and engineers engaged in research that addresses pragmatic designs, practices, and policies related to energy and resources, with a strong emphasis on market-based solutions.
www.rmi.org/rmi

Sierra Club
A nonprofit environmental advocacy organization founded in 1892 that combines legal action, information campaigns, and cooperative partnerships with industry to protect America's wild places.
www.sierraclub.org

Silicon Valley Toxics Coalition
A nonprofit organization engaged in research, advocacy, and grassroots organizing to promote human health and environmental justice related to the high-tech industry. Has advocated for electronics companies to reduce and eventually eliminate the use of toxic chemicals in the design and manufacturing of products and the implementation of extended producer responsibility at end of product life.
www.svtc.org/site/PageServer

Slow Food
With 100,000 members in 132 countries, a nonprofit member-supported organization that aims to counteract fast food and fast life and the disappearance of local food traditions, and raise awareness of how food tastes and how our food choices affect the rest of the world.
www.slowfoodusa.org

Surfrider Foundation

A nonprofit environmental organization dedicated to the protection and enjoyment of the world's waves and beaches through conservation, education, research, and activism.
www.surfrider.org

Sustainability Consortium

Stewarded by Wal-Mart, a partnership of researchers from leading global universities, NGOs, governmental agencies, and business partners, created with the goal of establishing scientific standards to measure the sustainability of consumer products and ultimately developing scientifically valid and coherent product indexes to allow retailers compare consumer products.
www.sustainabilityconsortium.org

Sustainable Investment Research Analyst Network (SIRAN)

Supportive network for analysts taking an environmental, social, or governance approach to investment studies.
www.siran.org

Sustainable Packaging Coalition

Industry working group develops educational resources and tools on sustainable packaging. Featured projects and resources include a comparative packaging assessment tool, sustainable performance indicators and metrics, design guidelines for sustainable packaging, and environmental technical briefs.
www.sustainablepackaging.org

TNS Media Intelligence

Tracks competitive media expenditures and creative ads for advertising agencies, advertisers, broadcasters, and publishers.
www.tns-mi.com/aboutIndex.htm

United Nations Environment Programme

Founded in 1972 to coordinate and manage United Nations environmental initiatives, research, and policies.
www.unep.org

Wildlife Conservation Society

Founded in 1895, this organization manages 500 conservation projects in 60 countries aimed at saving wildlife.
www.wcs.org

Women's Voices for the Earth

Nonprofit organization that researches the health impacts of consumer products, including cosmetic and household cleaning products.
www.womenandenvironment.org

World Business Council for Sustainable Development

CEO-led global association of about 200 companies from more than 35 countries and 20 major industrial sectors. Provides a platform for companies to explore sustainable development, share knowledge, experiences, and best practices, and to advocate

business positions in a variety of forums, working with governments and non-governmental and intergovernmental organizations. Four key areas include energy and climate, development, the business role, and ecosystems.
www.wbcsd.org

World Resources Institute
Environmental think-tank working with business partners, governments, and civil society, with over 50 active projects focused on global climate change, sustainable markets, ecosystem protection, and environmentally responsible governance.
www.wri.org

Worldwatch Institute
Independent research organization led by Lester Brown focused on developing and disseminating data and strategies to address challenges of climate change, resource degradation, population growth, and poverty. Priority programs include Energy & Climate, Food & Agriculture, and Green Economy.
www.worldwatch.org

Zerofootprint
Zerofootprint Software applies technology, design, and risk management to reduce the world's environmental footprint and provides clients with tailored carbon management solutions. The Zerofootprint Foundation engages government, educators, and other not-for-profits to combat climate change.
www.zerofootprint.net

Certification and eco-labeling organizations

Aquaculture Certification Council
This certification recognizes aquaculture that meets social, environmental, and food safety standards.
www.aquaculturecertification.org

ASTM International
Originally known as the American Society for Testing and Materials, one of the largest voluntary standards organizations focused on technical standards for materials, products, systems, and services. ASTM has developed sustainability standards or has expertise in areas including soil, water, air quality, and waste management.
www.astm.org

Blue Angel
The official eco-label of Germany, covering 10,000 products and services. Awards made on single attributes representing greatest areas of impact per category.
blauer-engel.de

Bluesign
A global network of representatives from the scientific and political communities, trade and industry, and consumer and environmental organizations. The Bluesign standard ensures environmental responsibility, health and safety with the production of textiles.
www.bluesign.com

Carbon Trust

Provides Carbon Reduction label intended to help consumers better understand a product's carbon footprint.

www.carbontrust.co.uk

Center for Resource Solutions

A national nonprofit focusing on research and marketing of renewable energy options. Promotes the Green-e label for renewable energy.

www.resource-solutions.org

Cradle to Cradle Certification

Assesses a product's safety to humans and the environment and design for future life-cycles in the categories of materials, material reutilization, energy, water, and social responsibility. Products can be certified at four levels: Basic, Silver, Gold, Platinum.

www.c2ccertified.com

Eco Mark

Japan's voluntary multi-attribute eco-labeling program covering a wide range of consumer products.

www.ecomark.jp

EcoLogo

A multi-attribute environmental standard and certification mark founded in Canada but now available worldwide.

www.environmentalchoice.com

EPEAT

Not-for-profit organization managed and operated by the Green Electronics Council of the International Sustainable Development Foundation. Evaluates electronic products in relation to 51 total environmental criteria, identified in IEEE 1680 standards.

www.epeat.net

EU Ecolabel

A voluntary multi-attribute scheme administered by the European Eco-labeling Board with the support of the European Commission. Covers a wide range of products and services, including cleaning products, appliances, paper products, textile and home and garden products, lubricants, and services such as tourist accommodation.

www.eco-label.com

Fairtrade Foundation

UK member organization of Fairtrade Labelling Organizations International.

www.fairtrade.org.uk

Fairtrade Labelling Organizations International (FLO)

An international network of 24 designated nonprofits that are responsible for issuing licenses to use the "FAIRTRADE" label on products (includes Transfair [U.S.] and Fairtrade Foundation [UK]).

www.fairtrade.net

Forest Stewardship Council
Internationally recognized standard of responsible forestry.
www.fsc.org

Good Environmental Choice – Australia
Australia's voluntary multi-attribute environmental labeling program covering a wide range of products.
www.geca.org.au

Global Organic Textile Standard
Worldwide standard for organic textiles based on materials and processes used throughout production.
www.global-standard.org

Green Good Housekeeping Seal
Launched by *Good Housekeeping* magazine in 2009 to help consumers recognize products that have earned high ratings based on a wide range of environmental criteria and effectiveness.
www.goodhousekeeping.com/product-testing/history/welcome-gh-seal

Green Seal
One of the oldest independent nonprofit labeling organizations, develops standards for and certifies a wide range of environmentally responsible commercial and consumer products and services including cleaning aids, building and maintenance materials, and lodging properties.
www.greenseal.org

International Organization for Standardization (ISO)
Based in Geneva, Switzerland, ISO is a non-governmental network of national standards institutes of 163 countries and the world's largest developer and publisher of voluntary international standards. The ISO Catalogue includes more than 18,000 published International Standards, including ISO 14001 for corporate environmental management and ISO 14020 for eco-labeling.
www.iso.org

Marine Stewardship Council
Fish certified by this global program are from wild capture fisheries that practice sustainable fishing and protect the local ecosystems.
www.msc.org

National Standard for Sustainable Forest Management (Canadian Standards Association)
Products with this label comply with national and international environmental standards for forest management.
www.csa-international.org/product_areas/forest_products_marking

NSF International
Nonprofit organization founded in 1944 to certify products and write standards related to public health, safety, and the environment for food, water, and consumer goods.
www.nsf.org

Programme for the Endorsement of Forest Certification
The PEFC label can be found on wood and paper products from forests that are certified by an independent member of this international nonprofit association to be sustainably managed. Sustainable Forestry Program located in the U.S. is a member.
www.pefc.org

Protected Harvest
Agricultural products with this label come from farms with rigorous environmental growing standards.
www.protectedharvest.org

Rainforest Alliance
Independent certification of forestry and agricultural products along with verification of forest and farm projects that aim to reduce carbon emissions.
www.rainforest-alliance.org

Scientific Certification Systems
Develops standards attesting to the quality and sustainable production of various agriculture, manufacturing, and energy products.
www.scscertified.com

TransFair USA
A nonprofit that is the only third-party certifier of Fair Trade products for the U.S. The Fair Trade Certified label can be applied to coffee, tea and herbs, cocoa and chocolate, fresh fruit, flowers, sugar, rice, and vanilla. Certified farms practice environmentally sustainable farming methods and follow the Fair Trade community-oriented principles of fair labor conditions for workers.
www.transfairusa.org

ULEnvironment
A division of UL; certifies environmental claims and develops standards.
www.ulenvironment.com

United States Department of Agriculture
Through the National Organic Program develops, implements, and administers national production, handling, and labeling standards for organic agricultural products, including the USDA Organic label. Also home to the USDA BioPreferred government procurement program and voluntary consumer label.
www.usda.gov

United States Department of Energy
Maintains the Energy Guide for appliances, and co-manages the ENERGY STAR label (with U.S. Environmental Protection Agency).
www.energy.gov

United States Environmental Protection Agency
U.S. government agency that maintains the Design for the Environment (**www.epa.gov/dfe**), ENERGY STAR (**energystar.gov**), SmartWay transportation (**www.epa.gov/smartway**), and WaterSense (**www.epa.gov/WaterSense**) voluntary labels.

United States Green Building Council
Maintains the LEED (Leadership for Energy and Environmental Design) rating system
for sustainable building design and construction.
www.usgbc.org

Books

Business, design and sustainability

Companies on a Mission: Entrepreneurial Strategies for Growing Sustainably, Responsibly, and Profitably
Michael V. Russo (Stanford University Press, 2010)

The Clean Tech Revolution
Ron Pernik and Clint Wilder (Harper Collins Publishers, 2008)

Co-opportunity: Join Up for a Sustainable, Resilient, Prosperous World
John Grant (John Wiley & Sons, 2010)

Confessions of a Radical Industrialist: Profits, People, Purpose – Doing Business by Respecting the Earth
Ray C. Anderson (St. Martin's Press, 2009)

Driving Eco-innovation
Claude Fussler with Peter James (Pitman Publishing, 1996)

Ecological Intelligence: How Knowing the Hidden Impacts of What We Buy Can Change Everything
Daniel Goleman (Broadway Business, 2009)

The Green Marketing Manifesto
John Grant (John Wiley & Sons, 2008)

Green Recovery: Get Lean, Get Smart, and Emerge from the Downturn on Top
Andrew Winston (Harvard Business Press, 2009)

Hot, Flat, and Crowded: Why We Need a Green Revolution – and How It Can Renew America
Thomas L. Friedman (Farrar Straus & Giroux, 2008)

Life Cycle Assessment: Principles, Practice and Prospects
Ralph Horne, Tim Grant, and Karli Verghese (CSIRO Publishing, 2009)

Packaging Sustainability: Tools, Systems and Strategies for Innovative Package Design
Wendy Jedlicka (John Wiley & Sons, 2008)

Plan B 4.0: Mobilizing to Save Civilization
Lester R. Brown (Earth Policy Institute, 2009)

The Plot to Save the Planet: How Visionary Entrepreneurs and Corporate Titans are Creating Real Solutions to Global Warming
Brian Dumaine (Crown Business, 2008)

The Psychology of Climate Change Communication: A Guide for Scientists, Journalists, Educators, Political Aides, and the Interested Public
Center for Research on Environmental Decisions (Columbia University in the City of New York, 2009; free download at www.cred.columbia.edu/guide)

Strategy for Sustainability: A Business Manifesto
Adam Werbach (Harvard Business Press, 2009)

Sustainability by Design: A Subversive Strategy for Transforming Our Consumer Culture
John R. Ehrenfeld (Yale University Press, 2008)

The Sustainability Champion's Guidebook: How to Transform Your Company
Bob Willard (New Society Publishers, 2009)

Sustainable Energy – Without the Hot Air
David J.C. MacKay (UIT Cambridge Ltd., 2009; free download at www.withouthotair.com)

The Truth about Green Business
Gil Friend (FT Press, 2009)

Consumer books

50 Simple Things You Can Do to Save the Earth
John Javna, Sophie Javna, and Jesse Javna (Hyperion, 2008)

Big Green Purse: Use Your Spending Power to Create a Cleaner, Greener World
Diane MacEachern (Avery, 2008)

Generation Green: The Ultimate Teen Guide to Living an Eco-friendly Life
Linda Sivertsen and Tosh Sivertsen (Simon Pulse, 2008)

Green, Greener, Greenest: A Practical Guide to Making Eco-smart Choices a Part of Your Life
Lori Bongiorno (Perigee Trade, 2008)

Green Guide: The Complete Reference for Consuming Wisely
(National Geographic, 2008)

Gorgeously Green: 8 Simple Steps to an Earth-friendly Life
Sophie Uliano (Collins Living, 2008)

It's Easy Being Green: A Handbook for Earth Friendly Living
Crissy Trask (Gibbs Smith, 2006)

The Lazy Environmentalist: Your Guide to Easy, Stylish, Green Living
Josh Dorfman (Harry N Abrams, 2007)

Living Like Ed: A Guide to the Eco-friendly Life
Ed Begley Jr. (Clarkson N. Potter, 2008)

Ready, Set, Green: Eight Weeks to Modern Eco-living
Graham Hill and Meaghan O'Neill (Villard Books, 2008)

Simple Prosperity: Finding Real Wealth in a Sustainable Lifestyle
David Wann (St. Martin's Press, 2007)

Squeaky Green: The Method Guide to Detoxing Your Home
Eric Ryan and Adam Lowry (Chronicle Books, 2008)

Toolbox for Sustainable Living: A Do-It-Ourselves Guide
Scott Kellogg and Stacy Pettigrew (South End Press, 2008)

Worldchanging: A User's Guide for the 21st Century
Alex Steffen (Abrams, 2008)

Endnotes

Chapter 1

1 Natural Marketing Institute, *The LOHAS Report: 2009* (Harleysville, PA: NMI, 2009).
2 Focalyst, "It's Good to Be Green: Socially Conscious Shopping Behaviors among Boomers," Focalyst Insight Report; AARP Services and Focalyst, December 2007; https://www.focalyst.com/Sites/Focalyst/Media/Pdfs/en/CurrentResearchReports/698F1654.pdf; https://www.focalyst.com/Sites/Focalyst/Content/KnowledgeCenter, accessed September 16, 2010.
3 Randeep Ramesh, "Bhopal marks 25th anniversary of Union Carbide gas disaster," *The Guardian*, December 3, 2009; www.guardian.co.uk/world/2009/dec/03/bhopal-anniversary-union-carbide-gas, accessed September 16, 2010.
4 Known officially as the United Nations Conference on Environment and Development (UNCED).
5 Green Canary Sustainability Consulting, "New Research: 18- to 34-Year-Olds Key to Green Economy," Tuerff-Davis EnviroMedia; www.greencanary.net/news-item.php?id=693, accessed August 1, 2010.
6 The American College and University Presidents' Climate Commitment (ACUPCC) is about a global commitment to eliminate campuses' greenhouse gas emissions; www.presidentsclimatecommitment.org.
7 Sophia Yan, "Understanding Generation Y," *The Oberlin Review*, December 8, 2006; www.oberlin.edu/stupub/ocreview/2006/12/08/features/Understanding_Generation_Y.html, accessed August 1, 2010.
8 American Forest & Paper Association, "Facts About Paper," 2009; www.afandpa.org/FunFacts.aspx, accessed August 1, 2010.
9 Dan Shapley, "Green Election Issues 101," *The Daily Green*, August 28, 2008; www.thedailygreen.com/environmental-news/latest/green-elections-guide-47082517, accessed August 1, 2010.
10 League of Conservation Voters, "About LCV"; www.lcv.org/about-lcv, accessed August 1, 2010.

11 Beth Walton, "Volunteer Rates Hit Record Numbers," *USA Today*, July 7, 2006; www.usatoday.com/news/nation/2006-07-06-volunteers_x.htm, accessed August 1, 2010.

12 Gwynne Rogers, Natural Marketing Institute, email message to the author, March 29, 2010.

13 Tanya Irwin, "Study: Organic Products Selling Strong Despite the Economy," *MediaPost News*, May 4, 2009; www.mediapost.com/publications/?art_ aid=105371&fa=Articles.showArticle, accessed August 1, 2010.

14 Sustainable Life Media, "Sales in Organics Soar Over 17% Despite Recession," May 6, 2009; www.sustainablelifemedia.com/content/story/brands/sales_ in_organics_soar_over_17_percent_despite Recession, accessed August 1, 2010.

15 Jack Neff, "Why Burt's Bees CMO Won't Cut Spending in Recession," *Advertising Age*, May 13, 2009; adage.com/results?endeca=1&return=endeca& search_ offset=0&search_order_by=score&x=0&y=0&search_phrase=Why+Burt%27s+Bee s+CMO+Won%27t+Cut+Spending+in+Recession, accessed August 1, 2010.

16 John Murphy and Kate Linebaugh, "Honda's Hybrid Will Take On Prius," *Wall Street Journal*, October 1, 2008: B1.

17 Procter & Gamble, "Procter & Gamble Deepens Corporate Commitment to Sustainability," press release, March 26, 2009; www.pginvestor.com/phoenix. zhtml?c=104574&p=irol-newsArticle&ID=1270272, accessed September 16, 2010.

18 Procter & Gamble, "P&G Launches Initiative to Make Conservation of Natural Resources More User Friendly," press release, March 15, 2010; www.pginvestor.com/ phoenix.zhtml?c=104574&p=irol-newsArticle&ID=1402138&highlight=future%20 friendly, accessed September 16, 2010.

19 "Green Is The New Black," *Brandweek*, June 24, 2009; www.brandweek.com/bw/ content_display/news-and-features/green-marketing/e3i772f176924f862d41- ded85b4a202121f, accessed August 1, 2010.

20 Helen K. Chang, "Business: Coming Clean," *Plenty* 22 (June–July 2008); www. plentymag.com/magazine/business_coming_clean.php, accessed August 1, 2010.

21 www.openmic.org.

22 Sustainable Life Media, "Consumers Chuck Green Debate for Environmental Action," February 11, 2009; www.sustainablelifemedia.com/content/story/ brands/consumers_chuck_green_debate_for_environmental_action, accessed August 1, 2010.

23 Jeremy Lovell, "Global Warming Impact Like 'Nuclear War'," Reuters, September 12, 2007; www.reuters.com/article/environmentNews/idUSL1234809620070912, accessed August 1, 2010.

24 Bret Stephens, "Global Warming and the Poor," *Wall Street Journal*, August 4, 2009: A11.

25 U.S. Environmental Protection Agency, "Water Supply and Use in the United States," *WaterSense*, June 2008; www.epa.gov/watersense/pubs/supply.html, accessed 13 October 2009.

26 Leo Lewis, "Ecologists Warn the Planet Is Running Short of Water," *The Times*, January 22, 2009; www.timesonline.co.uk/tol/news/environment/ article5562906.ece, accessed August 1, 2010.

27 Sustainable Life Media, "86 of S&P 100 Have Corporate Sustainability Websites," July 23, 2008; www.sustainablelifemedia.com/content/story/strategy/86_of_s_and_p_100_have_corporate_sustainability_websites, accessed August 1, 2010.

28 Ibid.

Chapter 2

1 LOHAS, Naturalites, Conventionals, Drifters, and Unconcerneds are registered trademarks of the Natural Marketing Institute of Harleysville, Pennsylvania.

2 "Over Half of Consumers Factor Green Record into Buying Decisions," *Environmental Leader*, August 6, 2008; www.environmentalleader.com/2008/08/06/over-half-of-consumers-factor-green-record-into-buying-decisions, accessed August 1, 2010.

3 Amazon Green (www.Amazon.com/Amazon-Green) and Yahoo! Green (green.yahoo.com).

4 Sustainable Life Media, "Americans Buy Green to Save Green When Shopping for Electronics," April 17, 2007; www.sustainablelifemedia.com/content/story/brands/americans_buy_green_to_save_green, accessed August 6, 2010.

5 Daniel H. Pink, "Rise of the Neo-Greens," *Wired* 14.05 (May 2006); www.wired.com/wired/archive/14.05/neo.html, accessed August 1, 2010.

Chapter 3

1 Renewable Energy Certificates, also known as renewable energy credits, are tradable commodities representing proof that a certain amount of electricity used in production was generated from an eligible renewal energy source, again not under their domain (Source: www.epa.gov/greenpower/gpmarket/rec.htm).

2 "Certified B Corporation," B Lab; www.bcorporation.net, accessed August 11, 2010.

3 "Fighting Dirty, "an interview with the founders of Method green home-care products by Sarah van Schagen, March 14, 2008: www.grist.org/article/fighting-dirty, accessed August 15, 2010.

4 The jugs in question being the large, handled bottles that rival brands use rather than the small pump bottles of Method.

5 Katie Molinari, Method Products Inc., telephone interview, July 22, 2009.

Chapter 4

1 Several multi-attribute eco-labeling programs have been developed in various countries around the world for this purpose.

2 D. Sabaliunas, "Tide Coldwater: Energy Conservation through Residential Laundering Innovation and Commercialization," presented at the *10th Annual Green Chemistry and Engineering Conference,* Capital Hilton, Washington, DC, June 26–30, 2006; acs.confex.com/acs/green06/techprogram/P27314.HTM, accessed October 19, 2010.

3 U.S. Environmental Protection Agency, "Life-Cycle Assessment (LCA)"; www.epa.gov/nrmrl/lcaccess.

4   "PepsiCo Reveals Method for Calculating Carbon Footprint of Products," *Environmental Leader*, October 5, 2009.

5   Glenn Rifkin, "Saving Trees is Music to Guitar Makers' Ears," *New York Times*, June 7, 2007: C4.

6   Earthworks No Dirty Gold Campaign, "Dirty Gold's Impacts"; www.nodirtygold.org/dirty_golds_impacts.cfm, accessed August 1, 2010.

7   Earthworks No Dirty Gold Campaign, "Tiffany & Co. Stakes Bold Position on Mining Reform," press release, March 24, 2004; www.nodirtygold.org/stdnt_alternatives.cfm, accessed August 1, 2010.

8   Tiffany & Co., "Sources and Mining Practices: Our Views on Large-Scale Mining," 2009; www.tiffany.com/sustainability/mining.aspx, accessed August 1, 2010.

9   Tiffany & Co., "Our Environmental and Social Commitments," 2008; www.tiffany.com/sustainability, accessed August 1, 2010.

10 Cure Recycling, "Recycle Printer Cartridges," Earthtone Solutions Inc.; www.earthtonesolutions.com/recyclecartridgesinkjet.html, accessed August 1, 2010.

11 Emma Ritch, "Pumping up the Value of Recycled Plastics," Cleantech Group LLC, May 8, 2009; cleantech.com/news/4439/hp-lavergne-improve-value-recycled, accessed August 1, 2010.

12 Sustainable is Good, "Recycline Wins Forbes Boost Your Business Contest," December 17, 2007; www.sustainableisgood.com/blog/2007/12/recycline-wins.html, accessed August 1, 2010.

13 Jenny Hoponick, "Nonylphenol Ethoxylates: A Safer Alternative Exists to This Toxic Cleaning Agent," Rep. Sierra Club, Jersey Coast Anglers Association, November 2005.

14 Organic Trade Association, "U.S. Organic Sales Grow by a Whopping 17.1 Percent in 2008," press release, May 4, 2009; www.organicnewsroom.com/2009/05/us_organic_sales_grow_by_a_who.html, accessed August 1, 2010.

15 Emily B. York, "Safeway to Roll out House Brands to Grocery Stores Nationwide," *Advertising Age*, August 6, 2008; adage.com/article?article_id=130191, accessed August 1, 2010.

16 "Safeway Aims to Expand O Organics, Eating Right Lines Beyond Its Store Shelves," *Nutrition Business Journal: Strategic Information for the Nutrition Industry | Nutrition Industry Research*; nutritionbusinessjournal.com/retail/news/07-15-safeway-exapand-o-organics-eating-right-beyond-store-shelves, accessed 6 August 2010.

17 Sarah F. Gale, "Earth's Best: A Food Every Mother Could Love," *Organic Processing Magazine*, July–September 2006; www.organicprocessing.com/opjs06/opjs06enterprise.htm, accessed August 1, 2010.

18 Paulette Miniter, "Organic-Food Stocks a Natural Choice in Slowdowns," *SmartMoney*, February 28, 2008; www.smartmoney.com/investing/stocks/organic-food-stocks-a-natural-choice-in-slowdowns-22626, accessed August 1, 2010.

19 WWF, "Agriculture and Environment: Cotton. Environmental Impacts of Production on Water Use," WWF International, 2009; www.panda.org/what_we_do/footprint/agriculture/cotton/environmental_impacts/water_use, accessed August 1, 2010.

20 *Nikebiz*, "Nike Responsibility"; www.nikebiz.com/responsibility/considered_design/environmentally_preferred.html, accessed August 1, 2010.

21 Nicole Peyraud, "Mainstream Green," *Yogi Times*, September 2007: 38-39.

22 Organic Exchange, "OE 2009 Organic Market Report: Global Organic Cotton Grows 35%, Hits 4.3 Billion in 2009," press release, August 16, 2010; organicexchange.org/oecms/OE-2009-Organic-Market-Report-Global-Organic-Cotton-Grows-35-Hits-$4.3-Billion-in-2009.html, accessed October 1, 2010.

23 UNICEF, "Child Labor," March 6, 2008; www.unicef.org/protection/index_childlabour.html, accessed August 1, 2010.

24 BBC News, "Women Face Bias Worldwide – UN," April 5, 2008; news.bbc.co.uk/2/hi/europe/7331813.stm, accessed August 1, 2010.

25 Department for International Development, "Fairtrade Olive Oil Offers Economic Lifeline for Palestinian Farmers," press release, February 2009; collections.europarchive.org/tna/20100423085705/http://www.dfid.gov.uk/Media-Room/Press-releases/2009/Fairtrade-olive-oil-offers-economic-lifeline-for-Palestinian-farmers, accessed August 1, 2010.

26 Fairtrade Foundation, "Global Fairtrade Sales Increase by 22%," press release, June 8, 2009; www.fairtrade.org.uk/press_office/press_releases_and_statements/jun_2009/global_fairtrade_sales_increase_by_22.aspx, accessed August 1, 2010.

27 Ben Cooper, "The Just-Food Interview – Sophi Tranchell, Divine Chocolate," *Just-Food*, March 5, 2009; www.just-food.com/article.aspx?id=105703&d=1, accessed August 1, 2010.

28 Clearly So, "Divine Chocolate"; www.clearlyso.com/company.jsf?id=172, accessed August 1, 2010.

29 Andrew Cleary, "Cadbury Brings in Fairtrade Dairy Milk as Ethical Foods Prosper," Bloomberg.com, July 22, 2009; bloomberg.com/apps/news?pid=20601130&sid=a10orRl3z8Dw, accessed August 1, 2010.

30 TransFair USA, "Ben & Jerry's Goes Globally Nuts for Fair Trade"; www.transfairusa.org/content/about/ppr/ppr_100218.php, accessed October 1, 2010.

31 Amy Pellicane, Clarins, email to author, August 18, 2010.

32 Clarins, "Sustainable Development"; www.clarins.com.my/social_sustainabledevelopment.php, accessed October 1, 2010.

33 Ibid.

34 Ibid.

35 Clarins, "Clarins We Care"; my.clarins.com/clarins-cosmetics/about-clarins/commitment-to-beauty/clarins-we-care/178, accessed October 1, 2010.

36 Clarins, "The ClarinsMen Award"; int.clarins.com/clarins-cosmetics/about-clarins/commitment-to-beauty/environmental-protection/the-clarinsmen-award/174, accessed October 1, 2010.

37 Julia R. Barrett, "Phthalates and Baby Boys: Potential Disruption of Human Genital Development," *Environmental Health Perspectives* 113 (2005): A542.

38 Paul Brown and Keris KrennHrubec, "Phthalates and Children's Products," National Research Center for Women & Families, November 2009; www.center4research.org/2010/04/phthalates-and-childrens-products, accessed August 1, 2010.

39 Industrial Designers Society of America, "Nike Considered Boot," 2005; www.idsa.org/content/content1/nike-considered-boot, accessed August 1, 2010.

40 Reena Jana, "Nike Quietly Goes Green," *Bloomberg BusinessWeek*, June 11, 2009; www.businessweek.com/magazine/content/09_25/b4136056155092. htm?campaign_id=rss_tech, accessed August 1, 2010.

41 Susan Piperato, "Marmoleum & Green on Display," *New York House*, July 2009; www.metrogreenbusiness.com/archive/article.php?issue= 39&dept=57, accessed August 1, 2010.

42 Forbo, "Forbo Group Annual Report 2009," March 10, 2010; www.forbo.com/ default.aspx?menuId=33, accessed August 16, 2010. Currency information converted from CHF to USD using 2009 rate of 1.03 provided in Forbo report.

43 Environmental Health Association of Nova Scotia, "Guide to Less Toxic Products" (Halifax, Nova Scotia: EHANS, 2004; www.lesstoxicguide.ca/index. asp?fetch=household, accessed August 1, 2010).

44 Seventh Generation, *Spheres of Influence: 2007 Corporate Consciousness Report* (Burlington, VT: Seventh Generation, 2008; www.svg2007report.org/flash. html#/-2, accessed August 1, 2010).

45 Martin Wolf, Director of Product and Environmental Technology, Seventh Generation, telephone interview, August 13, 2008.

46 Rich Pirog and Andrew Benjamin, "Checking the Food Odometer: Comparing Food Miles for Local Versus Conventional, Produce Sales to Iowa Institutions" (Ames, IA: Leopold Center for Sustainable Agriculture, Iowa State University, July 2003; www.leopold.iastate.edu/pubs/ staff/files/food_travel072103.pdf, accessed August 1, 2010).

47 Paul Martiquet, "More to Eating Local," Vancouver Coastal Health Authority, April 16, 2008; www.nscg.ca/Services/archive.cfm?id=261, accessed July 10, 2009.

48 Natural Marketing Institute, *LOHAS Consumer Trends Database 2009* (NMI, 2010).

49 U.S. Department of Agriculture, Agricultural Marketing Service, "Farmers Markets and Local Food Marketing," USDA, Agricultural Marketing Service, October 10, 2009; www.ams.usda.gov/AMSv1.0/ams.fetchTemplate Data.do?template=T emplateS&navID=WholesaleandFarmersMarkets&leftNav=WholesaleandFarme rsMarkets&page=WFMFarmersMarketGrowth&description=Farmers%20Marke- t%20Growth&acct=frmrdirmkt, accessed August 1, 2010.

50 Wal-Mart, "Wal-Mart Commits to America's Farmers as Produce Aisles Go Local," press release, July 1, 2008; walmartstores.com/FactsNews/ NewsRoom/ 8414. aspx, accessed August 1, 2010.

51 Wal-Mart, "Locally Grown Fact Sheet," *Live Better Index*, Wal-Mart; www. livebetterindex.com/savemoreprod.html, accessed August 6, 2010.

52 Erica Erland, Maxwell PR, email message to the author, November 20, 2009.

53 Kettle Foods Inc., "Sustainability," November 13, 2009; www.kettlefoods.com/ about-us/sustainability, accessed August 1, 2010.

54 Cyrus Farivar, "Pulling the Plug on Standby Power," *The Economist*, March 9, 2006; at Global Technology Forum, globaltechforum.eiu.com/index. asp?layout=rich_story&channelid=3&categoryid=10&title=Pulling+the+plug+on +standby+power&doc_id=8293, accessed August 1, 2010.

55 Bosch, "Life is Better with Bosch," 15 July 2009: 91; www.bosch-home.com/Files/ bosch/us/us_en/literaturerequests/bosch_full_line_winter_08lr.pdf, accessed September 30, 2010.

56 Bosch, "New Bosch Washer and Dryer Line Fits Your Lifestyle, Pampers Your Clothes for the Next Wave in Laundry Care," press release, November 2003; www.bosch-press.com/tbwebdb/bosch-usa/en-US/PressText.cfm?CFID=707&C FTOKEN=714c9f97d9380b9-9964A3F4-B5A3-413F-9367- DE1036D275FA&Search=1&id=160, accessed October 1, 2010.

57 Bosch, "Life is Better with Bosch": 9.

58 Rebecca Smith and Ben Worthen, "Stimulus Funds Speed Transformation toward 'Smart Grid'," *Wall Street Journal*, September 20, 2009: Marketplace, B1.

59 World Business Council for Sustainable Development, "Reducing Mobile Phone No-load Energy Demand: Nokia," June 18, 2008; www.wbcsd.org/Plugins/ DocSearch/details.asp?DocTypeId=24&ObjectId=MzA0MTM, accessed August 1, 2010.

60 U.S. Environmental Protection Agency and U.S. Department of Energy, "Find a Car: 2010 Toyota Prius"; at Fueleconomy.gov, www.fueleconomy.gov/feg/ findacar.htm, accessed July 10, 2009.

61 Matthew Dolan, "Ford Device Stretches Gallons," *Wall Street Journal*, October 29, 2008: D10.

62 United Nations Environment Programme, *Global Environment Outlook 4 (GEO4): Environment for Development*, 2007: 148; www.unep.org/geo/geo4/ report/geo-4_report_full_en.pdf, accessed October 1, 2010.

63 Ibid.

64 Ibid.

65 American Water Works Association, "Water Use Statistics," Drinktap.org; www. drinktap.org/consumerdnn/Default.aspx?tabid=85, accessed August 1, 2010.

66 TreeHugger, "Dual Flush Toilet by Caroma," March 1, 2005; www.treehugger. com/files/2005/03/dual_flush_toil_1.php, accessed August 1, 2010.

67 Sustainable Solutions, "Thinking Bathrooms," 24 July 2009.

68 Sharon Nunes, "Smarter Water and Energy Conservation Policies," *Environmental Leader*, July 22, 2010; www.environmentalleader.com/2010/07/22/smarter-water-and-energy-conservation-policies, accessed August 26, 2010.

69 Stokke Global, "Tripp Trapp Highchair," 2009; www.stokke-highchair.com/en-us/ tripp-trapp-highchair.aspx, accessed August 1, 2010.

70 Emily Arnold and Janet Larsen, "Bottled Water: Pouring Resources Down the Drain," Earth Policy Institute, February 2, 2006; www.earthpolicy.org/ Updates/2006/Update51.htm, accessed August 1, 2010.

71 Campaign to End Bottled Water, "Bottled Water is a Serious Problem," Wellness Enterprises, July 24, 2009; www.endbottledwater.com/TheProblem.aspx, accessed August 1, 2010.

72 Arnold and Larsen, "Bottled Water: Pouring Resources Down the Drain."

73 Springwise, "Reusable Envelopes for Reply Mail," March 7, 2008; springwise. com/marketing_advertising/reusable_envelopes_for_reply_m, accessed August 1, 2010.

74 Ibid.

75 Jim McLain, "Patagonia Seeks to Recycle Used Capilene Products into New Clothing," *Environmental News Network*, August 23, 2005; www.enn.com/top_ stories/article/2402, accessed August 1, 2010.

76 Patagonia, "Capilene Baselayers are the Best Option for High-Sweat Activities and Wet Conditions"; www.patagonia.com/web/us/patagonia.go?slc=en_US&sct=US&assetid=10148, accessed October 1, 2010.

77 Toray, "Toray, Patagonia to Jointly Work on Chemical Recycle of Nylon 6," press release, December 12, 2007; www.toray.com/news/eco/nr071212b.html, accessed August 1, 2010.

78 VerTerra, "Company"; www.verterra.com/company.php, accessed October 1, 2010.

79 Michael Dwork, CEO, VerTerra, email message to the author, November 4, 2009.

80 Jeff Borden, "SunChips Lets the Sun in: How Frito-Lay Embraced Green and Grounded its Brand Identity," *Marketing News*, September 30, 2009: 10.

81 Ibid.

82 SunChips, "SunChips Bags"; www.sunchips.com/resources/pdf/sunchips_bags.pdf, accessed August 1, 2010.

83 GenPak, "Environmentally Friendly Food Packaging"; harvestcollection.genpak.com, accessed October 1, 2010.

84 Biodegradable Products Institute, "The Compostable Label"; www.bpiworld.org/BPI-Public/Program.html, accessed October 1, 2010.

85 Biodegradable Products Institute, "FAQ"; bpiworld.org/Default.aspx?pageId=190434, accessed October 1, 2010.

86 Reuters, "Dutch Government Blocks PlayStation One," *CNet News*, December 4, 2001; news.cnet.com/Dutch-government-blocks-PlayStation-One/2110-1040_3-276584.html, accessed August 1, 2010.

87 Philips Lighting Company, "Lighting the Future" (Somerset, NJ: Philips Lighting Company, 2008; www.lighting.philips.com/us_en/environmentandsustainability/downlad/sustainability_brochure.pdf, accessed August 1, 2010).

88 Philips Lighting Company, "Alto Lamp Technology" (Somerset, NJ: Philips Lighting Company, 2009; www.wescodist.com/healthcare/docs/alto_brochure.pdf, accessed August 1, 2010).

Chapter 5

1 Joyce Cohen, "Brushing Innovations, Built on Titanium," *New York Times*, November 13, 2007: F6.

2 Soladey, "How It Works"; www.soladey.com/about.htm, accessed July 15, 2010. Author's note: a life-cycle assessment is needed to understand the relative impacts of their system versus conventional brushing.

3 Tina Butler, "Taking Care of Business: Diapers Go Green," Mongabay.com, April 2, 2006; news.mongabay.com/2006/0402-tina_butler.html, accessed August 1, 2010.

4 Ibid.

5 Industrial Designers Society of America, "SIM from Tricycle," 2006; www.idsa.org/content/content1/sim-tricycle, accessed August 1, 2010.

6 Maggie Overfelt, "Product Samples that Save Money (and the Earth)," CNNMoney.com, October 24, 2006; money.cnn.com/magazines/fsb/fsb_archive/2006/10/01/8387304/index.htm, accessed August 1, 2010.

7   Industrial Designers Society of America, "SIM from Tricycle."
8   Overfelt, "Product Samples that Save Money (and the Earth)."
9   Michael Hendrix, "Waste Not," *Innovation*, Fall 2006: 94-96.
10 Katie Fehrenbacher, "Why the Kindle Is Good for the Planet," *Earth2Tech*, August 19, 2009; earth2tech.com/ 2009/08/19/why-the-kindle-is-good-for-the-planet, accessed August 1, 2010.
11 Associated Press, "Israel Gets First Plugs For All-Electric Car Network," MSNBC. com, December 8, 2008; www.msnbc.msn.com/id/28113041, accessed August 1, 2010.
12 Mara Der Hovanesian, "I Have Just One Word For You: Bioplastics," *BusinessWeek*, June 30, 2008: 44-47.
13 The Coca-Cola Company, "The Coca-Cola Company Introduces Innovative Bottle Made from Renewable, Recyclable, Plant-Based Plastic," press release, May 14, 2009; www.thecoca-colacompany.com/presscenter/nr_20090514_ plantbottle.html, accessed August 16, 2010.
14 Brian Dumaine, "Feel-good Plastic that Fades Away," *Fortune*, April 29, 2010; money.cnn.com/2010/04/29/technology/feel_good_plastic.fortune/index.htm, accessed August 20, 2010.
15 Natureworks, "Many New Products Launch for the Foodservice Industry," LLC Ingeo News, June 13, 2009; www.natureworksllc.com/news-and-events/ ingeonews/ingeonews-v6-issue4.aspx, accessed October 1, 2010.
16 Steve Davies, Director of Communications and Public Affairs, NatureWorks, email message to the author, November 14, 2009.
17 Anna Burroughs, "Are Biodegradable Plastics Good for the Environment?" Associated Content, August 15, 2006; www.associatedcontent.com/article/51038/ are_biodegradable_plastics_good_for.html, accessed August 1, 2010.
18 NatureWorks LLC, "NatureWorks Discovers There Is No Technical Barrier for Recycling Plastic Bottles Made from Plants," press release, February 23, 2009; www.natureworksllc.com/news-and-events/press-releases/2009/02-23- 09-sorting-recycling.aspx, accessed October 1, 2010.
19 Amy Westervelt, "Explosive Growth for LED Lights in Next Decade, Report Says," SolveClimate, May 13, 2010; solveclimate.com/blog/20100513/explosive-growth- led-lights-next-decade-report-says, accessed August 27, 2010.
20 "The Home Depot Sells Ecosmart LED Lamps Made by Lighting Science Group," *LEDs Magazine*, May 2010; www.ledsmagazine.com/products/22332, accessed August 27, 2010.
21 Joe Mullich, "Mainstreaming Alternative Energy," *Wall Street Journal*, May 6, 2008: A12-13.
22 Michael S. Davies, "Understanding the Cost of Solar Energy," *Green Economet- rics*, August 13, 2007; greenecon.net/understanding-the-cost-of-solar-energy/ energy_economics.html, accessed August 1, 2010.
23 Mullich, "Mainstreaming Alternative Energy."
24 "Solio Solar Charger Product Comparison Chart"; www.solio.com/charger/solio- charger-comparison-chart.html, accessed August 9, 2010.
25 Voltaic Systems Inc., "Voltaic Solar Bags and Solar Chargers"; www.voltaicsystems.com.
26 Reware, "Products"; www.rewarestore.com/product/beachtote.html.

27 Martin LaMonica, "Quiet Wind-turbine Comes to U.S. Homes," *CNET News*, October 28, 2008, updated with correction February 6, 2009; news.cnet.com/8301-11128_3-10075828-54.html, accessed August 1, 2010.

28 Warren McLaren, "Ventura: Human Powered Digital Watches," Treehugger.com, April 5, 2006; www.treehugger.com/files/2006/04/ventura_human_p.php, accessed August 1, 2010.

29 Collin Dunn, "AladdinPower Hand Generator," Treehugger.com, December 2, 2005; www.treehugger.com/files/2005/12/aladdinpower_ha.php, accessed October 1, 2010.

30 Tylene Levesque, "Human-Powered Gyms in Hong Kong," *Inhabitat*, March 8, 2007; www.inhabitat.com/2007/03/08/human-powered-gyms-in-hong-kong, accessed August 1, 2010.

31 Windstream Power, "Bike Power Generator"; www.windstreampower.com/Bike_Power_Generator.php, accessed August 1, 2010.

32 GM Volt, "Chevy Volt Exact Launch Date Will be Mid-November 2010, Tens of Thousands in 2011," April 20, 2009; gm-volt.com/2009/04/20/chevy-volt-exact-launch-date-will-be-mid-november-2010-tens-of-thousands-in-2011, accessed August 16, 2010.

33 Chevrolet, "Chevy Volt: The Future is Electrifying"; www.chevrolet.com/pages/open/default/fuel/electric.do?evar23=fuel_solutions_landing%20page, accessed August 1, 2010.

34 Jeff Sabatini, "Honda Sees a Hydrogen Future," *Wall Street Journal*, November 30, 2007: W7.

35 Ibid.

36 Ibid.

37 Tom Mutchler, "Commuting in a Honda FCX Clarity," ConsumerReports.org, January 26, 2009; blogs.consumerreports.org/cars/2009/01/commuting-in-honda-fcx-clarity-fuel-cell-car.html, accessed August 1, 2010.

38 Nissan Motor Company, *Nissan's Environmental Initiatives: Nissan Green Program* (Yokohama, Japan, February 2009).

39 Ibid.

40 Ibid.

41 Ibid.

42 Nissan USA, "Nissan LEAF: New Car," Nissan News: Technology, June 30, 2010; www.nissanusa.com/leaf-electric-car/news/technology#/leaf-electric-car/news/technology, accessed October 1, 2010.

43 Yoshio Takahashi, "Nissan Motor Turns Over a New Leaf, Going Electric," *Wall Street Journal*, August 3, 2009: B1.

44 Nissan Motor Company, *Nissan's Environmental Initiatives*.

45 Nissan-Global, "World First Eco Pedal Helps Reduce Fuel Consumption," August 4, 2008; www.nissan-global.com/EN/NEWS/2008/_STORY/080804-02-e.html, accessed October 1, 2010.

46 Nissan Motor Company, *Nissan's Environmental Initiatives*.

47 Ibid.

48 Ibid.

49 Shivani Vora, "Test-Driving Car-Share Services," *Wall Street Journal*, June 11, 2009: D2.

50 Zipcar, "Zipcar Announces Annual Low-Car Diet 'Call For Participants'," Zipcar Press Overview, June 24, 2010; zipcar.mediaroom.com/index. php?s=43&item=128, accessed August 11, 2010.

51 Zipcar, "Green Benefits"; www.zipcar.com/is-it/greenbenefits, accessed August 9, 2010.

52 Ibid.

53 Zipcar, "Zipcar Announces Annual Low-Car Diet 'Call For Participants'."

54 Steven Erlanger, "A New Fashion Catches On in Paris: Cheap Bicycle Rentals," *New York Times,* July 13, 2008: A6.

55 Tamar Lewin, "A Leading Publisher Announces a Plan to Rent Textbooks to College Students," *New York Times,* August 14, 2009: A10.

56 REC Solar Power Company, "Commercial Financing"; www.recsolar.com/ CommercialFinancing.aspx, accessed August 1, 2010.

57 Peter Maloney, "Pay for the Power, Not the Panels," *New York Times,* March 26, 2008: H1.

58 Netflix, "Netflix Passes 10 Million Subscribers, with 600,000 Net Additions since the First of the Year," Netflix.com, February 12, 2009; netflix.mediaroom.com/ index.php?s=43&item=307, accessed August 1, 2010.

59 Zonbu, "Zonbu's Zonbox Declared Greenest Computers for Consumers, Certified as First Consumer Device to Win Gold-Level Certification from EPEAT," July 6, 2007; www.zonbu.com/download/EPEAT-June-07.pdf, accessed August 1, 2010.

60 BASF Corporation, "PremAir Technology Destroys Ozone," August 21, 2007; www2.basf.us/corporate/news_2007/news_release_2007_00011.htm, accessed August 1, 2010.

61 BASF Corporation, "Yellow Cab Transforms into Smog-Eater for Taxi 07 Exhibit at New York Auto Show," April 4, 2007; www2.basf.us/corporate/news2007/040407_ Taxi07.htm, accessed August 1, 2010.

62 Reliance, "PUR Purifier of Water"; www.relianceproducts.info/index.html, accessed August 1, 2010.

Chapter 6

1 Jacquelyn A. Ottman, Edwin R. Stafford, and Cathy L. Hartman, "Avoiding Green Marketing Myopia: Ways to Improve Consumer Appeal for Environmentally Preferable Products," *Environment* 48.5 (2006): 22-36.

2 AFM Safecoat, "We Put Your Health First"; www.afmsafecoat.com, accessed October 1, 2010.

3 Rob Walker, "Sex vs. Ethics," *Fast Company*, June 2008: 74-78.

4 Ottman *et al.*, "Avoiding Green Marketing Myopia."

5 "Pepsi Cans Feature Recycling Info," *Environmental Leader*, April 27, 2008; www.environmentalleader.com/2008/04/27/pepsi-cans-feature-recycling-info, accessed August 1, 2010.

6 18Seconds.org; green.yahoo.com/18seconds.

7 Blue Planet Network, "Brita and Nalgene Partner to Challenge People to Make a Difference," August 21, 2007; blueplanetnetwork.org/news/brita_ nalgene, accessed August 1, 2010.

8   Aileen Zerrudo, Director of Communications, The Clorox Company, email message to the author, August 25, 2009.

9   Netflix, "Netflix Facts"; www.netflix.com/MediaCenter?id=5379#about, accessed August 1, 2010.

10 Nicole Rousseau, VP Retail Marketing, HSBC U.S., email message to the author, September 24, 2009.

11 Stonyfield Farm, "Meet our CE-Yo and his Team"; stonyfield.com/about_us/ meet_our_ceyo_and_his_team/index.jsp, accessed October 1, 2010.

12 Zipcar, "Zipcar Announces Annual Low-Car Diet 'Call For Participants'."

13 Philip W. Sawyer (ed.), "It's Not Easy Being Green: How to Improve Advertising with Environmental Themes," *Starch Tested Copy* 2.5 (1993): 5.

14 Don't Mess with Texas, "FAQs"; www.dontmesswithtexas.org/about/faq, accessed August 1, 2010.

15 Dawson M. Williams, "Car2Can Video Contest is 'Don't Mess with Texas' Campaign's Latest Anti-litter Initiative," *Dallas Morning News*, June 17, 2009; www. dallasnews.com/sharedcontent/dws/news/texassouthwest/stories/061709dnme tlittervideos.889ed007.html, accessed August 1, 2010.

16 Natural Marketing Institute, *Understanding the LOHAS Market Report* (Harleysville, PA: NMI, March 2008): 112.

17 "Reynolds Wrap Foil From 100% Recycled Aluminum," *Journal News*, June 6, 2009 (advertisement).

19 Cause Marketing Forum, "The Growth of Cause Marketing," 2010; www. causemarketingforum.com/page.asp?ID=188, accessed October 1, 2010.

20 Cone, "Cone Releases First Cause Consumer Behavior Study," October 1, 2008; www.coneinc.com/content1188, accessed July 20, 2010.

21 People, "Caught Caring: (RED), Bugaboo and Kelly Rutherford," People.com, September 14, 2009; celebritybabies.people.com/2009/09/14/caught-caring-red-bugaboo-and-kelly-rutherford, accessed August 13, 2010.

22 UNICEF, "International partnerships: IKEA Social Initiative," 11 May 2010; www. unicef.org/corporate_partners/index_42735.html, accessed August 13, 2010.

23 www.onepercentfortheplanet.org

24 Anya Kamentz, "Cleaning Solution," *Fast Company*, September 2008: 121-25.

25 "Clorox To Stop Using Chlorine," *Chemical & Engineering News*, August 16, 2010; pubs.acs.org/cen/news/87/i45/8745notw2.html, accessed October 1, 2010.

26 Andrew Adam Newman, "Tough on Crude Oil, Soft on Ducklings," *New York Times*, September 25, 2009: B6.

27 Rob Walker, "Big Gulp," *New York Times*, February 26, 2006; www.nytimes. com/2006/02/26/magazine/26wwln_consumed.html, accessed August 1, 2010.

28 Cone, "Cone Releases First Cause Consumer Behavior Study."

29 "Philips Launches 'A Simple Switch' Campaign," *Environmental Leader*, July 6, 2007; www.environmentalleader.com/2007/07/06/philips-launches-a-simple-switch-campaign, accessed August 1, 2010.

30 Emily Steel, "Taking Green Message to Great Outdoors," *Wall Street Journal*, October 2, 2007: B9.

31 United Nations Environment Programme, *Talk the Walk: Advancing Sustainable Lifestyles through Marketing and Communications* (UNEP, December 2005): 23.

32 Figures for June 30, 2010 from Internet World Stats, "World Internet Usage and Population Statistics"; www.internetworldstats.com/stats.htm, accessed August 1, 2010.

33 Jonathan Lemonnier, "Spending on Alternative Media Jumps 22%," *Advertising Age*, March 26, 2008; adage.com/digital/article?article_id=125950, accessed August 13, 2010.

34 No Sweat; www.nosweatapparel.com.

35 Beth Snyder Bulik, "What Your Favorite Social Network Says About You," *Advertising Age*, July 8, 2009; adage.com/digital/article?article_id=137792, accessed August 1, 2010.

36 "Role of Social Media in Sustainability Evolves," *Environmental Leader*, July 15, 2009; www.environmentalleader.com/2009/07/15/role-of-social-media-in-sustainability-evolves, accessed August 1, 2010.

37 Ibid.

38 Lauren Thaman, Associate Director, External Relations, Procter & Gamble, email message to the author, October 28, 2009.

Chapter 7

1 Emilia Askari, "USA: Ford CEO Says He's Green," *CorpWatch*, October 31, 2001; www.corpwatch.org/article.php?id=1453, accessed August 1, 2010.

2 As of February 24, 2010, General Motors officially announced their plans to "wind down" the Hummer business after the failure of the sale to a Chinese manufacturer. General Motors, "HUMMER Sale to Tengzhong Cannot be Completed. Wind Down of HUMMER Business to Begin," February 24, 2010; media.gm.com/content/media/us/en/news/news_detail.brand_gm.html/content/Pages/news/us/en/2010/Feb/0224_hummer, accessed August 12, 2010.

3 *Business Wire*, "Nine in 10 at U.N. Climate Change Conference Believe Greenwashing is a Problem," press release, December 9, 2007; www.businesswire.com/portal/site/google/?ndmViewId=news_view&newsId=20071209005061&newsLang=en, accessed August 1, 2010.

4 British Telecom, "Consumers Sceptical of Corporate Commitment to Sustainability," press release, January 4, 2007; www.btplc.com/News/Articles/Showarticle.cfm?ArticleID=11efc6a1-1df0-4189-a0f7-392c478a12bf, accessed September 29, 2008.

5 Bernie Becker, "Baseball Team Clashes with Environmentalist over Oil Company Advertising," *New York Times*, July 27, 2008; www.nytimes.com/2008/07/27/us/27stadium.html, accessed August 1, 2010.

6 Steve Jobs, "A Greener Apple," Apple Inc., September 14, 2008; www.apple.com/hotnews/agreenerapple, accessed August 1, 2010.

7 Burst Media, "Consumers Recall Green Ads," *Business Wire*, press release, April 14, 2008; www.businesswire.com/portal/site/google/?ndmViewId=news_view&newsId=20080414005857&newsLang=en, accessed August 1, 2010.

8 A certification rating provided by the B Lab nonprofit organization: www.bcorporation.net.

9 Patagonia, "The Footprint Chronicles"; www.patagonia.com/web/us/footprint/index.jsp?slc=en_US&sct=US, accessed October 1, 2010.

10 The Webby Awards; www.webbyawards.com/webbys/current.php?season=12, accessed October 1, 2010.

11 Natalie Zmuda, "Sigg Tries to Control Brand Damage after Admitting its Bottles Contain BPA," *Advertising Age*, August 31, 2009; adage.com/article?article_id=138712, accessed August 1, 2010.

12 Christopher A. Cole and Linda A. Goldstein, " 'Green' is so Appealing," *New York Law Journal*, September 15, 2008; www.law.com/jsp/nylj/PubArticleNY.jsp?id=1202424493387, accessed August 1, 2010.

13 "How to Avoid a Green Marketing Backlash," *Environmental Leader*, April 15, 2008; www.environmentalleader.com/?s=HOW+TO+AVOID+A+GREEN+MARKETING+BACKLASH, accessed August 1, 2010.

14 Mark Sweney, "Lexus Ad Banned for Claiming SUV is Environmentally Friendly," *The Guardian*, May 23, 2007, and as "Lexus ad Banned for Green Claims"; www.guardian.co.uk/business/2007/may/23/advertising.media, accessed August 1, 2010.

15 Reilly Capps, "Questioning How Biota Sprung a Leak," *Telluride Daily Planet*, April 16, 2008; www.telluridenews.com/archive/x121157044, accessed October 13, 2008.

16 BIOTA; www.biotaspringwater.com.

17 Christina Binkley, "Picking Apart Bamboo Couture," *Wall Street Journal*, November 12, 2009: D1.

18 "U.S. Green Council Debated," *Environmental Leader*, June 17, 2009; www.environmentalleader.com/2009/06/17/us-green-product-council-debated, accessed August 1, 2010.

19 Tim Bradshaw, "Complaint Upheld over Shell Advert," *Financial Times*, August 13, 2008; www.ft.com/cms/s/0/d08d0a66-68c1-11dd-a4e5-0000779fd18c.html, accessed August 1, 2010.

20 Mark Sweney, "Ad for US Cotton Industry Banned by ASA over Green Claims," *The Guardian*, March 12, 2008; www.guardian.co.uk/media/2008/mar/12/asa.advertising1/print, accessed August 1, 2010.

21 Dr. Anastasia O'Rourke, Co-Founder, Ecolabel Index, email to author, August 17, 2010.

22 Eve Smith, Brand Strategist, BBMG, email message to the author, December 3, 2009.

23 Emily Crumley, Manager, Chain of Custody, FSC, email message to the author, November 23, 2009.

24 Vanessa Gibbin, Brand, Advertising and Research, The Carbon Trust, email to author, May 12, 2010.

25 Joan Schaffer, Spokeswoman, USDA, telephone interview with author about USDA Organic, December 1, 2009.

26 Shelley Zimmer, Manager of Environmental Affairs, HP, email message to the author, December 1, 2009.

27 International Association for Soaps, Detergents and Maintenance Products, *Promoting Sustainable Consumption of Household Laundry Detergents in Europe: Washright, a Unique Industry Campaign* (Brussels: AISE, November 2002; www.washright.com/documents/Washright_11-2002.qxd.pdf, accessed August 1, 2010).

28 Michael Sanserino, "Peer Pressure and Other Pitches," *Wall Street Journal*, September 14, 2009: B6.

Chapter 8

1 Ian Austen, "Bottle Maker to Stop Using Plastic Linked to Health Concerns," *New York Times*, April 18, 2008; www.nytimes.com/2008/04/18/business/18plastic.html, accessed August 1, 2010.

2 Mark Ritson, "Bottled Water Brands Beware: Tap is Back," *Branding Strategy Insider* blog, November 7, 2007; www.brandingstrategyinsider.com/2007/11/bottled-water-b.html, accessed August 1, 2010.

3 Jennifer Lee, "City Council Shuns Bottles in Favor of Water from Tap," *New York Times*, June 17, 2008; www.nytimes.com/2008/06/17/nyregion/17water.html, accessed August 1, 2010.

4 International Bottled Water Association, "IBWA Launches Major Media Advertising Campaign," press release, August 2, 2007; www.bottledwater.org/content/ibwa-launches-major-media-advertising-campaign, accessed August 1, 2010.

5 Emily Bryson York, "Nestle, Pepsi and Coke Face their Waterloo," *Advertising Age*, October 8, 2007; adage.com/print?article_id=120986, accessed August 1, 2010.

6 Rebecca Wilhelm, "Bottling Trends: Bottled Water Industry Makes Strides," *Water & Wastes Digest*, April 2008; www.wwdmag.com/Bottling-Trends-article9117, accessed August 1, 2010.

7 Mike Verespej, "Nestlé Exec Counsels Bottled-Water Industry," *Plastics News*, July 7, 2008: 1.

8 Sustainable Life Media, "More Marketers Targeting Green-Conscious Kids," July 25, 2008; www.sustainablelifemedia.com/content/story/brand/more_marketers_targeting_green_conscious_kids, accessed August 1, 2010.

9 Briana Curran, Public & Community Relations Program Manager, Staples, email messages to the author, May 28, 2009 and September 2, 2009.

10 Vince Meldrum, "Robinson Students Address Invasive Species," Earth Force news, March 18, 2008; www.earthforce.org/content/article/detail/2083, accessed August 1, 2010.

11 Earth Force, "Staples Award Winners"; www.earthforce.org/section/thank_you/staples/staples_awards, accessed August 1, 2010.

12 Lynn Ascrizzi, "TerraCycle: Yogurt Cups, and More, Help Schools Raise Funds," Natural Resources Council of Maine, March 16, 2008; www.nrcm.org/news_detail.asp?news=2249, accessed August 11, 2010.

13 www.biggreenhelp.com

14 Joanna Roses, Sr. Director Communications, Nickelodeon, email message to the author, October 26, 2009; www.neafoundation.org/pages/educators/grant-programs/nea-foundation-green-grants, accessed July 21, 2010.

15 Jonas Risen, "Solar Decathlon – Technische Universität Darmstadt," Greenline, October 17, 2007; greenlineblog.com/2007/10/solar-decathlon-technische-universitat-darmstadt, accessed August 11, 2010.

16 www.nwf.org/campusecology/chillout

17 Jen Fournelle, Campus Program Coordinator, National Wildlife Federation, email message to the author, September 1, 2009.

18 Aria Finger, Chief Marketing Officer, DoSomething, email message to the author, October 1, 2009.

19 "SHRM Survey Asks How 'Green' is the American Workplace?" Reuters, January 16, 2008; www.reuters.com/article/pressRelease/idUS188509+16-Jan-2008-+BW20080116, accessed July 21, 2010.

20 Alcoa, "2008 Alcoa Worldwide Month of Service: Alcoa Employees to Make a Difference Where they Live and Work," press release, September 30, 2008; www.alcoa.com/global/en/community/foundation/news_releases/2008_mos.asp, accessed August 1, 2010.

21 Michael Barbaro, "At Wal-Mart, Lessons in Self-Help," *New York Times*, April 5, 2007; www.nytimes.com/2007/04/05/business/05improve.html, accessed August 1, 2010.

22 KaBOOM!, "KaBOOM Partner: The Home Depot," Kaboom.org, 2009; kaboom.org/about_kaboom/supporting_partners/meet_our_partners/partner_spotlight_home_depot, accessed 24 July 2009.

23 Erin Gunderson, Best Buy PR, email message to the author, September 2, 2009.

24 Jill Vohr, Marketing Manager, U.S. Environmental Protection Agency, email message to the author, December 8, 2009.

25 Ahmed El Amin, "Wal-Mart Unveils 'Green' Packaging Rating System," FoodProductionDaily.com, November 2, 2006; www.foodproductiondaily.com/content/view/print/104013, accessed August 1, 2010.

26 NatureWorks LLC, "KLM, the First Airline to Introduce the Environmentally Friendly Ingeo-Lined Cup," press release, June 16, 2009, updated November 11, 2009; www.natureworksllc.com/news-and-events/press-releases/2009/06-16-09-klm-cup.aspx, accessed August 1, 2010.

27 "Paper, Cardboard Packagers Launches 'Responsible Package' Initiative," *Environmental Leader*, October 8, 2009; www.environmentalleader.com/ 2009/ 10/08/paper-cardboard-packagers-launch-responsible-package-initiative, accessed August 1. 2010.

28 Brian M. Carney, "Bye Bye, Light Bulb," *Wall Street Journal*, January 2, 2008: A10.

29 Sustainable Housing Communities/U.S. Department of Housing and Urban Development (HUD), "Sustainable Housing and Communities," hud.gov, 2010; portal.hud.gov/portal/page/portal/HUD/program_offices/sustainable_housing_communities, accessed August 8, 2010.

30 Doris De Guzman, "Metabolix Targets Bioplastic Bottle," ICIS.com, October 8, 2009; www.icis.com/blogs/green-chemicals/2009/10/metabolix-targets-bioplastic-b.html, accessed August 11, 2010.

31 The National Environmental Directory, July 22, 2009; eelink.net/gaindirectories.html.

32 Conservation International, "McDonald's," 2009; www.conservation.org/discover/partnership/corporate/Pages/mcdonalds.aspx, accessed August 11, 2010.

33 Kimberly-Clark, "Kimberly-Clark Sets the Bar Higher for Tissue Products with Stronger Global Forest Policy," press release, August 5, 2009; investor.kimberly-clark.com/releasedetail.cfm?ReleaseID=401321, accessed August 1, 2010.

34 Lisa Bailey, Communications Manager, Americas, Marine Stewardship Council, email message to the author, August 27, 2009.

35 Rahul Raj, VP of Marketing, New Leaf Paper, email message to the author, September 2, 2009. Nicole Rycroft, Executive Director, Canopy, telephone interview with the author, July 30, 2009.

36 James E. Austin, Roberto Gutierrez, E. Ogliastri, and E. Reficco, "Capitalizing on Convergence," *Stanford Social Innovation Review* 5.4 (Winter 2007): 24-31.

37 American Museum of Natural History, "Climate Change"; www.amnh.org/exhibitions/climatechange, accessed August 1, 2010.

38 Cargill, "Cargill: Corporate Responsibility – Partnerships"; www.cargill.com/corporate-responsibility/partnerships/index.jsp, accessed August 12, 2010.

39 The Nature Conservancy, "The Home Depot"; www.nature.org/joinanddonate/corporatepartnerships/partnership/homedepot.html, accessed August 1, 2010.

Chapter 9

1 Timberland, "Creating Sustainable Change," March 5, 2009; www.timberland.com/corp/index.jsp?page=csr_civic_change, accessed August 8, 2010.

2 Alison Franklin, City Year, email to the author, June 28, 2010.

3 This case study was prepared by Jacquelyn Ottman using secondary sources and approved for publication by Cara Vanderbeck, Timberland, by email, August 2010.

4 Starbucks Coffee Company, "Starbucks Shared Planet Goals & Progress 2009"; www.starbucks.com/responsibility/learn-more/goals-and-progress, accessed August 12, 2010.

5 This case study was prepared by Jacquie Ottman using secondary sources and approved for publication by Ben Packard, Vice President, Global Responsibility, Starbucks, by email, March 18, 2010.

About the author

At age four, her siblings called her "Junkie Jacquie" when she dragged home treasures from the neighbor's trash. At age thirty-four, Jacquie pioneered green marketing by founding J. Ottman Consulting, Inc. Her mission: apply her in-depth consumer packaged goods expertise, with a creative bent for dreaming up new products and her finely honed strategic instincts, to help businesses develop and market the next generation of products designed with sustainability in mind.

With a client roster that includes over 60 of the Fortune 500, the USDA's BioPreferred and other U.S. government labeling programs, Ottman is a sought-after keynoter for conferences and corporate forums around the globe. She is a founding co-chair of the Sustainable Business Committee of the Columbia Business School Alumni Club of New York. She is also the former co-chair of the NYC chapter of O2, the global network of green designers, and was founding jury chair for the American Marketing Association's Special Edison Awards for Environmental Achievement in New Products.

In 2004, she spearheaded the IDSA-endorsed Design:Green educational initiative with the goal of jumpstarting eco-design education in the U.S. Underwritten with an Innovation Grant from the U.S. Environmental Protection Agency, Design:Green now continues as a course in the online Certificate in Sustainable Design program of the Minneapolis College of Art and Design.

The author of hundreds of articles on green marketing topics, she blogs at Jacquie Ottman's Green Marketing Blog (www.greenmarketing.com/blog), as well as for the *Harvard Business Review* and other websites.

Her three previous books on green marketing have been translated into five languages.

Ottman is a graduate of Smith College and lives in New York City. The widow of Geoffrey S. Southworth, an industrial recycler, she is the proud stepmother of his three children and two grandchildren.

Index

Page numbers in *italic figures* refer to illustrations